Unless WE Tell It . . .

It Never Gets Told!

Unless WE Tell It . . .

It Never Gets Told!

RODNEY L. HURST SR.

KiJas Press

Jacksonville, Florida

ISBN 978-0-578-17453-2

KiJas Press
P.O. Box 40351
Jacksonville, Florida 32219-3781

Acknowledgments

My sincere gratitude to the many persons who supported me throughout the writing of this book: those whom I talked with, those whom I asked for their opinions, those who read portions of the manuscript, those who offered comments, those who allowed me to quote them, and those who offered encouragement. Many of you understood my quest to tell these stories of Black history, the Civil Rights Movement, and the experiences of racism. I very much appreciate your faith in this endeavor.

My heartfelt thanks to the subjects of many of the individual chapters, who allowed me that special opportunity to talk with them about their great experiences and their exceptional lives.

My love and appreciation to my ever-growing family, and especially to Ann, my wife of nearly fifty years (December 10, 1966); to my sons, Rodney Hurst II and Todd Hurst; and to the two persons who make Ann and me gladly jump through grandparent's hoops, our granddaughters Marquiette and Jasmine.

And a very special thank-you to my editor and book designer, John Laursen of Press-22, in Portland, Oregon.

Preface

Maya Angelou once remarked, "There is no greater agony than bearing an untold story inside you." Sadly, this agony is routine to millions of Blacks, whose stories are often neither told nor heard, let alone published where they can be read by the world. My first book, *It was never about a hot dog and a Coke!* was my personal account of the 1960 Jacksonville Youth Council NAACP demonstrations and Ax Handle Saturday. The local press blacked out news of Ax Handle Saturday and the sit-ins that preceded that white race riot, leading to a false version of events that obscured the real truth of that infamous day. I wanted to tell the story and set the record straight before further "revisionist" history distorted the true history.

Stories of the historical achievements of great Black Americans —including Blacks in Jacksonville, Florida—are woefully unknown, as are many stories about the Civil Rights Movement. *Unless WE Tell It . . . It Never Gets Told!* tells some of those stories while also focusing on racism.

In the academic arena there is a saying, "If it is not written down, it did not happen," and Black history is seldom written on the pages of American history. Racism is also subject matter that does not make its way onto the pages of American history, and is often treated as a taboo subject or a four-letter word. Author and *Atlantic* columnist Ta-Nehisi Coates has said that, for Black people in America, racism is a physical experience of fear and violence. WE simply cannot afford to ignore stories about the legacy of Black history, and the legacy of the Civil Rights Movement any more. Those who tire of hearing about racism should ask yourselves, what if you were Black and had to live through the daily vulgarity of racism?

My own understanding of Black history and the Civil Rights Movement began at age eleven in Mr. Rutledge Henry Pearson's eighth-grade American history class at segregated Isaiah Blocker Junior High School in Jacksonville. Mr. Pearson, who was my mentor and the adviser of the Jacksonville Youth Council NAACP, would not teach his American history class from the textbook that during those days was approved for "Negro education," He simply told us to leave our textbook at home — a textbook that included only Booker T. Washington and George Washington Carver as Blacks who made a difference in the history of this country.

Note to American history teachers, white and Black: Do not expect your Black students to learn from your history class if you do not incorporate Black history. If I sit in a classroom and only read about the contributions made by white Americans and white Europeans, then the "learning field" is never level. It is downright dishonest that American history as portrayed in history textbooks essentially makes the statement that Blacks made no salient contributions to this country. My Black ancestors helped to develop this country before, during, and after slavery. You have to teach the truth without regard to what the textbooks proclaim. You are not teaching if you do otherwise.

Mr. Pearson wanted to arm us with the *real* truth, irrespective of what was "written down." Black History is who WE are. Racism is why WE fight . . . and why the Struggle must continue.

—Rodney Hurst
October 2015

To Ann Albertie Hurst, my beloved wife:
a caring and loving book "widow" more times than she will admit;
and a caring and loving wife, mother, aunt, and grandma all the time.

Contents

SECTION II
Confronting Racism

Unless WE Tell It . . .

It Never Gets Told!

One is astonished in the study of history at the recurrence of the idea that evil must be forgotten, distorted, skimmed over. We must not remember that Daniel Webster got drunk, but only that he was a splendid constitutional lawyer. We must forget that George Washington was a slave owner . . . and simply remember the things we regard as creditable and inspiring. The difficulty, of course, with this philosophy is that history loses its value as an incentive and example; it paints perfect man and noble nations, but it does not tell the truth.

—William Edward Burghardt "W. E. B." Du Bois
Sociologist, civil rights activist, Pan-Africanist, historian, author, and editor

INTRODUCTION

An Incomplete and Dishonest American History

We hold these truths to be self-evident, that all men are created equal, that they are endowed by their Creator with certain unalienable Rights, that among these are Life, Liberty, and the pursuit of Happiness.

—The Declaration of Independence

The poignant words above speak to the foundation of the United States of America—and, more important, to the proclamation of freedom and equality for its citizens.

Correction: for *some* of its citizens. America's founding fathers did not practice what it was that they wrote in the documents that laid the blueprints for this country. It is easy to see the hypocrisy of Thomas Jefferson, the acknowledged author of the Declaration of Independence and the father of the Constitution, writing these glorious words of freedom while at the same time he kept more than a hundred persons in chained bondage. Equality was not a true consideration. "Equality" was simply a word whose meaning rang hollow. Equality for Blacks meant chains and violence and degradation in the racist and well-defined institution of slavery. It is really quite extraordinary that this Christian country and its pious government allowed human beings to be held in chained bondage. But when you consider the economic advantage gained through free forced labor, Christianity was simply a ruse by American capitalism.

How flawed is a country whose founding documents speak of "freedom," yet that criminally holds a portion of its population in bondage and slavery?

How flawed is a country that passes racist laws, creates discriminatory governmental policies, and develops arcane societal categories designed to keep that same portion of its population in their place based on the color of their skin?

How flawed is a country whose history is built on "free" slave labor and the degradation of millions of human beings?

How flawed is a country that refuses to apologize for slavery and refuses to acknowledge the wrongs done to millions of its citizens?

How flawed is a country that creates and designs its own special brand of racism?

How academically pure, and historically and culturally informative it would be, to teach an honest American history!

How academically pure, and historically and culturally informative it would be, to find the names of the many Black Americans who impacted us as a nation in classroom textbooks!

Robert Kennedy said, "Truth is the token of trust." Not teaching the honest history of the role that Black Americans played in the development of this country keeps the playing field eternally uneven. The infrastructure of racism is rooted in dishonesty.

My eighth-grade American history textbook included the names of only three Black Americans: Crispus Attucks, without identifying him as being Black; Booker T. Washington; and George Washington Carver. As Black students—"Negro" and "Colored" were the racial terms at the time—we were expected to be grateful that their names were included at all. It should have been as important to read about Dr. Daniel Hale Williams as it was to read about

Eli Whitney; as important to read about Ida Wells-Barnett as it was to read about Betsy Ross; and as important to read about Granville Woods as it was to read about Benjamin Franklin.

Winston Churchill once said, "History is written by the victors." Apparently that is the overriding philosophy when you read segregated and racist textbooks of American history that give the impression that Blacks contributed nothing of substance to the development of this country.

Dr. Ja A. Jahannes, noted psychologist, educator, author, writer, composer, and social critic, recently commented, "The country is handicapped by news imposters who believe the anti-history and warped political theories of racist, white-supremacy textbooks of their high school days."

In American history, Mark Twain and Charles Dudley Warner came up with the term "the Gilded Age" to refer to the era of great economic and population growth in the United States during the post-Civil War and post-Reconstruction eras of the late nineteenth century. Gilded? Not for Blacks, not in this country. While the age was gilded for the rapidly growing white upper and middle classes, Blacks in the South faced one of the most racially oppressive periods in American history. Only slavery was comparatively worse.

This period is referred to as "the Nadir of Race Relations,"[1] by Dr. Rayford Whittingham Logan (1897–1982) in his 1954 book, *The Negro in American Life and Thought: The Nadir, 1877–1901.* An historian and Pan-African activist, Dr. Logan was one of the foremost Black scholars of the twentieth century, yet his career "demonstrated the difficulty African American scholars had in getting the predominantly white academic community to take their scholarship seriously." Dr. Logan was a professor of history at Howard University from 1938 until he retired in 1965; from 1942 until his retirement he was head of the department. In the late 1940s, Dr. Logan was the chief advisor to the National Association for the Advancement of

Colored People (NAACP) on international affairs. In 1980, he was awarded the NAACP's prestigious Spingarn Medal.

The "Nadir" lasted from the Compromise of 1877 through the first half of the twentieth century. America crafted and fine tuned the blueprint for vicious racism during the Nadir. White mob violence, organized racial terrorism, and rapidly spreading Jim Crow laws virtually eliminated all civil rights gains made during the period of Reconstruction that followed the Civil War. Those gains dissolved into nothingness in an amazingly short period of time.

I first read about the "Nadir of Race Relations" in Dr. James Loewen's excellently penned volume *Lies My Teacher Told Me: Everything Your American History Textbook Got Wrong.*[2] (I would meet Dr. Loewen in Jacksonville during the commemoration of the fiftieth anniversary of Ax Handle Saturday and the 1960 Jacksonville Youth Council NAACP sit-ins, in August, 2010.) In several of his books, Dr. Loewen details the impact of the "Nadir" following Reconstruction: the status of Blacks was negatively defined with visual iconic signs and symbols and violent examples of racism and segregation; Colored and White water fountain signs; Colored and White restroom signs; segregated schools; segregated restaurants; segregated hotels; segregated motels; segregated movie theatres; segregated doctor's offices; segregated buses and bus stations; segregated churches; segregated trains and train stations; segregated sports venues; segregated government offices at all levels; segregated public facilities; segregated beaches; horrific violent reprisals against Blacks for showing the slightest hint of wanting the guarantees of living in America; and perhaps the cruelest affront to freedom, having to pay in various ways for the right to vote.

"For a period of almost a hundred years after the Civil War," declared Robert Bruce Slater in the *Journal of Blacks in Higher Education,* "distinguished Black academics such as Logan were not acceptable as scholars at America's great institutions of higher learning." Black scholars were slighted because of blatant racism, and in part because they studied Black history at a time when the subject received little respect. Dr. Logan, explained reviewer Winthrop D. Jordan in the *Journal of Southern History*, "wrote and otherwise taught about the history of Black people in this country many years before it became fashionable to do so." James Loewen, a white historian, author, and sociologist, continues that honest history.

Yet history as it is usually told ignores those Blacks who fought for equality and justice against great odds while also fighting against the racism of America. Their history and the journey they started, the struggle they endured, continue to this day. Racist forces in America today would like to revise American history; to "pretty up" the abhorrent practices of slavery;[3] to romanticize the South's participation in the misnamed Civil War; to ignore the impact of Jim Crow laws; to conceal the obscenely violent acts perpetrated against the Civil Rights Movement; to return to the routine use of racial epithets; and to redefine the meanings of segregation and racism.

This ridiculous lack of honesty coincides with our country's apparent penchant to seek a return to its past racist attitudes. It is easier to think that relations are getting better when you are not feeling the brunt of racism.

Jim Lewis, an award-winning colleague and esteemed "news mentor" friend from my television news days (and a brilliant photographer), once commented to me that he did not know "which is worse—for people to knowingly make blatantly racist comments, or for them to be blissfully ignorant of the fact that their comments are racist."

Many of the signs are gone, making racism less overt; but that does not mean that it has disappeared, or that "equality is at hand" in what Dr. Maya Angelou refers to as "these, as yet, United States of America." In the final analysis, being Black and understanding being Black is a state of mind.

SECTION I

Real Stories About Blacks in Jacksonville, Florida

James Weldon Johnson, circa 1900.

1

James Weldon Johnson

I swear to the Lord
I still can't see
Why Democracy means
Everybody but me.

—Langston Hughes
Poet, activist, novelist, playwright, and columnist

American history simply cannot fathom the accomplishments of James Weldon Johnson, given the segregated era in which he lived. Civil rights activist, diplomat, author, politician, journalist, poet, educator, lawyer, songwriter, and one of the prime movers of the Harlem Renaissance, James Weldon Johnson was truly the embodiment of early vanguard Black pioneers. His inspiring and motivating leadership, his fight against racism, and his fight for equality during his years with the National Association for the Advancement of Colored People (NAACP) Johnson took Black activism and advocacy to a new level for the time. Not surprisingly, history overlooks Black pioneers like James Weldon Johnson.

Born in Jacksonville, Florida, on June 17, 1871, James William Johnson was the second of three children of Helen Louise Dilled and James Johnson.[1] (He changed his middle name from William to Weldon at age forty-two.) Johnson attended Edwin M. Stanton

School in Jacksonville through grade eight. With segregation the order of the day and no local schools for Blacks beyond eighth grade, Johnson's parents sent him to Atlanta, Georgia, to finish high school and attend college. After graduating from Atlanta University, Johnson returned to Jacksonville in 1894. The next year, seeking to educate Jacksonville's adult Black community, he founded the newspaper *Daily American*, the first such paper in this country. It lasted only a year, but gave him the opportunity to voice his position on racial issues. He later became the principal of Stanton School, where his mother had taught. Under Johnson, Stanton's educational mission changed with the addition of the high school years.

While serving as principal of Stanton, Johnson wrote the incomparable "Lift Ev'ry Voice and Sing." Asked to speak at an Abraham Lincoln birthday celebration, Johnson instead wrote a poem, probably his initial intent. But it was a poem unlike any that one would hear during that era of racism and discrimination. Deciding to change the poem to a song, he asked his brother, music professor John Rosamond Johnson, to write the music. The Johnsons intended "Lift Ev'ry Voice and Sing" to serve as a musical protest against the degrading conditions of Jim Crow and the bloody wave of racial lynching sweeping the country. James Weldon Johnson later recalled that near the end of the first stanza, when the following two lines came to him, "the spirit of the poem had taken hold of me."[2]

Sing a song, full of the faith that the dark past has taught us.
Sing a song, full of the hope that the present has brought us.

I am convinced that the country's insidious racism, and the known fact that on average three to five Blacks were lynched weekly, compelled James Weldon Johnson to pen such stirring lyrics expressing the plight of American Blacks. I might add that there is no mention of Abraham Lincoln. Julian Bond and Dr. Sondra Wilson reached similar conclusions in their book, *Lift Every Voice and Sing*.

(Actually, I guess I reached their conclusion.) They write, "Yet [the song's] message is ingeniously crafted and does not fuel the fires of racial hatred."

James Weldon Johnson later recalled the agony and ecstasy of creation as being like that of "a nervous father-to-be outside the delivery room." He recalled "pacing back and forth" on his front porch, "repeating the lines" of his song "over and over to myself." "The lines of this song," he said, "repay me in elation, almost of exquisite anguish, whenever I hear them sung."

Sociologist E. Franklin Frazier pointed out that in "Lift Ev'ry Voice and Sing," James Weldon Johnson "endowed the African American enslavement and struggle for freedom with certain nobility." Frazier further noted that Johnson expressed both an acceptance of the past and confidence in the future. Many of us consider "Lift Ev'ry Voice and Sing" the most inspiring song in American civil rights history. Each line, each verse, carries a message.

We have come over a way that with tears has been watered.
We have come, treading our path through the blood of the
    slaughtered.

Johnson's lyrics show his unswerving self-confidence and optimism, and his strong belief that the existing system, which was an unauthentic representation of the United States Constitution, could not endure.

During his time as Stanton's principal, Johnson became the first Black to take and pass the Florida bar exam, and, in 1901, the first licensed Black attorney in the state of Florida. Later that year, he decided to pursue a career in writing. Johnson resigned his post as principal in Jacksonville, and in 1902 he and John moved to New York, where they soon teamed up with Bob Cole to write songs for musicals. This partnership with Cole proved very successful, with the composition of more than two hundred songs for Broadway.

In 1904, Johnson served as treasurer of the Colored Republican Club. Understand that then—as opposed to now—Blacks were Republicans, loyal to the Republican Party because President Lincoln had freed the slaves. Later that year, Johnson went to work on Theodore Roosevelt's presidential campaign. Roosevelt would appoint Johnson as U.S. consul, first at Puerto Cabello, Venezuela, where he served from 1906 to 1908, and then in Nicaragua from 1909 to 1913. In 1910, during his time in Nicaragua, he married Grace Nail, the daughter of a wealthy real-estate developer. They had met years earlier in New York when Johnson was working as a songwriter. Grace Nail was the epitome of New York Black society, cultured and well-educated. She would later work with Johnson on several screenwriting projects.

Unable to secure a more desirable diplomatic post, Johnson resigned from his consulship. In 1916 Joel E. Spingarn, chairman of the NAACP board from 1913 to 1919, offered Johnson the post of field secretary for the NAACP. An effective organizer, Johnson was appointed executive secretary of the NAACP in 1920, and in this position he was able to bring attention to racism, lynching, segregation, and the emerging pattern of white mob assaults directed against Black communities.

James Weldon Johnson coined the phrase "Red Summer" to denote the bloody summer of 1919, which, with more than twenty-six race riots, was the year of the greatest racial violence in the nation's history. This national reign of terror saw racial confrontations, massacres, and lynchings throughout the country, all of them initiated by whites. During that summer there were anti-Black race riots in such cities as Chicago, Illinois; Elaine, Arkansas; Charleston, South Carolina; Knoxville and Nashville, Tennessee; Longview, Texas; Omaha, Nebraska; and Washington, D.C. Hundreds of Black people were killed in these riots; thousands were wounded; and thousands more were left homeless. These "Red Summer" riots were not limited to the South. In fact, one of the most violent episodes occurred in Chicago.[3]

I was not surprised when I read comments by Cameron McWhirter, author of *Red Summer*. In several radio and print interviews, he talked about the respect he gained for James Weldon Johnson while researching his book. McWhirter said of Johnson that "his most important civil rights work came during the Red Summer." That violent season, which Johnson later described in his memoir as "that summer when the stoutest-hearted Negroes felt terror and dismay" was, in many ways, the apex of this dynamo's impressive life.

McWhirter continued, "Johnson spent 1919 traveling coast-to-coast to deliver speeches on civil rights to packed audiences. He helped organize the NAACP's first national anti-lynching conference, and wrote dozens of commentaries on the violence for various publications. He met constantly with journalists and business leaders to advocate for equal rights. He forged a small but important coalition of White politicians sympathetic to Black rights. In reading his speeches from 1919, I was awed by Johnson's power and persistence. At times he sounded like Dr. King—and at times like Malcolm X. Often his speeches sounded like a mix of both, though Johnson delivered his words before either of those men was alive."

James Weldon Johnson also investigated the Tulsa, Oklahoma, race riot in 1921, the largest massacre of nonmilitary Blacks in the history of this country, which took place in an area called "Black Wall Street." That same year, while serving in the NAACP, Johnson supported Congressman Leonidas Dyer's anti-lynching bill, working tirelessly to get the Missouri congressman's bill passed. The Dyer Bill made it through the House of Representatives on January 26, 1922, and was given a favorable report by the Senate committee assigned to report on it in July of that year, but its passage in the Senate was halted by a filibuster. (The extent of lynchings during this period can be seen in statistics from the Tuskegee Institute, which recorded 3,446 lynchings of Blacks and 1,297 lynchings of whites between 1882 and 1968. The "white" category apparently included Mexican-Americans, Native Americans, and Asian-Americans.) With the demise of the federal anti-lynching bill, Johnson became disillusioned with the American political system, which led to his break with the Republican Party.

In 1930, James Weldon Johnson retired from the NAACP, and took a part-time teaching position at Fisk University in Nashville, Tennessee. He taught creative writing both at Fisk and at New York University. He also published his autobiography, *Along This Way*, in 1933 and a volume of poetry, *Saint Peter Relates an Incident*. The title poem of the latter work describes the opening of the Tomb of the Unknown Soldier, on Judgment Day. A crowd waits to see the honored but unknown military hero buried there, and is astonished when a Black man emerges. Johnson wrote the poem in response to unfair treatment that had been accorded to the mothers of deceased Black soldiers on a nationally sponsored trip to Europe.

According to the NAACP, "While W. E. B. Du Bois advocated intellectual development and Booker T. Washington advocated industrial training to combat racism, Johnson believed that it was important for Blacks to produce great literature and art. By doing so, Johnson held that Blacks could demonstrate their intellectual equality and advance their placement in America."

James Weldon Johnson was killed on June 26, 1938, when the car he was driving was struck by a train near his summer home in Wiscasset, Maine. His funeral in Harlem was attended by thousands.

I attended James Weldon Johnson Junior High School in 1954, during the days of overt Southern racism and segregated schools, which were personified in Jacksonville, Florida, by the Negro Education Division of Duval County public schools. Even at a young age I understood the Jim Crow laws of the South, yet I knew very little about this mighty Jacksonville giant whose name soared in the rafters of my junior high school.

Many decades later, I was invited to speak at a conservative Jewish temple in Jacksonville. It was quite an honor, according to those who would know, with the rabbi allowing me to speak during Friday-night services. I spoke about Black history, Jacksonville's civil rights history, and my book on these subjects. When the rabbi gave his concluding remarks, he commented that he had recently read my book, and had "enjoyed the read tremendously." (Authors like hearing that.) He went on to say that I made several references in the book to "Lift Ev'ry Voice and Sing," which stirred his attention. He apologized for his lack of familiarity with the song. He then commented that as he read the lyrics it occurred to him "how appropriate the words were to any oppressed people, including Jews." He was so inspired with the significance of the words that he proceeded to read aloud to his congregation each verse of "Lift Ev'ry Voice and Sing." He concluded the service and his comments with the final words of the song, "True to our God. True to our native land. Amen." How remarkable, I thought: we internalize James Weldon Johnson's words of faith and hope for Black people fighting racism, discrimination, and oppression, and the rabbi found Johnson's words of faith and hope appropriate for Jewish people fighting discrimination and oppression.

Over the years, Blacks stood when singing "Lift Ev'ry Voice and Sing," because it was referred to as "the Negro National Anthem." James Weldon Johnson, however, never thought of "Lift Ev'ry Voice and Sing" as an anthem, but as a hymn. When he became the first Black executive secretary of the national NAACP, "Lift Ev'ry Voice and Sing" was selected as the organization's official song and later denoted the "Negro National Hymn." Today, some of us still stand when we sing "Lift Ev'ry Voice and Sing," not because we have to, and not because it is referred to as the "Negro National Anthem"—or today as the "Black National Anthem"—but because of the majesty of this great masterpiece.

James Weldon Johnson spent his lifetime working to end discrimination in America. He certainly understood the fight for freedom and equality, and became a willing and active warrior in the fight. Yet the fight then, as it has been over the years, was not about might. It was about courageously challenging racism, segregation, and the prevailing Jim Crow laws of the day. Johnson was a staunch advocate of Black pride, empowerment, and equality. He took deserved pride in his accomplishments across a wide variety of careers: teacher, Broadway lyricist, poet, diplomat, novelist, and civil-rights leader. Johnson was a key figure, some say perhaps the key figure, in making the NAACP a truly national organization capable of mounting the attack that eventually led to the dismantling of the system of segregation by law.

I called a national organization seeking information related to the video trailer for *It was never about a hot dog and a Coke!* A Black female answered the phone. She was very cordial and very professional. I explained that for my trailer I wanted to use a recording of "Lift Ev'ry Voice and Sing." I asked her if I needed a mechanical licensing fee to use the song. After I gave her the name "Lift Ev'ry Voice and Sing" a second time, she also asked again for the name of the lyricist. I said, "James Weldon Johnson." When she asked for clarification on his name a third time, it dawned on me she was not familiar with James Weldon Johnson, nor was she acquainted with "Lift Ev'ry Voice and Sing." She left the phone for a few minutes and came back and told me the song was in the public domain, and a fee was not necessary. Again, she was very professional and courteous, but she did not know anything about either the writer or the song.

I did not want to give her a lesson on the phone and asked only that she research James Weldon Johnson's name and "Lift Ev'ry Voice and Sing" in her spare time.

Her not knowing of James Weldon Johnson was sad, and her obviously not knowing "Lift Ev'ry Voice and Sing" was equally sad. She was not taught. No one had told her. She did not know. This happens when Blacks are excluded from history. James Weldon Johnson's historical contributions to this country, his tremendous civil rights activism, his professional background, his literary contributions to this country, and his writing the moving masterpiece "Lift Ev'ry Voice and Sing" are more than enough to qualify his inclusion in American history textbooks. Telling the story is important; knowing the story is even more important.

The Ritz Theatre and Museum in Jacksonville, Florida, houses an outstanding animatronics presentation of "Lift Ev'ry Voice and Sing," featuring the voice of the late Ossie Davis as James Weldon Johnson. It is a must-see for anyone who visits Jacksonville.

Do you, by the way, know the words to "Lift Ev'ry Voice and Sing"?

On February 2, 1988, the U.S. Postal Service released a first-class commemorative stamp honoring James Weldon Johnson. The stamp was issued in the fiftieth anniversary year of Johnson's death, with the release date moved up from June 1988 to February, to mark Black History Month. His stamp is the eleventh in the Postal Service's *Black Heritage* series.

On May 14, 2014, James Weldon Johnson was inducted into the state of Florida's Civil Rights Hall of Fame. He is one of Jacksonville's brilliant native sons, though not appreciably nor adequately recognized in Jacksonville, the state of Florida, or these United States of America. James Weldon Johnson is a Black pioneer and a Renaissance man for the ages.

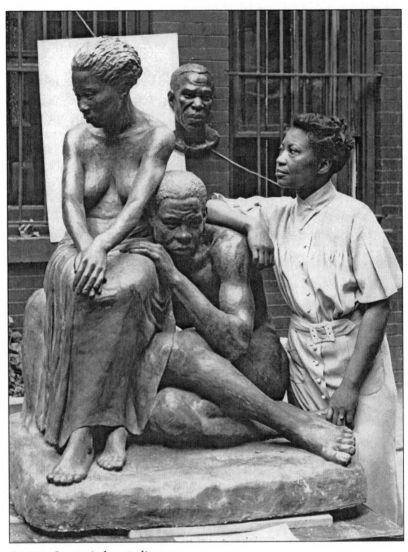

Augusta Savage in her studio, 1942.

2

Augusta Savage

Without a struggle, there can be no progress.

— Frederick Douglass
Social reformer, orator, writer, and statesman

Augusta Christine Fells was born on February 29, 1892, in Green
Cove Springs, Florida, about 30 miles from Jacksonville. An important African American artist, Savage began making art as a child.
Using the natural clay found in her community, she liked to sculpt
animals and other small figures. But her father, a Methodist minister, didn't approve of this activity, and did whatever he could to
stop her. Savage once said that her father "almost whipped all the
art out of me."[1]

Despite her father's objections, Savage continued to make sculptures. When the family moved to West Palm Beach, Florida, in 1915,
she encountered a new challenge, a lack of clay. Savage eventually
got some materials from a local potter and created a group of figures
that she entered in a local county fair. Her work was well-received,
winning a prize and the support of the fair's organizer, George Graham Currie. He encouraged her to study art.

After a failed attempt to establish herself as a sculptor in Jacksonville, Savage moved to New York City in the 1920s. She struggled financially throughout her life, but was able to study art at the

"The Harp," sculpture by Augusta Savage, 1938.

Cooper Union, which did not charge tuition. After a year, the school provided her a scholarship to help with living expenses. Savage excelled there, finishing her course work in three years instead of the usual four. During this time she married James Savage; they divorced after a few months, but she kept the name of Savage.

After settling in Harlem, Augusta established the Savage Studio of Arts and Crafts at 163 West 143rd Street, and used her studio to provide adults with art education. In 1937, she became the first director of the Harlem Community Arts Center, an institution funded by the Works Progress Administration (WPA).

Savage was commissioned to create a work for the 1939 New

York World's Fair, to commemorate the musical contributions of African Americans. She chose James Weldon Johnson's "Lift Ev'ry Voice and Sing" as her inspiration. Her work would become the famed sculpture "The Harp," in which the strings were represented by Black Americans and the soundboard was the arm and hand of God. "The Harp" was one of the most popular works of art at the World's Fair. Sadly, it was destroyed after the Fair closed, because Augusta did not have funds to have it cast in bronze, nor to move and store the piece.

After 1945, though no longer in the spotlight, Savage continued to teach sculpting and other art to both children and adults throughout New York.

Augusta Savage's sculptures focused on Black physiognomy, and uniquely reflected an aspect of African American culture. Her work influenced the careers of many now-celebrated artists, including Romare Bearden, Jacob Lawrence, and the photographers Morgan and Marvin Smith.

Bronze bust of James Weldon Johnson by Augusta Savage, 1939.

President Lyndon B. Johnson presenting Asa Philip Randolph with the Presidential Medal of Freedom on September 14, 1964.

3

Asa Philip Randolph

With a union, Black people can approach their employers as proud and upright equals, not as trembling and bowing slaves. Indeed, a solid union contract is, in a very real sense, another Emancipation Proclamation.

—A. Philip Randolph

In 2013 America commemorated the fiftieth anniversary of the March on Washington. It is challenging to appreciate the historical dynamic of that August Wednesday in 1963 even if you were there on that auspicious day and lived through it. The vision of A. Philip Randolph, the man who had the inspiration for the March on Washington and who went on to become its chief organizer, was as important as any speech made that day, including Dr. King's "I Have A Dream" oration. For, if one considers Dr. Martin Luther King to have been "the Drum Major for Justice," then Asa Philip Randolph certainly deserves the mantle of "the Band Director for Equality."

This dynamic national leader founded the Brotherhood of Sleeping Car Porters in 1925 and forged it into a formidable union. In the 1940s, Randolph arguably forced President Franklin Delano Roosevelt to implement equal federal job opportunities for Blacks by threatening a march on Washington, and later compelled President Harry S. Truman to integrate the military by again threatening a march on the nation's capital.

Asa Philip Randolph was born in Crescent City, Florida, on April 15, 1889, the second of two sons of African Methodist Episcopal minister James Randolph and his wife, Elizabeth.[1] Both James and Elizabeth were strong supporters of equal rights for Blacks. In 1891, the family moved to Jacksonville, Florida; although he had not been born there, A. Philip Randolph always considered Jacksonville his home.

Randolph grew up in poverty. Jacksonville had been open to African Americans in the nineteenth century, but early in the twentieth century the city joined other cities throughout the South in beginning to implement Jim Crow laws to segregate Blacks from whites. Although Asa's parents would not allow him and his brother James to ride the segregated streetcars or to use the segregated reading room at the public library, they emphasized the importance of education, and of reading and speaking correctly. Asa and James attended the Cookman Institute in Jacksonville, for years the only academic high school in Florida for Black male students. Asa Philip Randolph graduated in 1907 as his class valedictorian.

Randolph excelled in English, public speaking, and drama. He sang in the choir and was a standout baseball player. Since a lack of family finances precluded his attending college, Asa took odd jobs around Jacksonville. In April 1911 he moved to New York City, where he met and married Lucille Green, a schoolteacher who also owned a beauty salon. Although continuing to work, Randolph attended City College and became increasingly involved in politics and union activities.

In 1917, Randolph's advocacy magazine, *The Messenger*, campaigned against lynching, opposed U.S. participation in World War I by urging African Americans to resist being drafted to fight for a segregated society, and recommended that Blacks join unions.

Through his newspaper, Randolph reached thousands of Black workers and citizens in New York's Harlem. During World War I, Attorney General Mitchell Palmer, appointed by President Woodrow Wilson, called him "one of the most dangerous Negroes in America." (Oddly, although Palmer had previously associated with the progressive wing of the Democratic Party and had supported women's suffrage and the rights of trade unions, his views on civil rights changed drastically following his appointment as attorney general. *Time* magazine has called Palmer one of the worst presidential cabinet members of all time.)

In June 1925, a group of Pullman porters, the all-Black service staff of the Pullman sleeping cars, approached A. Philip Randolph and asked him to lead their new organization, the Brotherhood of Sleeping Car Porters.[2] By 1926, thousands of African Americans were working as Pullman and train porters, although few knew about the harsh conditions and menial pay. For working more than four hundred hours a month, Pullman porters were paid a little more than $60. They got by with tips, but in order to win those tips they had to perform tasks beyond those required by their already degrading jobs.

Randolph agreed to take the leadership in trying to better their conditions. His primary qualification for the job: he had a strong reputation for honesty. The porters trusted him, and the fact that he was not a Pullman company employee meant that the company could neither fire him nor buy him off. For the next ten years, he led a long and hard campaign to organize the Pullman porters. These Black men were being called upon to prove that "Black men are able to measure up"; the men never forgot that message, and in the end it served them well.

Their uphill battle was met with fierce and violent resistance from the Pullman Company, which was at that time the largest employer of Blacks in the country. Randolph and the Brotherhood persevered, however, winning the support of Black churches, Black newspapers, and the NAACP. By 1935, not only had the Brotherhood survived, but it had won an election supervised by the National Mediation Board, and the Pullman Company was finally forced to begin negotiations with the union. The same year, the American Federation of Labor reversed its previous position and voted to grant an international charter to the Brotherhood.

The negotiations with Pullman eventually resulted, in 1937, in a contract that netted $2 million in pay increases, a shorter work week, and overtime pay. This was the first contract ever signed by a white employer with a Black labor leader; Randolph called it the "first victory of Negro workers over a great industrial corporation." As one scholar wrote, "a small band of brothers—Black—had stood together and won against a corporation that had said it would never sit down and negotiate with porters."

A. Philip Randolph had become the most widely known spokesperson for Black working-class interests in the country. In January 1941, with President Franklin Roosevelt refusing to issue an executive order banning discrimination against Black workers in the defense industry, Randolph sent out a call for "ten thousand loyal Negro American citizens" to converge in a march on Washington, D.C. Support grew so quickly that soon he was calling for the participation of a hundred thousand marchers.

The purpose of planning a march on the nation's capital was to promote fair employment and equality for Black workers in federal jobs and the defense industry. With the country's entry into World War II looming on the horizon, Randolph and others foresaw the obvious contradiction in American forces battling racist Nazi soldiers abroad while Blacks were barred from opportunities at home because of the color of their skin. White workers in the early stages of the war benefited from huge government-funded contracts working in defense plants; Black workers, on the other hand, even Blacks

Asa Philip Randolph and Eleanor Roosevelt, 1946.

with proven skills, were told they could get jobs as janitors.

President Roosevelt's wife, Eleanor Roosevelt, was a staunch supporter of civil rights, and with her urging, and with the prospect of a hundred thousand people marching on Washington, President Franklin D. Roosevelt signed Executive Order 8802, declaring that "there shall be no discrimination in the employment of workers in defense industries or government because of race, creed, color, or national origin." Roosevelt also set up the U.S. Fair Employment Practices Commission to oversee the order.

Randolph continued to press for the rights of Black Americans. Following the passage of the Selective Service Act of 1947, he demanded that the government integrate the armed forces and founded the League for Nonviolent Civil Disobedience against Military Segregation, urging young men, both Black and white, to "refuse to cooperate with a Jim Crow conscription service." On July 26, 1948, President Harry Truman, threatened with widespread

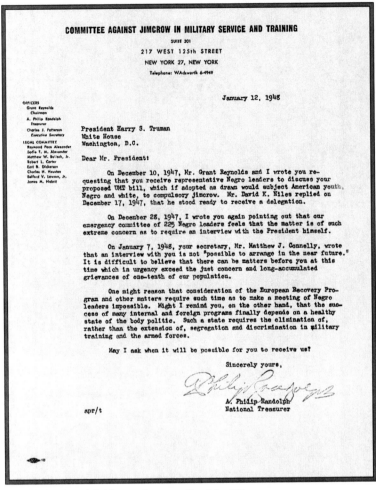

January 12, 1948

President Harry S. Truman
White House
Washington, D.C.

Dear Mr. President:

On December 10, 1947, Mr. Grant Reynolds and I wrote you requesting that you receive representative Negro leaders to discuss your proposed UMT bill, which if adopted as drawn would subject American youth, Negro and white, to compulsory jimcrow. Mr. David K. Niles replied on December 17, 1947, that he stood ready to receive a delegation.

On December 28, 1947, I wrote you again pointing out that our emergency committee of 225 Negro leaders feels that the matter is of such extreme concern as to require an interview with the President himself.

On January 7, 1948, your secretary, Mr. Matthew J. Connelly, wrote that an interview with you is not "possible to arrange in the near future." It is difficult to believe that there can be matters before you at this time which in urgency exceed the just concern and long-accumulated grievances of one-tenth of our population.

One might reason that consideration of the European Recovery Program and other matters require such time as to make a meeting of Negro leaders impossible. Might I remind you, on the other hand, that the success of many internal and foreign programs finally depends on a healthy state of the body politic. Such a state requires the elimination of, rather than the extension of, segregation and discrimination in military training and the armed forces.

May I ask when it will be possible for you to receive us?

Sincerely yours,

A. Philip Randolph
National Treasurer

apr/t

Asa Philip Randolph's 1948 letter to President Truman.

civil disobedience and needing the Black vote in his 1948 re-election campaign, ordered an end to military discrimination "as quickly as possible."

A. Philip Randolph also played a key role in the Montgomery Bus Boycott of 1955–1956. Contrary to popular belief—and to what is written in some historical accounts—the bus boycott was well-planned, and did not begin spontaneously simply because Rosa Parks was so tired that she would not move from her seat so that a white man could sit down. Edgar Daniel Nixon,[3] president of both

Unless WE Tell It . . . It Never Gets Told!

the Montgomery, Alabama, chapter of the Brotherhood of Sleeping Car Porters and the Montgomery branch of the NAACP, was one of the key leaders of the boycott. He knew that the effort would require extensive support, and selected Rosa Parks, secretary of the Montgomery NAACP, to be at the center of the legal "test case" because of her dignified demeanor and temperament. As shown in Jeanne Theoharis's book *The Rebellious Life of Mrs. Rosa Parks*, Rosa Parks was much more than merely a quiet seamstress who was so tired that she just had to sit down. Theoharis's absorbing portrayal provides a deeper understanding of the life of this civil rights icon and her lifetime of activism.[4]

Nixon asked Dr. Martin Luther King Jr., to lead the boycott. Because of the projected expenses for this large undertaking, he also contacted A. Philip Randolph for financial assistance with the effort. Randolph delivered more than $50,000 — the amount varies with some accounts — to help offset the costs related to the boycott, which lasted 381 days. According to Nixon, "without A. Philip Randolph, there would not have been a successful Montgomery Bus Boycott and no legacy of Dr. Martin Luther King Jr." Many consider Randolph to have been the true "Father of the Civil Rights Movement in the United States."

Randolph went on to organize and coordinate the celebrated March on Washington for Jobs and Freedom in 1963 — the occasion on which Dr. Martin Luther King Jr., gave his famous "I Have a Dream" speech. The planning and execution of the 1963 March on Washington stands as a testament to the extraordinary vision, political strategy, and determination of several organizations and key individuals, chief among them A. Philip Randolph and his chief lieutenant, Bayard Rustin, who together had first conceived of such an event back in the early 1940s.

Many consider the march of more than a quarter of a million people — some say as many as half a million — to be Randolph's

Asa Philip Randolph speaking at the 1963 March on Washington.

crowning accomplishment in the realm of civil rights. His call for civil disobedience to force an end to segregation helped convince the next generation of civil rights activists that nonviolent protests and mass demonstrations were the best way for the movement to mobilize public pressure.

By the summer of that year, the Council for United Civil Rights Leadership had formed, an umbrella group of member organizations that included the Southern Christian Leadership Conference (SCLC), the NAACP, the National Urban League, and the Student Nonviolent Coordinating Committee (SNCC), among others. Together these groups joined forces to raise funds to support the day-to-day efforts of Rustin and his production crew of dozens of college students.

In 1965 Randolph founded the A. Philip Randolph Institute, which to this day continues the struggle for social, political and economic justice for all working Americans.

Unless WE Tell It . . . It Never Gets Told!

Asa Philip Randolph died on May 16, 1979, at the age of ninety, after suffering from a heart condition and high blood pressure for several years. News of his death quickly spread throughout the civil rights community. Many expressions began pouring in from those who had drawn inspiration from this great man who had first begun to stir the conscience of the nation more than half a century earlier.

One of the first tributes came from Bayard Rustin. Standing in Mr. Randolph's library, where plaques, diplomas and other honors were stacked against the wall, Mr. Rustin, who at that time led the A. Philip Randolph Institute, declared: "No individual did more to help the poor, the dispossessed, and the working class in the United States and around the world than A. Philip Randolph." Rustin went on to say that, "with the exception of W. E. B. Du Bois, he was probably the greatest civil rights leader of this century until Martin Luther King."

Yet, as early as during World War I, Randolph's opponents had characterized him as "one of the most dangerous Negroes in America," on the basis of his proven power to create change. Because he wanted America to live up to its avowed goal of providing all of its citizens with the opportunity for "Life, Liberty, and the pursuit of Happiness," he was "dangerous." Norman Hill, president emeritus of the A. Philip Randolph Institute, said this: "Without A. Philip Randolph's principled leadership, the labor movement would not be the most integrated mass institution in American society."

My history teacher and my mentor, Mr. Rutledge Henry Pearson, introduced me to A. Philip Randolph in Jacksonville, Florida, in 1960, several days after Ax Handle Saturday. When I met Mr. Randolph I had a flashback to the time I first met Thurgood Marshall. Aside from being awestruck again, at age sixteen I realized I was again in the midst of civil rights greatness. After all the talk and conversations *about* Asa Philip Randolph, I am sitting and having a conversation *with* Mr. Randolph. His words were masterful. He spoke so authoritatively, as if he had been anointed from on high as a champion for civil rights. He congratulated the Jacksonville Youth Council NAACP and me as the Youth Council's president for standing up to discrimination, and congratulated Mr. Pearson as our adviser. I remember him saying how the Negroes must "stand together." Somehow, you always remember words that come from giants like A. Philip Randolph. Hearing his words would impress you at any age but especially if you are a "precocious sixteen year old" (the media's description of my younger self, not mine).

TONY HILL AND FLORIDA'S CIVIL RIGHTS HALL OF FAME

Anthony "Tony" Hill was only twenty-two years old when A. Philip Randolph died, yet he considers himself a Randolph "disciple." Hill, a long-time labor union activist, often says, "Everything I've tried to do in the labor movement has been in honor of him." Even in his life as an elected official, first as a Florida state representative and later as a Florida state senator, Tony said that he sought to emulate Mr. Randolph and to walk in his valiant footsteps, "motivated by Mr. Randolph's accomplishments and contributions over the years."

Hill began his labor career as a longshoreman with the International Longshoremen's Association, Local 1408, in Jacksonville. He became the secretary-treasurer of the Florida AFL-CIO, first elected in 1995 and serving through 2000. In April 2001, he was honored with the esteemed position of secretary-treasurer emeritus of the Florida AFL-CIO. In September 2001, because of his extraordinary commitment and service to the labor movement, he was inducted into the Florida AFL-CIO's Labor Hall of Fame, and presented with the A. Philip Randolph Award. Hill is the youngest inductee, and the first African American to receive this prestigious honor. When I asked Senator Hill what A. Philip Randolph meant him and to the labor movement, his response was: "He was our Moses."

Unless WE Tell It . . . It Never Gets Told!

Senator Hill co-sponsored the legislation to create the Florida Civil Rights Hall of Fame.

Florida Statutes. 760.065 Florida Civil Rights Hall of Fame. (1) It is the intent of the Legislature to recognize and honor those persons, living or dead, who have made significant contributions to this state as leaders in the struggle for equality and justice for all persons.

After being term-limited out, Hill served four years as Jacksonville's director of federal policy under Mayor Alvin Brown.

On February 3, 1989, the U.S. Postal Service, with its dedication of the A. Philip Randolph stamp, added Asa Philip Randolph's name as the twelfth individual to be honored in the *Black Heritage* series of commemorative stamps. In September of 2013 the U.S. Senate passed a resolution introduced by Senator Bill Nelson of Florida honoring the work of Mr. Randolph on the occasion of the fiftieth anniversary of the March on Washington and his commitment to a better America. On May 14, 2014, A. Philip Randolph was inducted into the state of Florida's Civil Rights Hall of Fame.

Throughout A. Philip's Randolph's years as a labor and civil rights leader, he rocked the foundations of racial segregation, pressuring presidents and corporations alike to recognize the need to fix the racist injustices heaped on Blacks. We remember this Black giant, this Black pioneer who wrote the book on Black civil disobedience in this country, this iconic and revered native son who considered Jacksonville his home, as "The Father of the Modern Civil Rights Movement."

Robert "Crow" Hayes, 1970.

4

Robert "Crow" Hayes

Until the lion gets to tell his story, the hunt will always glorify the hunter.

—African proverb

Bob Hayes never thought of himself as a pioneer. Pioneers seldom do. Yet during those days of racism and segregation in the 1950s and '60s, Bob's athletic prowess swelled the pride of a Black community and a segregated Matthew William Gilbert Junior Senior High School in Jacksonville, Florida, where Bob was a student.

Unequal and ridiculously underfunded budgets for Black schools during segregation ensured that Matthew William Gilbert High School did not have adequate facilities for classes, let alone adequate facilities for athletics. Gilbert struggled like most segregated Black schools to meet its most basic needs, with no gym of any consequence . . . nor high school track . . . nor baseball field.

Bob Hayes' most notable nickname in high school was "Crow." Said the late, revered, legendary coach Earl Kitchings: "Someone once asked me why we called him that. I said it was because he was black, he looked like a crow, and he could fly like a crow. It was an endearing nickname in the Black Community." Kitchings was Hayes' football coach at Matthew William Gilbert High School in 1958 and 1959. Bob Hayes was fast, real fast—so fast that it almost appeared as though he could fly, just as Coach Kitchings said. During those days, nobody could run like Bob Hayes. He was a football player with a sprinter's speed. Bob played football, baseball, and basketball, and ran track—a true four-letter athlete.

Unfortunately, the Black community had to read about Bob's high school athletic exploits in the segregated section of the *Florida Times-Union*, which described itself as "News For and About The Colored People of Jacksonville." Whites never read about Bob Hayes. White home deliveries did not include "News For and About the Colored People of Jacksonville."

Bob was the halfback on the 1958 Matthew William Gilbert High School football team, coached by Earl Kitchings, who saw his team finish with twelve wins and no losses to win the Black high school state championship of the Florida Interscholastic Athletic Association with a 14–7 victory over Dillard High School of Fort Lauderdale. I talked with Ervin Norman, one of Bob's teammates on that 1958 championship football team, to get his perspective. His first words to me were "Bob Hayes was the team sparkplug. If he got one step behind the defense, it was off to the races." Norman went on: "And, as coaches know and most football fans understand, speed kills."

Still mired in segregation some four years after the Supreme Court decision in *Brown vs. the Topeka, Kansas, Board of Education*, outlawing school segregation, Gilbert's accomplishments as an all-Black high school football team were easily ignored by the white media. Despite this discrimination and neglect, Matthew William Gilbert High School and its championship football team represented the total Jacksonville community well. In 2007, after fifty years of being shamefully overlooked, that 1958 team was finally recognized by the Florida High School Athletic Association (FHSAA), which proclaimed it as one of the best teams in state history and the best Florida football team of the 1950s.[1]

The Matthew William Gilbert High School 1958 State Championship football team; Bob Hayes, in jersey number 11, is in the second row from the top.

After graduating from Matthew William Gilbert in 1960, Bob Hayes attended Florida Agricultural and Mechanical University (FAMU) on a football scholarship. The halfback was Willie Galimore, who would later become a Chicago Bear. The quarterback was Charlie Ward, whose son, Charlie Ward Jr., would win the Heisman Trophy in 1993. The blocking fullback-tight end was Hewritt Dixon, later an Oakland Raider. Bob Hayes was a wingback in that vaunted backfield of celebrated coach Alonzo "Jake" Gaither, though he also took the field as a halfback and a receiver.[2]

Bob played at FAMU from 1961 to 1964. He averaged an incredible 34.3 yards per return as a freshman in 1961, led the team with eleven touchdowns as a junior in 1963, led the team in punt returns in 1962 and 1963, and led the team in kickoff returns all four years.

Bob's excellent football skills were there and on display in college, but it was his blazing track prowess that would make him legendary. Bob Hayes was the first person to break six seconds in the

Bob Hayes won the 100-meter dash at the 1964 Olympics in world-record time.

60-yard dash with his indoor world record of 5.9 seconds. In 1962, at a collegiate track meet in Miami, Hayes ran a new world record of 9.2 seconds for the 100-yard dash. In 1963, he broke his own record with a time of 9.1. He was the AAU 100-yard dash champion three years running, from 1962 to 1964, and in 1964 was the NCAA champion in the 200-meter dash. The FAMU 400-meter relay team of Robert Hayes, Robert Paremore, Robert Harris, and Alfred Austin would run the fastest time in the collegiate division in 1962 and 1963. Alfred refers to the team as "three Bobs and an Al."

In the 1964 Olympics in Tokyo, Japan, Bob won the 100-meter dash going away, in world-record time. This was an extraordinary achievement against the world's best sprinters.

Yet his greatest race—and arguably the greatest anchor leg in the history of the Olympic Summer Games—came a few days later, when Bob ran the anchor leg for the United States in the 4 x 100 relay. When Bob got the baton, the U.S. team was in sixth place, nearly six yards out of the lead. He took the baton from Dick Stebbins in the passing zone about five yards sooner than usual, and 112 yards from the finish line. The man they proclaimed the

"World's Fastest Human" had a mini United Nations in front of him. First, he had to catch Jamaica. Then Russia, Poland, France. Never mind winning the 4 x 100 relay—Hayes was worried about getting any medal for the United States.

But Bob Hayes, in the words of one observer, "exploded down the track in an eruption of speed never witnessed before or since." He blew past the field in about forty yards and went on to cross the finish line more than three yards clear of the nearest competitor, for a new world record of 39.0 seconds for the 4 x 100 relay. In that anchor leg, he had caught some of the finest sprinters in the world, and one of track and field's great debates is over how fast Hayes really ran that day. Track officials gave various estimates for his time, the slowest being 8.9 seconds but most being at 8.6 and 8.7. Hayes removed any doubt about which athlete would come to define speed for future generations.

Jocelyn Delecour, France's anchor leg runner, famously said before the relay final to Paul Drayton, Hayes' teammate on the open-

The U.S. 4 x 100 meter relay team being awarded the gold medal at the 1964 Olympics: Paul Drayton, Gerry Ashworth, Dick Stebbins, and Bob Hayes.

ing leg, "You can't win. All you have is Bob Hayes." Drayton was able to reply afterwards to Delecour, "Bob Hayes was all we needed."

Ralph Wiley, the revered sports columnist, would write, "The Bullet Man was behind five relay teams when he got the baton on the anchor leg of the 4 x 100-meter relay final in Tokyo. He made up nine meters on the field. Nine meters! He ran his leg in 8.6. That's not running. That's teleportation. That's *Star Trek*."[3]

Bob Hayes was drafted by the Dallas Cowboys as a seventh-round future pick in 1964. I was in the Cotton Bowl late that year, attending a Dallas Cowboys game as an airman of the U.S. Air Force stationed at Carswell Air Force Base, in Fort Worth, Texas. When the Cowboys announcer announced that "Bob Hayes, the World's Fastest Human" was at the game that Sunday, a tremendous yell—well, really a Texas holler—went up from the Cotton Bowl. Most of the crowd had no idea that Bob was a football player who happened to be fast. "The World's Fastest Human" would suffice that day; but soon and very soon Cowboy fans would find out what "World's Fastest Human" really meant. One serious problem for the Cowboys: they had very few quarterbacks on the roster who could get the ball to Hayes in practice. They also did not have defensive backs who could cover him in practice.

Then in 1965 the Cowboys drafted the gun-armed quarterbacks Craig Morton and Roger Staubach (although the latter first had an obligation to the Navy for four years.) When the Cowboys won the 1972 Super Bowl, Bob Hayes became the only person in the history of sports to have won both an Olympic gold medal and a Super Bowl championship ring. He still holds that distinction.

Bob Hayes died much too early at age 59, from several medical ailments, including complications of prostate cancer. More than five thousand people attended his funeral at Bethel Baptist Institutional Church on that Wednesday, September 25, 2002, a veritable who's

More than five thousand people attended Bob Hayes' funeral in 2002.

who in sports and the sports media from around the country. At his death, Bob had been passed over several times for induction in the National Football League Hall of Fame.

National columnist William Rhoden's article in the September 26, 2002, issue of the *New York Times* stated, "Bethel's Reverend Rudolph McKissick Jr., drew people from their seats multiple times during the 100-minute service. But the service was not only about what a great guy Hayes was . . . and it was not all about comforting the family. It was fervor directed at the news media and the invisible men who vote for inductees to the Pro Football Hall of Fame. McKissick was making a pre-emptive strike at the notion that a native son—a world-class football player and sprinter, a man who stumbled in life but got up and finished his race—would be barred from the Hall of Fame in Canton, Ohio. McKissick soared and condemned and preached an angry gospel about those who would judge. The highlight was when Reverend McKissick said the Pro Football Hall of Fame should be shut down for denying Hayes' admittance by focusing on his mistakes instead of his 371 catches for 7,414 yards (20.0 yards per catch) and 71 touchdowns."[4]

It took a few more years after the funeral, but God heard Reverend (later Bishop) Rudolph W. McKissick Jr. Bob Hayes was posthumously elected to the National Football League Hall of Fame in 2009. He was presented by Dallas Cowboys great and fellow Hall of Famer Roger Staubach, and was inducted by his son, Bob Hayes Jr. "Bob Hayes is part of the evolution of the NFL," said Staubach. "Bob had speed and he also had a football sense about him." Staubach would also say that, as long has Hayes was in the lineup, other teams had to make adjustments they would not ordinarily make.[5]

"I know one thing, and I played with him," commented Hall of Fame tight end Mike Ditka. "He changed the game. He made defenses and defensive coordinators work hard to figure out what you had to do to stop him."

Paul Zimmerman of *Sports Illustrated*, who had resigned from the NFL Hall of Fame committee because it snubbed Bob in 2004, wrote of Hayes after his passing: "They followed him into the NFL like rats following the Pied Piper. Olympic sprinters and hurdlers were handed a uniform and told to catch the ball and run away from people, just like Bob Hayes did. Speed is what Hayes brought into the league in 1965, more speed than anyone had ever seen on a football field. And when the rest of the NFL saw how he stretched defenses and forced them to go to all sorts of zones to try to stop him, general managers pored over copies of *Track & Field News* and sent out their invites."

Teams could not cover Bob with just one man and had to devise a zone defense, which meant each defensive back covering a specific area. Think about it; Bob Hayes' speed dictated the introduction of the "zone defense"—an entire new defense in the National Football League—just to cover him! And, as Matthew William Gilbert teammate Ervin Norman would say about Bob, "Speed kills."

Four times Bob was named first- or second-team All-NFL. Three times he led the Cowboys in receptions, including back-to-back titles in 1965 and 1966, when he caught a total of 110 passes for more than 2,200 yards and 25 touchdowns. Hayes was the second player in the history of the franchise to surpass 1,000 yards receiving in a single season, and he did that in his rookie year by finishing with 1,003 yards. During his rookie year, Bob led the team with 46 receptions and set franchise records for total touchdowns (13) and total receiving touchdowns (12). He finished his eleven-year career with 371 receptions for 7,414 yards and 71 touchdowns, giving him an impressive 20 yards-per-catch average (both his career touchdowns and his yards-per-catch average remain franchise records.) He also rushed for 68 yards, gained 581 yards and two touchdowns on 23 kickoff returns, and returned 104 punts for 1,158 yards and 3 touchdowns. His 7,295 receiving yards are the fourth most in Dallas Cowboys history. Bob Hayes is *still* the third leading touchdown-maker in Cowboys history with 76, behind Emmitt Smith and Tony Dorsett. He holds (or held) ten regular-season receiving records, four punt return records, and twenty-two franchise marks overall, making him one of the greatest receivers ever to play for the Cowboys.

When writing about a contemporary sports hero, a Black pioneer, and a friend, you open expanded avenues of anecdotes and stories. Some you seek out, while other stories come to you totally unsolicited. It is usually easy to find a former high school, college, or professional league teammate, or even a former coach to talk with about Bob Hayes, but occasionally you find those nuggets of genuine information that just make you smile.

Andria Daniels Lang is a friend who lived on Jacksonville's Eastside and attended Gilbert (as an underclassman) when Bob was there. While talking with Andria about her uncle, singer and celebrity personality Billy Daniels (the subject of another chapter in this book), Bob Hayes eventually became the focus of our conversation. Andria made several comments that struck me as being sincere, and a significant representation of the pride that Blacks had in Bob as an Olympian during those days of segregation. Knowing an Olympian, especially a hometown Olympian, was not an everyday occurrence. "When Bob went to the Olympics," Andria said, "he took his Eastside community with him." Andria was saying that Bob Hayes carried on his shoulders the hopes and dreams of Jacksonville's Black community generally, and the Eastside Black community specifically, "to do well" in the Olympics . . . and she was profoundly right! Talking with her about "Crow" after all this time—forty-seven years had passed since Bob went to the Olympics—I could sense the pride in her voice. I thought, how many of us know, really know, a world-class athlete who went to the Olympics . . . and who was expected to win a gold medal . . . and did . . . and in fact won two . . . and was a hometown hero?

Andria related a story about the community looking out for Bob during those days. Her dad was Edwin P. Daniels (brother of Billy Daniels) and a member of a men's club called the Eastside Community Club. When it was obvious that Bob would travel to Tokyo, Japan, and represent the United States in the Olympics, the club got busy raising money to help defray the costs of Bob's trip and to make sure he went "right." Going "right" meant having the proper attire to go out of town with friends and strangers. In the Black community during those days, some of us would never think about suitcases and house shoes and bathrobes until we were traveling and spending time with strangers, let alone white strangers. In addition to the days of segregation, those were also the days of true amateur athletics. No appearance fees, no special consideration from the many sportswear companies—at that time, as opposed to now, amateur meant amateur and there were no free clothes. Andria remembers the day when her daddy came home with J. C. Penney packages full of men's stuff. Everything in the bags was for

"Crow." He had house shoes, a bathrobe, underwear, tee shirts, and so on. Bob won his two gold medals of course, and also went to the Olympics the "right" way. Black men in his community saw to that.

Bob Hayes' return to Jacksonville as a triumphant Olympic champion native son with two Olympic gold medals should have been a major national news story. Yet it took an effort by then-reporter for the *Florida Times-Union* Jessie Lynne-Kerr to keep racism from rearing its head again, and to make sure that the Jacksonville paper did not relegate Bob's triumph to the newspaper's section of "News For and About the Colored People of Jacksonville."[6] (Jessie, who passed away on April 28, 2011, told me about her efforts when she attended one of my appearances at a book festival.)

Bob rode through downtown Jacksonville in a parade celebrating his triumphant return as a native son Olympic champion with two gold medals on a ribbon around his neck. But in Jacksonville, Florida, in 1964, this American hero still could not drink out of the whites-only water fountains downtown, or stay at a downtown hotel, or receive congratulations at a downtown restaurant. It did not matter how great his hometown adulation; it did not matter that he was revered by the international community as a track superstar, and Olympic champion; it did not matter that he now carried the title of "World's Fast Human." This was still the era of segregation, when the color of your skin trumped momentous personal and competitive accomplishments, and the recently passed civil rights bill made absolutely no difference.

Bob Hayes proved to the world that he was an athlete like nobody before him. This acclaimed athlete, who brought glory to a segregated Southern city in spite of itself; this "World's Fastest Human"; this internationally acclaimed track and field legend; this awe-inspiring, record-setting, NFL Hall of Famer; this magnificent native son from the Black Eastside Community of Jacksonville — Robert "Crow" Hayes remains one of a kind.

Dr. Mary McLeod Bethune in her home, circa 1930.

5

Dr. Mary McLeod Bethune

I leave you love. I leave you hope. I leave you the challenge of developing confidence in one another. I leave you respect for the use of power. I leave you faith. I leave you racial dignity.

> —Dr. Mary McLeod Bethune
> Founder, Bethune-Cookman College
> (now Bethune-Cookman University)

Before Dr. Johnnetta Cole (president emerita, Spelman and Bennett Colleges), Dr. Donna Oliver (former president, Mississippi Valley State University), Dr. Joyce Brown (president, State University of New York), Dr. Ruth Simmons (former president, Brown University), and Dr. Shirley Ann Jackson (president, Rensselaer Polytechnic Institute) — before these great Black female college presidents, there was Dr. Mary McLeod Bethune.

Dr. Bethune was one of the great educators of the United States — a leader of women, a distinguished adviser to several American presidents, and a powerful champion of racial equality. In Dr. Bethune's visionary insight, education was the key for Blacks in the world of tomorrow. Yet her path to the freedom of one's mind was filled with the routine racist stumbling blocks of her era.

Dr. Bethune was a visionary, with a mission to start a college for Blacks, literally "from scratch." She knew and understood that to make equality a reality, education, including an institution of higher education, must be a part of the solution. How did a Black female decide to found and develop a college in those ridiculously abhorrent days of racism and segregation, let alone find those who would contribute to underwrite her dream?

Mary McLeod Bethune, the fifteenth of seventeen children, was born in 1875 in Mayesville, South Carolina, to Samuel and Patsy McLeod.[1] Her parents were both former slaves, and most of her siblings had been born into slavery. Mary helped her parents on the family farm and when she was eleven years old entered a Presbyterian mission school. Later she attended Scotia Seminary, a school for African American girls in Concord, North Carolina, on a scholarship. After graduating from Scotia in 1893, she attended Dwight Moody's Institute for Home and Foreign Missions (now the Moody Bible Institute) in Chicago, hoping to become a missionary in Africa. When she was informed that she would not be able to follow this course because Black missionaries were not needed, she instead decided to teach. Bethune's first position as a teacher was for a brief time at her former elementary school in Sumter County.[2]

In 1896, she began teaching at Haines Normal and Industrial Institute, which was part of a Presbyterian mission in Augusta, Georgia. Haines had been founded by Lucy Craft Laney, a former slave who ran her school with a Christian missionary zeal. She emphasized character and practical education for girls, but also accepted the boys who showed up on the steps of her school eager to learn. Laney's mission was to help Black people to overcome the image of living with "shame and crime" through Christian moral education. Bethune spent only a year at Laney's school, but said of her experience, "I was so impressed with her fearlessness, her amazing touch in every respect, an energy that seemed inexhaustible, and her mighty power to command respect and admiration from

Unless WE Tell It . . . It Never Gets Told!

her students and all who knew her. She handled her domain with the art of a master."

Deeply influenced by Laney, Bethune adopted many of her educational philosophies, which included seeking to improve the conditions of Black people by educating primarily women: "I believe that the greatest hope for the development of my race lies in training our women thoroughly and practically."

While Mary was an instructor at Kindell Institute in Sumpter, South Carolina, in 1897-1898, she met Albertus Bethune, whom she later married. Coyden Harold Uggams (grandfather of entertainer Leslie Uggams), a visiting minister from Palatka, Florida, urged Dr. Bethune to move to Palatka and manage the new mission school he was starting. So in 1899 she moved to Florida with her son, followed by her husband. In Palatka she taught at the mission school and visited prisoners in the county jail, reading and singing to them. She tried to help the prisoners in any way she could, and worked to free those who were not guilty. Because money was tight, she supplemented the family income by selling life insurance for the Afro-American Life Insurance Company in Jacksonville, Florida.

Bethune began her career as an educator in earnest when she rented a two-story frame building in Daytona Beach, Florida, and embarked upon the difficult task of establishing a school for Black girls. Thus began the Daytona Educational and Industrial Training School for Negro Girls, founded in an era when most African American children received little or no education. Her school opened in October 1904, with six pupils—five girls and her own son. There was no equipment; crates were used for desks and charcoal took the place of pencils; and ink came from crushed elderberries. At first, Mrs. Bethune was teacher, administrator, comptroller, and custodian. Later she was able to secure a staff, many of whom worked loyally for many years. To finance and expand the school, Bethune and her pupils baked pies and made ice cream to sell to

Mary McLeod Bethune with students from her Daytona Educational and Industrial Training School for Negro Girls, 1905.

nearby construction gangs. In addition to her regular classes, Bethune organized classes for the children of turpentine workers. In these ways she satisfied her desire to serve as a missionary.

As the school at Daytona progressed, it became necessary to secure an adequate financial base, and Bethune began to seek financial aid in earnest. In 1912 she interested James M. Gamble of the Procter and Gamble Company of Cincinnati, Ohio, who contributed financially to the school and served as chairman of its board of trustees until his death.

In an era when not even African American men could vote, a frustrated Mary Bethune had to watch powerlessly as white-dominated organizations marched and protested nationwide. But in 1920, after passage of the Nineteenth Amendment, the time for action had come. Bethune believed that if African American women were to vote, they could bring about change. Riding a bicycle she had used when she was raising money for her school, she went door to

Unless WE Tell It . . . It Never Gets Told!

door raising money to pay the poll tax. Her night classes provided a means for African Americans to learn to read well enough to pass the literacy test. Soon a hundred potential voters had qualified. The night before the election, eighty members of the Ku Klux Klan confronted Bethune, warning her against preparing Black citizens to vote. Bethune did not back down, and the men left without causing any harm. The following day, Bethune led the procession of a hundred African Americans to the polls, all voting for the first time.

The story of her defiance of the Klan spread, and soon she was in demand as a speaker for the rights of African Americans. Meeting many prominent people was in some ways an eye-opener for her. She met W. E. B. Du Bois, and after hearing him comment that, because of his race, he couldn't even check out one of his own books from a Southern library, she made her own school library available to the general public, the only free source of reading material for Blacks in Florida at that time.[3]

In 1923, Bethune's school for girls merged with a school for boys, the Cookman Institute of Jacksonville, Florida. Established in 1872, the Cookman Institute was the first—and for a long time the only—institution of higher education for African Americans in the state of Florida. Specializing in the religious and academic preparation of teachers, it was among the first of America's many historically Black colleges and universities. The Cookman Institute, then located at Beaver and Hogan streets, had been founded by the Reverend Samuel Darnell, who had originally moved to Jacksonville to serve as pastor of Ebenezer Methodist-Episcopal Church. Named for another Methodist preacher, the Reverend Alfred Cookman of Ocean Grove, New Jersey, whose gift helped establish the school, the Cookman Institute was acclaimed for the scope of its rigorous curriculum.

Under the leadership of Reverend Darnell, the school served thousands of young Black men and women until it was destroyed in the great Jacksonville fire of 1901. Before rebuilding, the school changed locations in order to be a little farther from the center of town. Reverend Cookman, a friend of Reverend Darnell, helped raise money to rebuild the school at its current site, and after rebuilding, the enrollment was about two hundred and fifty. The Cookman Institute for Boys had classes in all the elementary grades and in the four high school grades. There were special courses in normal training, music, domestic science, sewing, and public speaking, and eventually they added sewing, shoemaking, printing, business, and agriculture.

When Bethune's Daytona school and the Cookman Institute merged, the new coeducational school became known as Bethune-Cookman Collegiate Institute. A year later, the Institute became affiliated with the United Methodist Church; by 1931 it had evolved into a junior college named Bethune-Cookman College. In 1941, the Florida Board of Education approved a four-year baccalaureate program offering liberal arts and teacher education. Bethune stepped down as president in 1942, although she returned to the presidency for a year in 1946.

In 1930, journalist Ida Tarbell included Mary McLeod Bethune on her list of America's greatest women, ranking her at number ten. Dr. Bethune worked for the election of Franklin D. Roosevelt in 1932, and became a member of Roosevelt's "Black Cabinet," an informal group of policy advisors who shared the concerns of Black people with the Roosevelt administration while at the same time spreading Roosevelt's message to the Black population, most of whom had traditionally been Republican voters.

In 1935, Dr. Bethune received the NAACP's coveted Spingarn Medal, a symbol of distinguished achievement. She gained national recognition in 1936, when President Franklin D. Roosevelt appointed her director of African American affairs in the National Youth Administration and a special adviser on minority affairs; she served for eight years, supervising the expansion of employment opportunities and recreational facilities for Black youth throughout the United States. She also served as a special assistant to the Secretary of War during World War II, and in the course of her government assignments she became a close friend of Eleanor Roosevelt.

Dr. Mary McLeod Bethune was the only Black woman present at the founding of the United Nations in San Francisco in 1948, representing the NAACP with W. E. B. Du Bois and Walter Francis White. In 1949 she became the first woman to be given the Medal of Honor and Merit, Haiti's highest award, presented at the Haitian Exposition. She was the U.S. emissary to the induction of President William V. S. Tubman of Liberia in 1949. She later served as president of the prestigious National Association of Colored Women's Clubs and founded the National Council of Negro Women.

Upon her death, in May 1955, columnist Louis E. Martin said, "She gave out faith and hope as if they were pills and she some sort of doctor." Not only is her home at Bethune-Cookman University in Daytona Beach a National Historic Landmark, but her house in Logan Circle in Washington, D.C., is preserved by the National Park Service as a National Historic Site. You will find a sculpture of her in Lincoln Park in Washington, D.C.

Dr. Bethune often used the flower garden to illustrate the principle of equality. "Flowers are many colors", she would say, "but they all grow together in harmony in the garden." In Holland, she was given bulbs of the black tulip and in Switzerland she saw a black rose for the first time. She was captivated by it. She ordered black roses for the Bethune campus. The black rose became her trademark, and people started calling her "the Black Rose."

Markeisha Coney Powell teaches in the Duval County public school system. I asked her why she decided to attend Bethune-Cookman College. "At seventeen years old, I knew that in order to accomplish anything in life, college was mandatory, so I decided to take the hour-long journey from Jacksonville to Daytona Beach, Florida, and Bethune-Cookman College. Once I enrolled there, I could feel and see the life and richness of the institution everywhere; signs, posters, and great pictures of history. Not to mention *the house*—the home that had belonged to Mary McLeod Bethune. It was beautiful, enriched with history and stories, and even Dr. Bethune's original clothing, laid out upon her bed. Bethune-Cookman exposed me to the history and legacy of a historic institution of higher education and exposed me to the history and legacy of a great visionary. Notwithstanding a person's resources, it is almost a shame not to attend college when you fully understand what Dr. Bethune went through so that many of us could have a college education. She was such a great lady, a great person, and a great advocate for education and young people."

Arthur Ray Brinson, former president of the National Alumni Association of Bethune-Cookman: "Dr. Bethune was not my attraction to Bethune-Cookman College per se. There was not a long line of college recruiters beating down my door with scholarship offers when I graduated from Carver Heights High School in Leesburg, Florida. In fact, Johnson Junior College (now Lake Sumpter Community College), which had just opened in Leesburg, and Bethune-Cookman were my only options. I received enough money to attend college via scholarships provided by my high school principal, S. T. E. Pinckney, who was an associate trustee at Bethune-Cookman. After I enrolled in 1965, I started to learn more about this phenomenal woman, and quite frankly fell in love with her. She was one of the most influential and powerful women of her time. She is at the top of my list of the greatest Americans in the history of this country! Although arguably lacking in political and technical knowledge, she knew the human spirit well, and she knew that all people were God's chosen and deserved the best the world had to offer. She knew how to go after what she believed in. She was an exemplary orator, a skilled negotiator, and a person of tremendous integrity."

Without the insight of this heroic visionary who saw the need for an institution to educate "Negro boys and girls," thousands of this country's best minds would not have been trained, and their resulting accomplishments would not have been realized. What astronomical odds she faced and overcame to found Bethune-Cookman College. I have cited comments from former students as an example of how graduates of Bethune-Cookman feel about Dr. Bethune. Sure, alumni throughout the country can say that about their colleges, except, no other college was founded in the early twentieth century, during days of appalling racism and segregation, by a Black female determined to help young Black college students brighten the future of this country's leadership.

Bethune-Cookman celebrated its hundredth anniversary in 2004, and three years later achieved university status with the launching of a master's degree program in transformative leadership. The university currently sits on 82.2 acres in Daytona Beach, located on Mary McLeod Bethune Boulevard (formerly Second Avenue). There are now forty buildings, serving to help educate more than three thousand students from almost every state in the United States and thirty-five countries. The university offers thirty-five majors in six major colleges: arts and humanities, business, education, nursing, social science, and science engineering. The university's website states that "the vision of the founder remains in full view over one hundred years later. The institution prevails in order that others might improve their heads, hearts, and hands."[4]

In 1985, the U.S. Postal Service issued the eighth stamp in its *Black Heritage* series in honor of Dr. Mary McLeod Bethune.

Dr. Johnnetta Betsch Cole, 2009.

6

Dr. Johnnetta Betsch Cole

We are for difference: for respecting difference, for allowing difference, for encouraging difference, until difference no longer makes a difference.

—Dr. Johnnetta Cole

If you had all the money necessary to start a college or a university, you would do two things. The second thing you would do is to acquire the land and build the necessary buildings. The first thing you would do is to pray that Dr. Johnnetta Betsch Cole is available to be the president of your new college, and that she would accept the job. For, with the regal educational splendor of Dr. Johnnetta Cole, you would have the very best.

Johnnetta was born in Jacksonville, Florida, where her family had long been established as leaders of the Black community. In 1901 her great-grandfather, Abraham Lincoln Lewis, cofounded the Afro-American Life Insurance Company in Jacksonville; Johnnetta's mother, Mary Betsch, and her father, John Betsch, were both employed by "the Afro." Mary Betsch had worked as an English teacher and registrar at Edward Waters College prior to becoming a vice-president of Afro-American Life Insurance.

As a child, Johnnetta Betsch met such influential Blacks as Mary McLeod Bethune, and she studied Black history in a public library named for her own great-grandfather. She was bright and talented, and began college through an early admissions program at Fisk University in 1952.

While at Fisk, she had frequent contact with Arna Bontemps, a noted writer who also held the job of Fisk's librarian. Seeing this respected author in a work setting was important to Johnnetta because, as she later wrote in a column for *McCall's* magazine, "When our . . . heroes are portrayed as bigger than life, living, working, accomplishing beyond the realm of the normal, when they are depicted as perfect human beings, they are placed so far from us that it seems impossible that we could ever touch them or mirror who they are in our own lives."

In 1953 Johnnetta transferred to Oberlin College, where her sister, MarVyne, was majoring in music. She would later earn a master's degree and a Ph.D. in anthropology from Northwestern University.

In 1970 Dr. Cole became the director of the new Black Studies Department at Washington State University, at the time one of only two university departments for Black Studies in the country. She taught in the Department of Anthropology at the University of Massachusetts Amherst from 1970 to 1983, also serving as associate provost of undergraduate education from 1981 to 1983 and playing a pivotal role in the development of the university's W. E. B. Du Bois Department of Afro-American Studies. In 1983 she joined the faculty of Hunter College, where she directed the Latin American and Caribbean Studies Program, and she continued at Hunter College while serving on the graduate faculty of the City University of New York.

In 1987 Dr. Cole made history by becoming the first African American woman to serve as president of Spelman College. At her inauguration as the college's seventh president, Bill Cosby and his wife, Camille, made a gift of twenty million dollars to Spelman, the largest single gift from individuals to any historically Black college or university.

From the year Dr. Cole took office, Spelman's freshman classes have had the highest SAT averages of any of the historically Black colleges or universities. In 1992 *U.S. News & World Report* gave Spelman a coveted number-one rating in its annual survey of "Best College Buys," and also ranked Spelman the number-one regional liberal arts college in the South. That same year, Johnnetta Cole was named to President-elect Bill Clinton's transition team as the Cluster Coordinator for Education, Labor, and the Arts and Humanities.

In 1996 *Money* magazine listed Spelman as the best historically Black college, the best women's college, and the seventh-best college of any kind in the United States. Under Dr. Cole's leadership, the college completed a capital campaign that brought in 113.8 million dollars, at that time the largest sum that had ever been raised by a historically Black college or university.

After ten outstanding years as president of Spelman, Dr. Cole returned to teaching in 1998, as Presidential Distinguished Professor of Anthropology, Women's Studies, and African American Studies at Emory University.

In 2002 Dr. Cole accepted an appointment to serve as the president of Bennett College for Women in Greensboro, North Carolina. Like Spelman, Bennett is a historically Black college; Spelman and Bennett are the only two institutions in the United States that focus specifically on the higher education of African American women.

Dr. Cole has conducted research in Africa, the Caribbean, and the United States, and has authored and edited several books—including her 1993 volume, *Conversations: Straight Talk with America's Sister President*, and two textbooks used in classrooms throughout the country—as well as scores of scholarly articles. She is now president emerita of both Bennett College for Women and Spelman College, the only individual to have served as president of the United

States' two historically Black colleges for women. She is also professor emerita at Emory University.

In addition to her academic duties, Dr. Cole has served on the boards of directors of Home Depot, Merck & Co., Inc., and Nations-Bank South, and was the first woman elected to the board of Coca-Cola Enterprises. From 2004 to 2006, she was chair of the board of United Way of America, the first African American to serve in that position. She is a fellow of the American Anthropological Association and the American Academy of Arts and Sciences, serves on the boards of trustees of the American Association of Art Museum Directors and of Gregory University in Uturu, Nigeria, and is a member of the Scholarly Advisory Board for the Smithsonian Institution's National Museum of African American History and Culture, the construction of which will be completed on the National Mall in 2016. She was appointed the director of the Smithsonian National Museum of African Art in March 2009.

Dr. Cole has been awarded sixty-one honorary degrees, and is the recipient of awards from a broad spectrum of civic and cultural organizations too numerous to list. She is a member of Delta Sigma Theta Sorority, Inc., the Links, Inc., and the National Council of Negro Women. In 2012, in Uturu, Nigeria, His Royal Highness Eze Cyril Ibe conferred upon Dr. Cole an Igbo chieftaincy title of ADAOHA (Daughter of All). In a nationally televised ceremony at Washington, D.C.'s Warner Theater in February 2015, Dr. Johnnetta Betsch Cole was presented with Black Entertainment Television's Honors 2015 Education Award for her lifelong work.

Dr. Cole is married to James D. Staton Jr., and is the mother of three sons and a stepson, and the grandmother of three grandchildren. Dr. Cole's late sister, MaVynee Betsch was an opera singer, an environmentalist, and an activist, who was known as "the Beach Lady." Her brother, John Thomas Betsch Jr., is a jazz musician in Paris, France.

Unless WE Tell It . . . It Never Gets Told!

An Interview with Dr. Johnnetta Cole

In 1970, while working at the Public Broadcasting Service Channel 7 (WJCT) in Jacksonville as one of the thirteen original Corporation for Public Broadcasting Fellows, I interviewed Dr. Cole when she visited her family in Jacksonville en route to her appointment as the director of the new Black Studies Department at Washington State University. Now, more than four decades later, I was interviewing her again. I started our conversation by asking Dr. Cole to look back over those years.

RH: *Compare your developing the Black Studies Program at Washington State then and the state of Black Studies today. Is there still a need for Black Studies?*

Dr. Cole: If we did not have Black Studies or African American Studies, we would need to invent it. We still do not have sufficient attention to the complexity and the diversity of the African American experience. So the job is not done.

RH: *What do you say to young Black students who say history is boring, yet know very little about Black history? How do you teach them Black history?*

Dr. Cole: I rather think there is no such thing as an ineducable child or adult. But there is such a thing as a non-effective teacher. In fact, Black history or any history can be boring. And unfortunately, when teachers do not somehow feel the passion of the subject matter, it is hard for the students to feel it. When you want to teach our young people that history matters, one way you teach history is to ask students whether they have any interest in being remembered. You should try and personalize history. Or pose the question, "Is what you are doing today anyway connected with what you did yesterday?" Instead of screaming at our young people about how they should be respectful of all these folk who went before them, personalize it and ask them if they would really wish to cease to be. Because to ignore Black history, you are asking that an entire race of people and their experiences cease to be.

RH: *What is unique about Spelman College and Bennett College and how do you ask someone for twenty million dollars?*

Dr. Cole: The word "unique" is misused at times, but Spelman and Bennett are indeed unique as the only two institutions of higher education for Black women in the United States. They are in a special place. [Dr. Cole referred me to one of her favorite books, a Black Women's Studies text entitled *But Some of Us Are Brave: All the Women Are White, All the Blacks Are Men.*] There is distinctiveness about this coming together of race and gender that produces African American women. Here we have two institutions of higher education that have as their mission the education of these women—as W. E. B. Du Bois would say, these women of "the darker hue."

RH: *How do you ask for twenty million dollars? [As mentioned above, Dr. Bill Cosby and his wife, Camille, gave twenty million dollars to Spelman College when Dr. Cole was president, the largest gift that has ever been given to a historically Black college or university.]*

Dr. Cole: I did not ask for the twenty million dollars, which is the extraordinary part of the gift. Dr. Bill Cosby called my office. I was on the way to a senior staff meeting and my assistant, Ms. Jackie Marshall, stopped me and said, "I know you are running late Dr. Cole, but you might want to take this call from Dr. Cosby." I picked up the phone, and, after exchanging pleasantries, Dr. Cosby said that he and his wife, Camille, had watched me and Dr. Henry Ponder, the president of Fisk University, on television last night. I jokingly told him that I watch him on television; he doesn't watch me on television.

I then remembered that Dr. Ponder and I had taped an interview several weeks earlier. I said to Dr. Bill that I was not sure that

I, as an alumna of Fisk, had ever thanked him and Dr. Camille for their gift of two and a half million dollars to Fisk University. It had saved Fisk.

His next words were, "Well, Camille and I were wondering, do you think you can use twenty million dollars at Spelman?" Now I was still focusing on the Fisk gift. My next words were, "Dr. Bill, two million for Spelman?" His next words were, "Girl, can't you hear? I said twenty million!" I was flabbergasted. His gift broke all the rules of development, and of soliciting.

RH: *What are the trials and the future of historically Black colleges and universities?*

Dr. Cole: Well, I am not prepared to make a prediction, but these are unusually challenging times for our institutions. The road had never been easy. But now when we are in an economic downturn and when raising money for any not for profit group is difficult, our historically Black colleges and universities are really feeling the pinch. What I can imagine is that one of these days we will all wake up and become more creative. We are going to do things that we have not been willing to do before. For example, perhaps consider some mergers of two or three struggling institutions into a larger university system with different campuses. We are just going to have to get creative.

RH: *Your accomplishments and awards are many, and there are those who would prefer having dinner with you as easily as any international dignitary or celebrity, including President Obama. Who would you like to have dinner with . . . if there is anyone left . . . and why?*

Dr. Cole: I would choose to have dinner with the three women who shared the 2011 Nobel Peace Prize. [The Nobel Peace Prize for 2011 was awarded to three women from Africa and the Arab world in acknowledgment of their nonviolent role in promoting peace, democracy and gender equality. They were the first women to win the prize since Wangari Maathai of Kenya was named as the laureate in 2004. Most of the recipients in the award's 110-year history have been men, and the 2011 decision seemed designed to give impetus to the fight for women's rights around the world.] Two of these women have a special place in my heart because they are Liberian, and I did my doctoral fieldwork in Liberia. They are Liberian President Ellen Johnson Sirleaf and peace activist Ms. Leymah Gbowee. The third, of course, is Tawakkol Karman of Yemen, a pro-democracy campaigner. What compels me to want to have dinner with the two Liberian women is their relation to grassroots organizing, including the community work of Ms. Gbowee and the political understanding and sophistication of President Sirleaf, who is the only female president of any of the fifty-five countries of Africa.

And while I know the experiences of women of color must be understood within the context of their particular country and culture, these women can teach us so much about change, about leadership, about the place of spirituality in our lives, and about the role of transforming a nation.

RH: *If you were president for a day—notwithstanding the blatant obstructionism—what would be your "One Day Agenda"?*

Dr. Cole: The first thing I would do is acknowledge to myself and to anyone listening that, while a day matters, change is not so much an event, but a process. Change can be launched—and even culminated—in a day, but it takes a much longer journey to get to where one needs to be. So I would walk into my day with pretty humble expectations.

But one of the things I would want to do, is make it clear that no president, no matter what country, no matter what stage of a country's development, no president alone can do what needs to be done. You can be as charismatic and political savvy as the late

Nelson Mandela, you can be as wealthy as the Sultan of Oman . . . you can hold a position of great power like President Barack Obama . . . but we have got to understand that although presidents are necessary, they are not sufficient instruments by themselves for positive change. Maybe I would just spend my day trying to get that message across, and the next day we could get down to our collective agenda.

RH: *What is left on your lifetime achievement list of "Things To Do"?*

Dr. Cole: That's tough, because I have been incredibly blessed to do with others what I have done so far. My list is not a long list. I have to struggle to see what is on it. I think before I would take on incredible never-done-before things, I would like to do even better the things I have already been doing. Figure out how my community service can be even more effective. Figure out how I can use with others that powerful force called education. Figure out how I can be a better mom, grandmom, wife, sister, friend. So I think I would like to stay on my current path and walk it more effectively.

RH: *Taking the title of one of your books, what is your "Boldest Dream for America"?*

Dr. Cole: It is hard to respond to that question without being rhetorical. But it is certainly that American would live up to what she said she would do and absolutely what she has the possibility to be. And while some days that seems to be a fleeting dream, there are other days when I see that happening.

RH: *What can or should we expect from the National Museum of African Art?*

Dr. Cole: Everybody ought to expect a lot. This is a museum for everybody. If one would just go back far enough, no matter your color, your so-called race, your gender, your sexual orientation, your age, your physical ability or mental ability, your nationality if you go back far enough . . . you are an African. Africa is the only place that can honestly claim to be the cradle of all humanity. This is not my agenda; it should be everyone's agenda.

Some folk are either not aware that Africa is the place of the first tool, the first language, the first art, the first human—or they don't care. Then I would have to say the National Museum of African Art would help people to care. Secondly, and in addition to making the Museum a place everybody owns, we need to continue to do our work through exhibitions, education, and outreach to help people rethink how they think about Africa. Because the number of misconceptions and the amount of ignorance is startling, we have a lot of work to do, but it is happening.

RH: *Many have described America as "post-racial," with a blind eye to racism and existing discriminations. What is your response to a "post-racial America"?*

Dr. Cole: Let me say, "I wish it were so!" Frankly, I think it is quite naive to assume that the long-held and deeply entrenched patterns of racial inequality in our country would just go away as a result of the election of the first African American to the presidency of the United States. At the same time, I do not want to minimize the significance of the fact that for the first time in the history of the USA, there is an African American family in the White House—a place that was built in part by enslaved Black folks.

As I listened to Dr. Cole's answers to my questions, I thought I would be foolish to try and paraphrase what she had said rather than to repeat her answers word for word. Her eloquent responses did not require a lot of follow-up questions by me. I conducted the interview listening to every word as a good interviewer should and was rather proud of myself. I thoroughly enjoyed every minute of my interview with Dr. Cole.

Dr. Cole is not only the voice of wisdom; she is also a voice of education, a voice of knowledge, a voice of leadership. It is quite easy to see why Dr. Johnnetta Betsch Cole is a Black pioneer and a Black she-ro, with a voice that has had an impact on this country and an intelligence that has played a role on the international stage.

Her life is a testament and a testimony to the hymn "May the works I've done speak for me." Her works shout volumes. Her works shout to the highest rooftops. Her prodigious works shout to every mountaintop you can name . . . to the Alleghenies of Pennsylvania . . . to the snowcapped Rockies of Colorado . . . to the curvaceous slopes of California . . . to Georgia's Stone Mountain . . . to Tennessee's Lookout Mountain . . . even to every hill and molehill of Mississippi . . . and to every mountainside that Dr. King talked about in his "I Have A Dream" speech on the National Mall in Washington, D.C., in 1963.

Dr. Johnnetta Betsch Cole is what the Civil Rights Movement was all about: to give our greatest and our best an opportunity to lead this country. In spite of the "dark hue" of her skin, she took her opportunity to "walk through the door" many years ago, and in the process positively impacted our young people, our future brain trust. She continues to give her very best, and for that we are all eternally grateful.

Thurgood Marshall in front of the Supreme Court, mid-1950s.

7

Brown vs. Board of Education
and the Struggle for School Integration

We conclude that, in the field of public education, the doctrine of "separate but equal" has no place. Separate educational facilities are inherently unequal. Therefore, we hold that the plaintiffs and others similarly situated for whom the actions have been brought are, by reason of the segregation complained of, deprived of the equal protection of the laws guaranteed by the Fourteenth Amendment.

— Chief Justice Earl Warren,
   reading from the unanimous decision in
   Brown vs. the Topeka, Kansas, Board of Education

No one issue produced heroes and achievements—as well as negative and virulent racist reactions—like the fight over school integration. When the U.S. Supreme Court issued its monumental ruling on school segregation in *Brown vs. the Topeka, Kansas, Board of Education* on May 17, 1954, with a unanimous (9–0) decision stating that "separate educational facilities are inherently unequal," school integration started its determined journey into public education.

The key holding of the Court was that, even if segregated Black and white schools were of equal quality in facilities and teachers, segregation by itself was harmful to Black students and unconstitutional. The justices found that a significant psychological and social disadvantage was dealt to Black children from the nature of segregation itself, drawing on research conducted by Kenneth Clark, assisted by June Shagaloff. This was vital because the question was not whether the schools were "equal," which under *Plessy vs. Ferguson* they nominally should have been, but whether the doctrine of "separate but equal" was constitutional. The justices answered with a strong "no."

The Court also held that school segregation violated the Equal Protection and Due Process clauses of the Fourteenth Amendment. The following year the Court ordered desegregation "with all deliberate speed." Although school desegregation cases were different in different places, the vitriolic reactions were very much the same.

THURGOOD MARSHALL

Born in Baltimore, Maryland, Thurgood Marshall graduated with honors from Lincoln University in Pennsylvania. His exclusion from the University of Maryland School of Law due to racial discrimination marked a turning point in his life. As a result, and although offered a scholarship to Harvard Law School, he instead opted to attend the Howard University Law School, graduating first in his class in 1933.[1]

Attorney Charles Hamilton Houston, who became known as "The Man Who Killed Jim Crow," and who played a role in nearly every civil rights case before the Supreme Court between 1930 and the 1954 *Brown vs. Board of Education* decision, persuaded Marshall to leave private law practice and join the NAACP legal staff in New York. In 1939, Marshall became the first director of the NAACP Legal Defense and Educational Fund, Inc.

Between 1934 and 1961, Marshall traveled for the NAACP across the United States, and principally throughout the South. He represented clients whenever a dispute involved questions of racial justice—from trials for common crimes to appellate advocacy—raising the most intricate matters of constitutional law. These cases include *Smith v. Allwright* (1944), which invalidated the so-called white primary (the practice of barring blacks from the Democratic Party primary in Texas where that party controlled state government); and *Shelley v. Kraemer* (1948), which prohibited state courts from enforcing racially restrictive real estate covenants. His advocacy and worked earned him the title of "Mr. Civil Rights."

Thurgood Marshall argued thirty-two cases before the U.S. Supreme Court, prevailing in twenty-nine of them. In 1950, as an attorney for the NAACP, he brought two important cases before the Supreme Court, each involving racial segregation at the college level. He successfully convinced the Court that both the University of Texas and the University of Oklahoma had violated the Constitution by denying fair treatment, respectively, to black applicant Heman Sweatt and student George McLaurin. Later, in 1954, Marshall and the NAACP pulled together five class-action lawsuits under the title *Brown et al. vs. Board of Education of Topeka et al.*, each calling for an end to segregation at the pre-college level.

In 1965, President Lyndon B. Johnson appointed him to be Solicitor General, and in 1967 nominated him to a seat on the Supreme Court. Thurgood Marshall was approved by the Senate as the first Black Justice of the U.S. Supreme Court, a position which he held for a quarter of a century, retiring in 1991. Marshall died in 1993.

DAISY BATES AND THE LITTLE ROCK NINE

On the morning of September 23, 1957, under escort from the U.S. Army's 101st Airborne Division, nine Black students entered all-white Central High School in Little Rock, Arkansas. Three weeks earlier, Governor Orval Faubus had directly questioned the authority of the federal court system and the legitimacy of desegregation.

Daisy Bates, below right, and the Little Rock Nine, 1960.

He then joined local whites in resisting integration by surrounding the school with troops of the Arkansas National Guard to prevent its federal court-ordered racial integration. The nine Black students—"the Little Rock Nine," recruited and led by civil rights pioneer Daisy Bates—were blocked by the guardsmen from entering the school. The courageous students of the Little Rock Nine were: Ernest Green (who in 1958 would be the first Black student to graduate from Central High School), Carlotta Walls Lanier, Minnijean Brown Trickey, Jefferson Thomas, Elizabeth Eckford, Terrence Roberts (later to become Dr. Terrence Roberts), Gloria Ray Karlmark, Thelma Mothershed-Wair, and Melba Pattillo Beals.

After a tense standoff, President Dwight D. Eisenhower federalized the Arkansas National Guard and sent a thousand army paratroopers to Little Rock to enforce the court order and to escort the nine students into the school. This event, broadcast across the nation and world, was the first important test for the implementation of the U.S. Supreme Court's historic *Brown vs. Board of Education* decision of 1954, and Arkansas became the symbol of state resistance to integration. The crisis at Little Rock's Central High School forced the nation to resolve to enforce Black civil rights in the face of massive Southern defiance during the years following the *Brown* decision, and it showed America that the U.S. President could and would enforce court orders with federal troops. One of the Nine later remembered, "After three full days inside Central, I knew that integration is a much bigger word than I thought."

Born in 1914, Daisy Lee Gatson grew up in the small Arkansas town of Huttig.[2] In 1942 she married L. C. Bates (1901–1980), a newspaperman who had attended Alcorn A&M College (now Alcorn State University) in Mississippi, and Wilberforce University in Ohio. L. C. Bates had worked for newspapers in Colorado, Missouri, California, and Tennessee, and after the two were married, they settled in Little Rock. There they established the weekly *Arkansas State Press*, the first issue of which appeared on May 9, 1941.

This newspaper became the largest and most influential Black paper in the state. In 1952 Daisy Bates was elected president of the Arkansas State Conference of NAACP branches, and it was in this capacity that she became the advisor to the Little Rock Nine. (I had the good fortune to first meet Mrs. Bates in Jacksonville in 1958 when she spoke to an NAACP mass meeting.) Because of their involvement in the integration of Central High, advertiser boycotts and the consequent loss of revenue forced the couple to close the *Arkansas State Press* in 1959. In 1960, L. C. Bates became NAACP field director for the state, a post that he held until his retirement in 1971.

In the 1980s Little Rock paid high tribute—both to Daisy Bates and to the new era she helped to initiate, by naming the Daisy Bates Elementary School after her. The state of Arkansas designated the third Monday in February as an official state holiday: "George Washington's Birthday and Daisy Gatson Bates Day."

Daisy Bates died on November 4, 1999. She was the first—and to this day is still the only—Black person to lie in state in the Arkansas Capitol, the building once occupied by Governor Orval Faubus. On that same day, the Little Rock Nine were honored at the White House by President Bill Clinton, the first U.S. President from Arkansas. Daisy Bates is featured on the 2009 *Civil Rights Pioneers* issue of U.S. postage stamps.

DONAL GODFREY AND IONA GODFREY KING

The school desegregation case in Jacksonville, Florida, was originally referred to as the Braxton case because it was initiated by plaintiff Sadie Braxton on behalf of her children, Sharon and Daly Braxton. It was filed in federal court in 1960 by Jacksonville NAACP attorney Earl M. Johnson. In August 1962, U.S. District Judge Bryan Simpson found that the Duval County school system was segregated, and ordered the School Board to submit a plan to bring about integration.

In September 1963, a year after Judge Simpson issued the order to integrate the Jacksonville school system, Iona Godfrey King enrolled her son, Donal, in Lackawanna Elementary School. Donal was one of thirteen Black first-graders to enter formerly all-white Jacksonville schools that year as a result of the order to desegregate schools. Although he was the only Black student at Lackawanna Elementary, Mrs. King was not part of a concerted desegregation effort. She simply felt that sending her son to his neighborhood school was the reasonable thing to do. "My child had a right to go to a public school that was five blocks away," Iona said. "He's an American. Why can't he go to the nearest school?" Donal Godfrey remembers his mother walking him to school that first day and the biting comments that came with that walk. "Where do you think you're taking that little Black boy?" was something Godfrey said he heard from the street. Police detectives would end up later having to walk Godfrey to and from school.[3]

Outside the school, a group of ten women picketed Donal for a week after the start of school year. "I can remember the first day where there were a few parents asking questions like, 'Where do you think you're taking this little Black boy . . . this little nigger? What do you think you're doing?'" recalled Donal. "I didn't understand all the hoopla around it. I took it as something not being right but I needed to go to school." In his classroom, Donal sat in the last row of his white classmates. He remembers his teacher reading such stories as "Little Black Sambo." But Donal never mentioned any of this to his mother. "I knew nothing of the heckling and harassment to and from school," she later told me.

Other than teasing, little else happened to him during the first six months of school. Then the family became a target. "I remember people calling [and] hanging up. [They said] 'you need to take the nigger out of school or something is going to happen,'" said Donal. This went on until February 1964, when a bomb ripped through the Godfreys' Gilmore Street home. Iona Godfrey King said that they believed that the bomb was intended to be placed near their bedrooms but, luckily, was placed on the opposite side of the house and did not kill or injure them. Even so, it was chillingly reminiscent of the bomb placed under the bedroom of Harriette and Harry T. Moore on Christmas night, 1951, in Mims, Florida, which murdered the couple on their twenty-fifth wedding anniversary.[4]

On March 12, 1964, a two-count indictment was returned against William Rosecrans and five co-defendants. The first count charged that on September 1, 1963, and continuing to the date of the indictment, they, in violation of Title 18 U.S.C. § 241, did conspire "with each other and with divers other persons to the grand jury unknown to injure, oppress, threaten and intimidate one Donal Godfrey, a negro citizen of the United States, and other persons similarly situated, in the free exercise and enjoyment of a right secured to them by the Constitution of the United States, namely, a right to attend the Lackawanna Public School and other public schools in Duval County, Florida, pursuant to a permanent injunctive decree of the United States District Court for the Middle District of Florida."[5]

U.S. District Judge Bryan Simpson sentenced Rosecrans, a member of the Indiana Ku Klux Klan and an associate of the local Klan, to seven years in prison after he pled guilty in the bombing. Five Jacksonville men were tried; not surprisingly, one was acquitted and mistrials were declared in the other cases.

Donal, who was six at the time, left Lackawanna Elementary immediately after the bombing, but eventually returned to complete fifth and sixth grades. He graduated from Robert E. Lee High School and eventually left Jacksonville in 1977, when he joined the military. Godfrey, his wife and family, and his mother, Iona, now live in Africa, where he works for the U.S. State Department.

In December of 1969, after years of failing to desegregate the system, the School Board was ordered by U.S. District Judge William A. McRae to reassign teachers so that each school would have 70 percent white faculty and 30 percent Black faculty. Judge McRae, with help from the Florida Desegregation Center at the University of Miami, drew a desegregation plan that paired and clustered elementary schools. This first phase of the McRae Plan took three neighborhood elementary schools, two white and one Black, and put them in a cluster assigning specific grades to each school. Out of six years, every student would be bused four years, and would attend their neighborhood school for two years. By this strategy, the McRae Plan spread the burden of court-ordered busing between the Black community and the white community. Blacks felt that the McRae Plan was fair; many whites said it was not. Jacksonville's desegregation case was ultimately transferred to U.S. District Judge Gerald Bard Tjoflat, who "redrew" Jacksonville's desegregation plan. In June of 1971, armed with a U.S. Supreme Court decision allowing the use of busing, Judge Tjoflat ordered massive busing to integrate Duval County's public school classrooms. Unlike the

McRae Plan, many Blacks felt the Tjoflat Plan placed the entire burden of busing on the Black community. Pairing and clustering went out the window, as did assistance from the University of Miami's Florida Desegregation Center.

One philosophy espoused about desegregation plans over the years was that putting the burden of busing on the Black community would make it more likely that whites would accept the plan. The Tjoflat Plan placed a disproportionate amount of busing on Black children and included comments in its rationale about how therapeutic it was for Black children to leave their segregated ghetto environment, take a daily bus ride to the suburbs, see how their white student counterparts lived in the suburbs, and have the pleasure of crossing the St. Johns River on their busing round trip. No one has ever dealt with how intellectually dishonest and disingenuous that claim was, and no one has ever explained how the long daily bus ride experience was supposed to be good for Black students. If it were beneficial for Black students to visit the suburbs, it should have been just as beneficial for white students to visit the inner city.

Ruby Bridges

Ruby Bridges was six years old when her parents agreed to a request from the NAACP to allow her to integrate the public school system of New Orleans, Louisiana. This momentous event occurred in 1960, six years after the *Brown* decision and three years after Little Rock. Ruby was the first Black student to attend William Frantz Elementary School, as well as the first Black student to attend an all-white elementary school located in the South.[6]

Ruby Bridges was one of several kindergartners to take an entrance test in the spring of 1960, and she scored one of the highest grades on that school board exam. She was the only Black student assigned to William Frantz Elementary that fall. Ruby's father did not want her to attend Frantz, feeling that Ruby being the student to integrate the school would lead to problems for her as well as for the family. Ruby's mother, however, felt strongly that Ruby should be involved. She understood the impact her daughter's role would have on Blacks in the future. She won the argument in the end.

On November 14, 1960, Ruby recalls that there was a huge crowd of people surrounding the school, but she thought it was because of Mardi Gras. She entered the school escorted by U.S. marshals past an angry mob of whites protesting her being at Frantz Elementary. She spent her first day in the principal's office with her mother, while parents of white students pulled them out of school, refusing to allow their children to sit in the classroom with a Black child, let alone be educated alongside her.

The next day, the crowd had grown larger and was even angrier. "I tried not to pay attention to the protestors," Bridges said in her book, *Through My Eyes*. She could not, however, miss the sight of a

Ruby Bridges had to be escorted to and from William Frantz Elementary School by federal marshals, 1960.

Black doll in a coffin, which scared her, and she did see the woman who threatened to poison her. People were shouting and throwing things. She did not understand initially that the things being yelled were directed towards her, for the offense of being a Black child daring to enter "their" school.

The forces of intolerance dictated that Ruby Bridges would be the sole student in her class. She was taught by a white teacher, Mrs. Barbara Henry, originally from Boston, Massachusetts, whose husband was stationed at Keesler Air Force Base in Biloxi, Mississippi. She became Ruby's teacher, and Ruby was her only pupil for the entire year. Ruby and Mrs. Henry became very close, but Mrs. Henry's decision to teach Ruby caused her to be ostracized from the rest of the staff, who let her know how much they did not appreciate her olive branch to this little "colored" girl.

Every day, Ruby continued to walk through the hostile, jeering crowd. This brave young six-year-old had to endure physical threats on a daily basis. As a result of the woman having threatened to poison her, the U.S. marshals, dispatched by President Eisenhower to oversee her safety, allowed Ruby to eat only food that she brought from home. As the school year progressed, Ruby slowly started to have some interaction with white students, and it was through this, and through hearing the comments of the protestors, that she finally became aware of the racism that was directed at her. As she recounts in her book, "'I can't play with you,' the boy said. 'My mama said not to because you're a nigger.' At that moment, it all made sense to me. I finally realized that everything had happened because I was Black."

Ruby's mother suggested that she begin praying on her way to school, so Ruby did his. In one particular uplifting moment, Ruby stopped in the middle of the crowd and appeared to be talking to herself. When Mrs. Henry asked her what she was doing, Ruby told her that she had forgotten to say her prayers that morning. So, following her mother's advice, she stopped prior to entering the building to say her prayers.

Much of what her father had anticipated would happen to Ruby and to the family did happen. Her father lost his job. Her grandparents, sharecroppers living in Mississippi, were sent off the land. There were many death threats to Ruby and to the family. They were supported, however, by the Black community, who would help Ruby's father get a new job, babysit, watch the house to protect it, and walk behind the marshals' car.

At the conclusion of the year, Mrs. Henry was not asked to return to William Frantz Elementary. She moved back to Boston to raise her family in a place where she felt things were "normal." She never forgot about Ruby. She kept a picture of the girl with so much courage on her bureau in her bedroom. Mrs. Henry and Ruby Bridges were reunited after Ruby became an adult.

In 1963, Norman Rockwell confronted the issue of prejudice head-on with one of his most powerful paintings. Inspired by the story of Ruby Bridges and school integration, the image featured a

"The Problem We All Live With," painting by Norman Rockwell, 1963.

President Barack Obama, Ruby Bridges Hall, Norman Rockwell Museum director Laurie Norton Moffatt, and museum president Anne Morgan, viewing Norman Rockwell's "The Problem We All Live With" hanging in a West Wing hallway near the Oval Office in 2011.

young African American girl being escorted to school by four U.S. marshals amidst signs of protest and fearful ignorance. The painting, with the word "nigger" scrawled on the side of a street building where Ruby would walk with her federal marshal escort, was published in *Look* magazine. It ushered in a new era in Rockwell's career, and remains an important national symbol of the struggle for racial equality. Rockwell received letters of praise from *Look* readers, as well as criticism for making such direct social commentary in his illustrations. He would revisit the theme of civil rights in several other illustrations from the period.

President Bill Clinton awarded Ruby Bridges the Presidential Citizens Medal in 2001. In 2006, a new elementary school was dedicated to Ruby in Alameda, California. In 2007, the Children's Museum of Indianapolis opened an exhibition that chronicled the lives of Ruby Bridges, Ryan White, and Anne Frank. At the request of President Barack Obama, Rockwell's iconic portrait of Ruby's walk to school was on display throughout the summer of 2011 outside the Oval Office in the White House.

Ruby Bridges Hall now serves on the board of the Norman Rockwell Museum, and in 1999 founded the Ruby Bridges Foundation to promote the values of tolerance, respect, and appreciation of people's differences. She commended Rockwell for having "enough courage to step up to the plate and say I'm going to make a statement, and [doing] it in a very powerful way."

Ruby Bridges' bravery motivated and inspired a young student in Jacksonville to write about her for a class project in seventh grade world history. When Tatyiana Hayes was an eleven-year-old student at James Weldon Johnson Magnet School she decided to write about Ruby Bridges as a classroom assignment after her teacher listed "the story of Ruby Bridges" as one of several potential classroom research projects. (I was that same age when I enrolled in Mr. Pearson's eighth-grade American history class, and the story about Ruby Bridges would become one of my favorite civil rights stories.)

Tatyiana's parents, Reverend and Mrs. Stavius Powell, who are personal friends of mine, told me of Tatyiana's decision. They did not know at the time that I was writing another book, what it would entail, or the chapter subjects. With her parents' permission, I talked to Tatyiana about Ruby Bridges. I asked her why she decided to write about Ruby Bridges. She told me that after hearing about Ruby Bridges and what she did at her age, she wanted to write about her and research her life. I asked her if she understood racial segregation. Tatyiana told me that racial segregation is separating people for not being the same color as others. Schools were racially segregated, and whites were taught that they were better than Blacks. It was discrimination, and whites did not want Blacks in their schools. They did not want to go to school with Black people.

I asked Tatyiana what impressed her after studying Ruby Bridges' story. She said although Ruby was very young, she was very brave

Tatyiana Hayes.

and not afraid. I asked Tatyiana, "What did you learn about Ruby Bridges that you did not know before you completed your report?" She said she did not know about the threats on Ruby's life or the threat to poison her. Then she said, "Mr. Hurst, discrimination is just plain wrong."

I finally asked her how she would solve the problems of race relations in this country today, and what equality is. Tatyiana said, "Black people and white people should talk and communicate their feelings. They should try and work out their problems. Everybody is the same. Skin color should not be a difference." From the mouths of babes! During Tatyiana's 2011–2012 seventh-grade school year, she was elected vice-president of the student council. She is now a student at William Marion Raines High School.

Unfortunately, as the United States observes the sixtieth anniversary of the landmark 1954 *Brown vs. Board of Education* Supreme Court decision, which helped outlaw racial segregation in American schools, the realization is sinking in that segregated schools are not just remnants of history. Many schools in this country are still effectively segregated—and, even where this is not the case, the effects of segregation still reverberate in our new century.

Charlie E. Cobb Jr., 2008.

8

Charlie E. Cobb Jr.

In my writings, I have focused on the economic, political, and cultural dimensions of racism, suggesting its permanence because of the social stability it provides in a system that contains great disparities in income and wealth. But I want to raise the possibility of a deeper foundation growing out of an undeniable fact. Most racists are also Christians."

    — Attorney Derrick Albert Bell Jr.

      First tenured African American professor of law

        at Harvard University, author, *Critical Race Theory*

Charlie Cobb is truly an icon of the Civil Rights Movement. He is one of the organizers of Freedom Summer in Mississippi. His is not a household name, but it should be.

I met Charlie several years ago after he and his wife, Ann, moved to Jacksonville. He is a friend, and I proudly claim him now as an honorary native of Jacksonville. I knew about Charlie prior to meeting him. Certainly, his superlative background and reputation preceded him. He is a civil rights legend.[1]

In 1962, Cobb became a field secretary in the Mississippi Delta region for the Student Nonviolent Coordinating Committee (SNCC), for whom he wrote the original proposal for the Mississippi Freedom School, an education initiative that was launched during Freedom Summer in 1964. As a field secretary for SNCC, Charlie was a grassroots organizer; he lived in the homes of the people he worked with, as did other SNCC field secretaries, staying with sharecroppers, janitors, cooks, maids, factory workers, and day laborers and learning their perspective firsthand.[2]

According to Charlie, this concept had a lot to do with the influence of Ella Baker, one of the great persons in the civil rights struggle. As Charlie put it, Ms. Baker taught us to organize from the bottom up, rather than from the top down. I sat down with Charlie to talk about his experiences and asked his motivation to join the Civil Rights Movement. Charlie began:

"I watched the initial stages of the student part of the Civil Rights Movement on television. When the sit-ins happened in 1960, I was a senior in high school in Massachusetts. For the first time I saw young people my age or younger involved in challenging segregation, and that was my initial interest in the movement. Up until then, in fact, when I watched news about the movement, I thought that this was something that only adults did.

"I was preparing to go to college and had been accepted to Howard University. After I got to Howard, I read a story in the student newspaper about Howard students and their involvement in the sit-ins and the Freedom Rides. While I was reading it, someone handed me a leaflet saying that a bus would be leaving from campus at an appointed time to carry students to a sit-in demonstration in Baltimore, Maryland, about fifty miles away. There were three sort of "radical" student groups on Howard's campus. One was the Howard NAACP college chapter, which was recognized as a Howard student organization; the other two were Howard's Nonviolent Action Group, which included Stokely Carmichael, and Bayard Rustin's Young People's Socialist League. Those latter two were not recognized as official college organizations. As a freshman, though, I did not know any of these groups or the people in the groups. I decided to take the bus ride, which is how I met some members of the Non-violent Action Group. I decided to hang with them during this excursion into protest. But I am thinking they are going to picket, not necessarily to sit in. So I go to check out this 'stuff.'

"When we get to Baltimore, Juanita Jackson Mitchell, the daughter of key Maryland NAACP leader Lilly Jackson (and the wife of NAACP stalwart Clarence Mitchell), decided she wanted to extend the sit-ins beyond Baltimore to Annapolis, which is the home of the U.S. Naval Academy. Juanita was one of the first Blacks to graduate from the University of Maryland Law School and was often the attorney for arrested protesters. She asked for volunteers and the Nonviolent Action Group, the group I am with, volunteered to go to Annapolis. There everybody walks into Antoinette's Pizza, a segregated restaurant frequented by midshipmen, and the group of about six or seven sat down.

"I was not planning to sit in, but now I feel that I have no choice; I've been talking to these guys and so I sit too. Soon we are asked to leave. We don't leave, and the restaurant calls the police. When the police arrive to arrest us, they ask us to stand and march to the

Stokely Carmichael, Charlie Cobb, and George Greene, 1963.

Charlie E. Cobb Jr.

paddy wagon. Everyone stands, but then they go limp. I had never seen any of this before; all of this is new. They were the veterans at this. . . . I was seventeen or eighteen years old. Even without any training, I recognized their strategy of making it hard for the police to get all of us out of the restaurant; so I grabbed the biggest person in the group and wrapped my arms around her to also make it hard and was dragged out along with everybody.

"I had been at Howard barely two months and I wind up in jail. None of this was in my plans.

"I would later get involved on a regular basis with the Nonviolent Action Group, the Student Nonviolent Coordinating Committee, and the Congress of Racial Equality (CORE), because these groups were in touch with what was going on in the South. I was invited by CORE to Houston, Texas, for a youth civil rights training workshop and given money for a bus ticket to get there. I decided I would take the opportunity to also see the portions of the South I kept reading about and seeing on television. I bought a bus ticket from Washington, D.C., through Virginia, the Carolinas, Georgia, Alabama, Mississippi, Louisiana, and on into Texas. I come from a civic and politically activist family, so my parents had no trepidation about my involvement.

"I decided to get off the bus in Jackson, Mississippi, because of the wave of sit-ins there. We had our sit-ins in Virginia and Maryland, but I could not quite get my brain around these students "sitting in" in Mississippi. Of course, at that time Mississippi was considered the worst place in the world for a Black person. For me, although my grandparents came from the state, Mississippi was wholly associated with Emmett Till. I wanted to meet students brave enough to sit in in Mississippi. I asked around and eventually got a "headquarters" location for the sit-in demonstrations. When I got there and met the students, I told them that I had wanted to meet them, and that I was on my way to a civil rights workshop in

Houston. Lawrence Guyot, a big hulking guy, a recent graduate of Tougaloo College, and one of the leaders of the demonstrations — he would later become the chairman of the Mississippi Freedom Democratic Party—walked over to me and asked, in a voice full of contempt and disdain, what sense it made to go to Texas for a civil rights workshop when I was standing there in Mississippi. I understood his challenge and I never made it to Houston."

Of his many experiences, Charlie told me about Ruleville, Mississippi, a small city in Sunflower County, the home county of U.S. Senator James Eastland. Sunflower County had a population of about twenty thousand and was 67 percent Black. Ruleville had about eleven hundred people and 80 percent were Black. But only about a hundred Blacks were registered in the entire county.

Charlie said he had been in Ruleville two days and was walking down one of the roads with two of the guys helping with voter registration. "A car pulled up and a white guy gets out of the car with a gun drawn. He was the mayor. He also was a justice of the peace, owned the town's hardware store, and headed the local White Citizens' Council. Pistol in hand, he ordered us to get in his car and brought us to his hardware store, where he ranted about our being from New York and being 'Communists' and told us to get out of town. The leader of our little threesome, Charles 'Mac' McLaurin, responded and in an argumentative fashion said we were in Sunflower County to encourage and help people register to vote. 'The U.S. Constitution gives us the right to do this,' Mac told him. The mayor's unforgettable response: 'That law ain't got here yet.' Mayor Charles Dorrough was going to leave us at the hardware store, but Mac was adamant about the mayor returning us to the spot where he picked us up. The mayor did so."

While still in Ruleville and Sunflower County, Charlie met civil rights icon Fannie Lou Hamer, who lived on a plantation outside of Ruleville.

Charlie continued: "We were taking a group of about seventeen persons to register and had to take them to the courthouse in Indianola, the county seat. We were using a bus that transported plantation workers; and, yes, they were still called plantations. Mrs. Hamer was one of those persons. She lived on the Marlow plantation. We get to Indianola and, of course, whites do not want them to register. They proceeded to take 'slow' to another level. We were there in plenty of time but had to wait and wait and wait. No particular reason, and while we were waiting, they simply closed the courthouse. We had no choice but to leave. When we got to the edge of town, the police pulled the bus over and arrested the driver for driving 'a bus of an illegal color.' It is the end of the day and you do not want to be on the road at night in Mississippi as civil rights workers with persons who want to register to vote, so we had a dilemma.

"Of course, we could not let anyone else drive the bus because they would be arrested for the same thing. It was a dangerous situation and the people on the bus also recognized the danger. They were exposed. Then from the back of the bus we heard this voice singing the freedom songs—'This Little Light of Mine,' 'Woke up This Morning with My Mind Stayed on Freedom.' It was Mrs. Hamer. There was just something about her singing that shored up the group. So we appointed a spokesperson to talk with the police to see what could be done to work something out and to try and get everyone back to their homes. The police officer said there was a fine and it was one hundred dollars, which was serious money in 1962. So we took a collection of those on the bus, those with SNCC, and we come up with forty-six dollars! That was it for about eighteen or nineteen persons. So the spokesperson goes to the policeman and said, 'We have forty-six dollars and if that is not enough you will have to arrest all of us because that is all we have.' Amazing comments considering our situation, yet these were comments not from us but from the persons we were taking to register . . . natives of Ruleville—sharecroppers and farmers and domestic workers. The police officer accepted the forty-six dollars. We never knew if that money ever made it to the county office . . . and really did not care.

"When Mrs. Hamer got back to the plantation where she worked and lived with her family, Mr. Marlow is there. The word had spread in this little small city and county about those who tried to register to vote. Mr. Marlow told Mrs. Hamer that if she persisted in registering to vote, he would fire her and she would have to leave the plantation where she had worked and lived for eighteen years with her husband and her children. Mrs. Hamer was employed on the plantation as a sharecropper, a cotton picker, and a timekeeper. She was the timekeeper because she was better educated than most with her third-grade education. She responded to Marlow, 'I didn't go there to register for you. I went to register for myself.' Mr. Marlow told her to get off the plantation that evening. She was forty-six years-old and became SNCC's oldest field secretary."

Charlie went on to tell me that he never planned to stay in Mississippi, but he did where he found himself working with Guyot and others trying to get Blacks registered to vote.

"I figured I had the summer before I had to return to school. But I hadn't realized that, when you start doing something like this, you just can't suddenly stop and leave. People's biggest fear was that if they did something you asked, like try and register to vote, when the inevitable reprisals—violent and economic—came, you could go back home—to Washington, D.C., in my case—and they could not go anywhere, could not leave."

We talked about Mrs. Hamer, and, although there are many who know of her leading the Mississippi Freedom Democratic Party in 1964, few know about a savage beating she took the year before. Charlie gave me this account: "On June 3, 1963, after returning from a civil rights workshop in South Carolina, Fannie Lou Hamer and

Charlie E. Cobb Jr.

Fannie Lou Hamer, a leader of the Mississippi Freedom Democratic Party, speaking before the Credentials Committee of the Democratic National Convention in Atlantic City, August 22, 1964.

other civil rights workers arrived in Winona, Mississippi, by bus. They were ordered off the bus and taken to the Montgomery County jail. Later that night while in jail, three white men came into her cell with two Black prisoners. They made her lay down and ordered the Black prisoners to beat her with a blackjack. They savagely beat her until they got tired. When she was released three days later, it took her more than a month to recover, but we never felt she ever fully recovered. Though she died fourteen years later apparently of breast cancer, she continually had kidney complications from the beating she sustained that night in 1963, which I am convinced contributed to her death."

I asked Charlie about the legacy of the Civil Rights Movement. He said there are several. "First, you can struggle against great odds, as evidenced by the Mississippi Freedom Democratic Party forcing the creation of a two-party system in the South. Sit-ins, and the student sit-in movement, not only challenged the infrastructure of racism but empowered the free speech movement at many traditional universities, and is where the roots of Black Studies departments can be found. The Civil Rights Movement changed people, their lives and the eventual paths they would take. The civil rights experience literally changed lives."

He also felt that the Civil Rights Movement saw the emerging leadership of young Black high school students and Black college students, who took the initiative fighting segregation and racism through direct-action demonstrations. Black students established going to jail for a principle, which at the time was quite new and revolutionary. Finally, he commented that Black World War II veterans were a very important part of the movement—Medgar Evers, Vernon Dahmer, Aaron Henry, to name a few. Fighting for freedom in foreign countries and then coming home to bigotry and blatant Jim Crow laws did not resonate at all.

Charlie began his journalism career in 1974 as a reporter for WHUR Radio in Washington, D.C., and in 1976 joined the staff of National Public Radio as a foreign affairs reporter, bringing to that network its first regular coverage of Africa. He helped to establish the NPR's first coverage of African affairs. After leaving National Public Radio, Cobb worked as a correspondent for the PBS show *Frontline* from 1983 until 1985. In 1985 he became the first black staff writer for *National Geographic* magazine. He was a member of *National Geographic*'s editorial staff from 1985-1997. Charlie is one of the founders of the National Association of Black Journalists and on July 24, 2008, the National Association of Black Journalists honored Charlie and his work by inducting him into its Hall of Fame.

He is the co-author, with civil rights organizer and educator Robert P. Moses, of *Radical Equations: Civil Rights from Mississippi to the Algebra Project.*

His book *On the Road to Freedom: A Guided Tour of the Civil Rights Trail* establishes and demonstrates, how history, generally speaking, emerges from specific identifiable places: ordinary places such as neighborhoods and communities, the places where people live their everyday lives. The book goes on to show how the Civil Rights Movement emerged from specific places such as Selma and Birmingham in Alabama, Memphis, Baltimore, Charleston, and Marion in Georgia. *On the Road to Freedom: A Guided Tour of the Civil Rights Trails* serves as the guide for a new, educational DVD series created by the United Methodist Publishing House; Charlie is one of the series' narrators.

Cobb's newest book, *This Nonviolent Stuff'll Get You Killed: How Guns Made the Civil Rights Movement Possible*, was published in 2014. Charlie makes the point that the Civil Rights Movement, often lauded for its commitment to nonviolence, perhaps could not have achieved some of its goals without the age-old tradition of armed Black self-defense.[3]

THIS
NONVIOLENT
STUFF'LL
GET YOU
KILLED

How Guns Made the Civil Rights Movement Possible

CHARLES E. COBB JR.

In June 2014, Charlie spent several weeks in Mississippi with SNCC colleagues as they commemorated the fiftieth anniversary of the Mississippi Freedom Summer. Charlie Cobb currently is the first activist-in-residence of the SNCC Legacy Project, a partnership between Duke University and SNCC. The SNCC Legacy Project is designed to document SNCC's major role in the struggle for freedom and to allow young activists to draw on the hard-won experiences and wisdom of those who marched before them.

Charlie is a part of the heritage of the Student Nonviolent Coordinating Committee, the freedom movement, and the Civil Rights Movement. Like many veterans of the Civil Rights Movement, he understands that America's founding fathers did not have the equality of Black citizens in mind when they originated the country's founding documents. Many will argue that America still does not. Yet you fight anyway. Charlie understands the unpaid debt. Experiences from the Civil Rights Movement eternally affect your life. I did not have to ask Charlie; I knew from my experiences. Charlie Cobb Jr., has spent a lifetime simply working to get America to pay its debts. They remain overdue.

Norma White, 2002.

9

Dr. Norma Ruth Solomon White

Without education, there is no hope for our people, and without hope, our future is lost.

—Charles Hamilton Houston

Norma Ruth Solomon White blazed a path where no female—and certainly no Black female—in Jacksonville, Florida, had trod. She was a pioneer then, as she is now.

Music and education were always component parts of Norma's family. During the days of segregation, her mother, Mrs. Ruth Solomon, taught education in a one-room schoolhouse in an area called Cosmo, in the eastern part of Jacksonville's Black Arlington community at that time. She was literally the teacher and the principal and the counselor and everything in between.

Mrs. Solomon wanted her daughter to play the piano, and Norma started taking piano lessons at age seven. She enjoyed the piano, but something else grabbed her interest. Her father played the trombone in a local band, and that trombone looked much more interesting to the young girl than just playing the piano. When her father wasn't home, Norma would get his trombone and go through the imaginary mechanics as if she were playing it. She was fascinated, and that lit the spark that would ignite her desire to play in a high school band.

By the middle of junior high school, Norma was taking piano lessons and music theory from Mrs. Alpha Hayes Moore, considered by many Blacks to be one of Jacksonville's notable Black patrons of the arts. When Norma enrolled in Stanton High School in 1948 as a tenth-grader, and then auditioned for the school band, her perseverance in taking those piano lessons and studying the music theory came in handy. Nevertheless, Mrs. Moore pushed Norma to concentrate on the piano. Forty members made up Stanton's band during her first year under coach James "Bubbling" Small, who tripled as the band director, head football coach, and athletic director. When Coach Small asked Norma what instrument she wanted to play in the band, she said the violin. He acted as if he hadn't heard her, and told her to have her mother purchase an alto horn from the pawn shop. Although Norma had never played an alto horn, Mrs. Solomon went to the pawn shop and purchased one. Because of Norma's ability to read music, she became an alto horn player in the Stanton band.

Norma was so excellent an alto horn player before the year was over that Coach Small, appreciating her ability to read music and recognizing her emerging music ability, asked her to move to the baritone horn. This time Mrs. Solomon did not have to make a trip to the pawn shop, since the school already had a baritone horn that Norma could play.

Kernaa McFarlin became Stanton's band director in the 1949–1950 school year. After mastering playing the baritone horn, as she had with the alto horn, Norma eventually became section leader. It was heady stuff for a Black female band member, who as a female would have been expected to play the flute or the piccolo or the clarinet, and who had come to the band wanting to play the violin. During Mr. McFarlin's first year, Stanton's band expanded to sixty-five members and now needed more space for its rehearsals. He moved some of the band's rehearsals from the school auditorium to the

Unless WE Tell It . . . It Never Gets Told!

Eartha M. White Building, in the next block on Ashley Street. The marching band held its rehearsals at Wilder Park on Davis Street.

During her high school summers, Norma accompanied her mother to New York City, where Mrs. Solomon was working on her master's degree at Columbia University. Southern colleges and universities did not admit Blacks, so those who would have been their potential "customers" had to go elsewhere. Mrs. Solomon, as with any Black person in academia seeking a graduate degree, had to do so by attending a college or university outside the South. For Mrs. Solomon and other Duval County schoolteachers who were accepted into academic graduate programs, the Duval County school system paid their tuition expenses. Segregation was indeed expensive, and its practice exacted financial costs.

In New York for those summers with her mother, Norma attended a summer session at Rhodes College Preparatory School and, for two years, the summer program in Juilliard's music division. The college preparatory school at Rhodes was considered to have exceptional, dedicated teachers whose academic expectations for their students were high. With its excellent reputation, the school drew students from all over the world. Many Rhodes graduates went on to Ivy League schools, to Seven Sisters schools, or to other prestigious institutions around the country and the world. Now defunct, the school is often commonly referred to as "Rhodes School" or simply "Rhodes." According to Dr. White, "Rhodes accelerated my academic learning curve. I was already a good student at Stanton; my session at Rhodes made me a very good student." Of course, Juilliard is well known to be the veritable crème de la crème of fine arts schools, and Norma's experience there likewise enhanced her understanding of music theory and her growing musical skills.

Mrs. Solomon and Mrs. Moore wanted Norma to attend Howard University, at that time widely considered to be foremost among the historically Black colleges and universities. Norma herself wanted to attend Howard, and Mrs. Moore, of course, still wanted Norma to take up piano at Howard. Done deal, right?

Well, not quite. Images of Norma Solomon matriculating at Howard University changed when Dr. William Foster, the legendary director of the "Marching 100" band at Florida Agricultural and Mechanical College (FAMC, now Florida Agricultural and Mechanical University, FAMU), came to Norma's parents' house at the invitation of Mr. McFarlin. When Dr. Foster walked into their living room he was not there just to talk, but came prepared to offer Norma a band scholarship, thereby making her the first female member of the famed FAMC band. Howard University quickly fell out of contention and any consideration of studying the piano in college simply vanished.

The first female in the FAMC Marching and Concert Band completed FAMC graduation requirements in three and half years, and graduated in 1955. Norma then set her sights on returning to Jacksonville and interning under her mentor Mr. McFarlin at New Stanton High School, the new Black high school in Jacksonville. Imagine her shock when she received her intern assignment, and discovered that it was at Isaiah Blocker and not at New Stanton. Isaiah Blocker, which was a junior high school, did not have a band! But, Norma thought, "Since this is just a college internship and not an actual teaching assignment, whatever the mix-up, we'll straighten it out." She later found out that the principal of Isaiah Blocker Junior High School, William Harper, had specifically asked for her to be placed there as an intern. At the time, little did Norma know that Mr. Harper had big plans for her and her obviously gifted musical skills. The centerpiece of those big plans was for her to help to establish the Isaiah Blocker Junior High School band.

Not giving up on an assignment to Stanton and the opportunity to work with Kernaa McFarlin, and seeking to get her assignment "straightened out," Norma paid the requisite visit to Dr. John Irving Elias Scott, who, as superintendent of Negro education for the Duval County school system, assigned all the Black teachers. Mr. Harper, though, recognized Norma's talents. He kept his voice in Dr. Scott's ear, and his interference bore fruit. Norma was dispatched to Isaiah Blocker Junior High School, and, as an intern during the 1954–1955 school year, given the onerous yet satisfying responsibility for creating the junior high school band. Task number one was for her to help establish interest and meet with parents. Her second task was to explain what is required to establish a junior high school band. This entailed additional tasks: purchasing band uniforms, purchasing instruments, solidifying support from both parents and the community, and setting up the band's rehearsal schedules. And all of this for an intern! Her job did not permit her to be a clock-watcher, because she had to perform all of these endeavors after the regular school day.

In 1955, Norma Solomon became the first female band director in the Duval County school system. Her impact was immediately felt. Interest in the band went through the proverbial roof. The number of students wanting to play in the band significantly increased.

New Stanton High School's Marching Blue Devil Band under Mr. McFarlin quickly became known as one of the best high school bands in the South, arguably in the country. Isaiah Blocker Junior High School's Band, under Norma Ruth Solomon, became known as the Junior Blue Devil Band, with some even feeling that Isaiah Blocker's junior high band was better than most high school bands. Norma would serve as Isaiah Blocker's band director from 1955 to 1964, and then continue on until 1967 as the band director for Darnell-Cookman Junior High School, when Isaiah Blocker exchanged missions with Darnell-Cookman Elementary School. (Isaiah Blocker reverted back to an elementary school and Darnell-Cookman became a junior high school).

A particular moment of pride on the day in 2007 when Norma had the pleasure of pinning her granddaughter Danielle.

Music was important, but education was every bit as important, if not more. Norma, as her mother had before her, applied to and was accepted in Columbia University's graduate program. Just as her mother had, she had her tuition paid by the Duval County school system. Norma received her master's degree from Columbia in 1959.

In 1952, Norma became a member of FAMC's chapter of the Alpha Kappa Alpha Sorority, Inc. Forty-six years later, in 1998, she became the twenty-fifth international president at the AKA meeting held in Chicago, Illinois, making her the titular head of two hundred thousand sorority members nationally and internationally, including Germany, Korea, and Japan.[1]

Ebony magazine recognized her as one of the hundred most influential Blacks in this country. The theme for her administration was "Blazing New Trails," and it embraced six target areas: leadership development, education, health, the Black family, economics, and the arts. White also initiated the sorority's "On Track" after-school program which targeted at-risk students in grades three through six to prepare them for middle school. During Norma Solomon White's administration, Alpha Kappa Alpha Sorority, Inc., built ten schools in South Africa.

White is Alpha Kappa Alpha's first supreme basileus to be part of a mother-daughter legacy. She does take pride in being the first female band director and the first Black female band director in Jacksonville, the first female member of the FAMC "Marching 100," and the twenty-fifth supreme basileus, but her proudest moment was "pinning" her granddaughter, Danielle, as an AKA. Danielle is the daughter of Marcel White, Norma's son with her former husband, Alvin White.

In 1999 Norma Solomon White received an honorary doctorate from her alma mater, Florida Agricultural and Mechanical University. In 2014 the Florida Education Association honored Dr. Norma Solomon White with the Mary McLeod Bethune Human Relations in Education Award.

Norma White fought discrimination on many fronts, yet she made her commitment to the fight with very little fanfare. Her quiet and brilliant strength makes her a role model for many today. She exemplifies supreme quality.

Dr. Arnett E. Girardeau, 1990.

10

Dr. Arnett E. Girardeau

I learned that courage was not the absence of fear, but the triumph over it. The brave man is not he who does not feel afraid, but he who conquers that fear.

—Nelson Mandela

There is no learning curve to fighting racism. You recognize racism, and you fight it or you don't fight it. If you are Black and you lived in the United States in the 1940s, the '50s, and the '60s, you understood racism up close and very personal. Sometimes you fought racism and segregation by showing up somewhere where your Black face was not expected. You fought the vestiges of segregation and racism, because racism was then, and is now, an insidious "monument" to virulent discrimination based on the color of a person's skin.

Dr. Arnett E. Girardeau is one of a number of unsung civil rights pioneers who fought racism to combat the notion that discrimination and segregation should continue as a way of life in this country. He has continued his unselfish and at times self-sacrificing fight for many years.

Arnett Elyus Girardeau was born in Jacksonville, Florida, three months prior to the stock market crash of 1929, the beginning of the Great Depression. Although his father did not have a steady job for almost ten years, his mother worked as a classroom teacher and enabled her six children to survive and the family to stay together. Arnett, being the youngest child, remembers those difficult days during his early childhood. He recalls his family being poor but even so remaining cohesive and totally supportive of one another. He began developing his work habits as a twelve-year-old bag boy at the local grocery chain Daylight Store, which was the only supermarket in the Black community. Two years later, he and his close friend, Harry Alexander, began working on weekends as busboys in the Seminole Hotel's coffee shop.

Girardeau joined the Boy Scouts of America in February 1942, at age twelve, and at age seventeen earned the rank of Eagle Scout with four fellow Black Eagle Scouts. It was the first time in Jacksonville, Florida, that five Scouts from a Black church—Ebenezer Methodist Church, Troop 51—achieved the Eagle Scout rank at the same court of honor.

The year after Arnett's brother Otis returned from the war and entered Howard University, Arnett and his brother Emmett were also accepted to attend Howard. Arnett graduated from Howard in 1952, and later that year was drafted into the U.S. Army. On his drive home from Howard, just outside of the small town of Raeford, southwest of Fayetteville, North Carolina, Arnett was involved in a car accident. An eleven-year-old white girl was crossing the highway, and, while trying to avoid an oncoming truck, she plowed into the side of Arnett's car. A hostile crowd of whites quickly gathered— angry and ready to attack him because it appeared to them that "this Nigger boy" had injured "a white girl."

This was three years before the murder of Emmett Till. But, with the history of Black men being lynched in the South, Arnett said he really felt that the mob was prepared to kill him and that he "was dead for sure." Fortunately for him, a white local soft drink distributor witnessed the accident and spoke up on his behalf; and, because of the white man's status in the community, and his willingness to step forward, Girardeau was neither lynched nor held for prosecution. Shaken, he left North Carolina as quickly as possible, and then spent the rest of his trip to Jacksonville thinking about what might have happened to him. Frightening as it was, this incident would begin his preparation for a life fighting the politics of vicious racism.

Military orders assigned Girardeau to Camp Gordon (now Fort Gordon), in Augusta, Georgia. He completed High Speed Telegraphy School, and was later chosen to teach at the school. He also attended Non-Commissioned Officer Military Leadership School and, as the leader of the group, became the first Black at Camp Gordon to receive the American Spirit Honor Medal. (This medal, established in 1950 by the Citizens Committee for the Army, Navy, and Air Force, Inc., is awarded to a single recruit in each basic training cycle who demonstrates outstanding leadership qualities. Although it is a private award, selection is determined by drill instructors and a board of officers.)

After years of working with Dr. Girardeau in the community and in the political arena, and with obvious personal interest, I asked him when it was that he really committed himself to the Civil Rights Movement. He thought about the question, and said, "It was on August 28, 1960 . . . the day after Ax Handle Saturday." Dr. Girardeau said that he had always felt that Ax Handle Saturday and the sit-in demonstrations that day changed his life and his perspective on life. "I attended the mass meeting at St. Paul AME Church. On that day, following Ax Handle Saturday, sitting in St. Paul AME, I committed to the struggle. The day before, I had looked into the eyes of angry white Klansmen filled with hatred and contempt, who wanted to harm us because we were Black and because we dared seek service at 'their' lunch counter."

He continued, "Until that fateful day, I had been in school in Washington, D.C., and, because the federal government is always the center of news there, my routine was Howard University and home. I had obviously heard of lunch counter sit-ins, but dental school was my primary interest. It was the hostilities of August 27, 1960, that sealed the deal for me.

"I had experienced segregation and discrimination all of my life and hated the manner in which whites could so easily deprive Blacks of their rights. While at Camp Gordon in 1952, I volunteered to serve in Korea, in order to leave Georgia, where racist white policemen were daily beating Black soldiers with impunity. I willingly volunteered for 'suicide service' in Korea, because I felt that, if I were treated as I had seen other Black serviceman mistreated by white policemen in Augusta, I would have reacted in such a manner that I would be either be killed outright or lynched by a white mob. I preferred dying in Korea fighting on the battlefield to dying on the streets of Georgia at the hands of a white policeman. Instead of Korea, I received orders to Austria, which probably saved my life.

"That was eight years prior to 1960 and Ax Handle Saturday. Jacksonville's sit-in demonstrations, the Jacksonville Youth Council NAACP, and my classmate Rutledge Pearson gave me the opportunity to fight racism, segregation, and discrimination. When I joined the NAACP, I dedicated myself to this cause and this struggle for the next half-century of my life. When you dedicate to a cause like civil rights, you knowingly and willingly lose your individuality. The movement takes over your life and dictates circumstances. My journey of committal to the Civil Rights Movement had taken eight years—from 1952 to 1960—but now it was in full force."

In 1964, Dr. Robert Hayling, a leader of the St. Augustine Civil Rights Movement and a fellow dentist and friend of Dr. Girardeau, was viciously beaten by the Ku Klux Klan. Fearful of the treatment or lack thereof that he might receive in St. Augustine's hospitals because of his civil rights activities, friends saw to it that Hayling was taken to Brewster Hospital—a segregated but not segregating

Black hospital in Jacksonville—in a hearse provided by Leo Chase, a Black funeral director in St. Augustine. Hayling received emergency medical treatment by Black doctors at the hospital, which saved his life. Those Black doctors also maintained their professional medical care of Dr. Hayling until he was healthy enough to return home, and Dr. Girardeau provided extensive oral surgery. All medical and dental care was provided to Dr. Hayling at no cost.

The life of Arnett Elyus Girardeau has been one of commitment and service to the Jacksonville community. Dr. Girardeau was elected to the Florida House of Representatives in 1976, where he served as a member of the Corrections Committee, and as the chairman of the Justice Model and Correctional System Subcommittee. He was one of founding members of the Florida Conference of Black State Legislators, serving as both vice-chairman and chairman.

Dr. Girardeau was elected to the Florida Senate in 1982 as Florida's first Black senator since Reconstruction. In 1989 Senator Girardeau became the first—and so far only—Black person to serve as pro tempore of the Florida Senate.[1]

While in the Florida legislature, Dr. Girardeau created the Sub-Saharan African Scholarship Program, which led to a number of African students getting an American college education.

Nothing exemplifies Dr. Girardeau's commitment to his community, as well as his devotion to historical fair play and integrity, more than his work to ensure that Blacks in north Florida would have the opportunity to elect a Black to the U.S. Congress. The year was 1992. Following the census of 1990, as is the custom every ten years, the Florida legislature was charged with the responsibility of redrawing boundary lines for congressional districts, and Dr. Girardeau was appointed chairman of the Senate Subcommittee on Congressional Redistricting. He spent countless hours working with his Florida Senate colleagues, with the Senate staff, and with his own legislative staff working on drawing fair boundary lines for

Senator Arnett Girardeau during his tenure as chairman of the Florida Senate Subcommittee on Congressional Redistricting in 1990.

Florida's District Three of the U.S. House of Representatives. Finally, after months of work, and after that work had withstood several challenges, the court and the Department of Justice approved new lines for Congressional District Three. We need to know and remember that this did not just happen. It required great integrity and strenuous effort for Arnett E. Girardeau to become the architect of the first Congressional seat in Jacksonville to which it would be possible for a Black person to be elected. In 1992 Corrine Brown was elected to Congress from the Third Congressional District (now the Fifth Congressional District), giving Jacksonville and north Florida their first Black member of Congress since Reconstruction.

Dr. Girardeau's community service is equally trailblazing. As a dentist with a successful practice, Dr. Girardeau continued to give to his community. He served on the board of Greater Jacksonville Economic Opportunity, Inc., Jacksonville's anti-poverty program. He organized several community-based organizations in Jacksonville, including the Black Community Coalition, which, as its name

Unless WE Tell It . . . It Never Gets Told!

implies, was an alliance of community-based organizations who joined together to fight discrimination and support efforts for civil and political change in Jacksonville and the Black community. Over the years, Dr. Girardeau served as vice-president of the Jacksonville branch of the NAACP, president of the Community Urban Development Council, president and vice-president of United Jacksonville, a member of the Jacksonville Housing Authority, a member of the Citizens Against Crime steering committee, president of the Black Community Coalition, a member of the 1969 Mayor's Task Force on East Jacksonville Civil Disorder, and a founding member of the Jacksonville Home Town Plan Advisory Committee.

Dr. Girardeau is married to Dr. Carolyn Girardeau, who is retired from the Duval County public school system. They have a daughter Arnetta, and a son, Arnett Jr.

Dr. Arnett Girardeau's gait is perhaps a bit slower now, but his continual resolve to work for civil rights in his community has not lessened. His life has been one of unselfish service to his fellow man and woman, helping the helpless and the voiceless in the Jacksonville community and the state of Florida—a life defined by his compassion, his commitment, and his integrity.

Clanzel T. Brown, 1977.

11

Clanzel T. Brown

The truth is that there is nothing noble in being superior to somebody else. The only real nobility is in being superior to your former self.

    —Whitney Young
      Executive director of the national Urban League,
      1961–1971

The name of Clanzel Thornton Brown Sr., will not appear in most critical histories of the Civil Rights Movement in this country generally, nor in Jacksonville, Florida, specifically, but it should. His influence in Jacksonville, and in this country, was certainly felt when he served as executive director of the Jacksonville Urban League, and it is still felt today.

    Clanzel was more than a friend to me. He was a close confidante with whom I spent many hours discussing Jacksonville's myriad problems and their possible solutions. It is difficult writing about a friend who gave so much to his community, and one who died much too early. It is more difficult recalling the memories of what that friend meant to the community he served. But I am not writing about Clanzel T. Brown because he was a friend. I am writing about Clanzel T. Brown because of what he represented to the Jacksonville community and this country.

Clanzel was convinced that the key to achieving social parity and civil rights for Blacks was fighting for economic inclusion, educational achievement, and civic engagement, long before civic engagement became the buzzword it is today. It was said that, "Clanzel had but one enemy—and that enemy was poverty." Clanzel was one of this country's unsung warriors in the "War on Poverty." Those of us who worked for the anti-poverty program, or worked with that program, or worked in other community programs fighting poverty, would laughingly invoke Billy Preston's words from his epic hit, "Nothing from Nothing" when he sang "I'm a soldier in the War on Poverty." If many of us, like Ervin Norman, Dr. Harold Childs, Earl Sims, and Jacqueline Jackson, were considered soldiers and officers in that war, then Clanzel Brown, like Moses Freeman and Alton Yates (former executive directors of Jacksonville's anti-poverty programs), were War on Poverty generals.

Over the years Urban League directors in this country were thought of as somewhat conservative, as opposed to being on the front lines of the Civil Rights Movement, and they were also considered somewhat single-task-oriented, with jobs as their priority. Clanzel saw a much larger picture.

Clanzel Thornton Brown Sr., was born in Rome, Georgia, on November 17, 1933, one of nine children of Judson Lee and Blanche Brown. He spent his formative years in Jacksonville, attended the city's public schools, and graduated from Stanton High School in 1950. Brown served in the U.S. Army as a paratrooper during the Korean conflict. After completing his military service, he attended Florida A&M University and earned a bachelor of science degree in sociology in 1956. In 1960 Brown married childhood friend Annie Virginia Butts, a childhood friend and fellow FAMU alumna. Together they raised five children, Clanzenetta, Clanzel II, Clanzerria, Clanzedric, and Annie's daughter Ava Johnson.

Clanzel earned his master's degree in social work in 1975 at

Clanzel Brown, 1975.

Morehouse College while he was executive director of Jacksonville's Urban League, where he began as a volunteer. In addition to his career at the Urban League, Brown was a lifelong member of the NAACP, the first Black to serve on the Jacksonville Downtown Development Authority, the first vice-chairman of the City of Jacksonville's original Human Relations Commission, and a volunteer leader working with more than thirty organizations, including Jacksonville Community Council, Inc., and the Jacksonville Chamber of Commerce. Brown was the recipient of a host of honors, including the Humanitarian Award from the northeast Florida affiliate of the National Conference of Christians and Jews in 1981.

Clanzel's passion was to improve the lives of Jacksonville's Black citizens during the civil rights struggle of the 1960s, '70s, and '80s. During his tenure at the Urban League, he created programs that encouraged and recruited Blacks to apply for jobs in the City of Jacksonville's police and fire departments; he was a moving force

Clanzel T. Brown

to add Blacks to the construction industry by developing the Jacksonville Hometown Plan (funded in part by the U.S. Department of Labor); he developed many pioneering youth programs; he established one of the premier housing programs in the country; and he spearheaded the Urban League's "State of Black Jacksonville Report" in 1977, using research and data as instruments for measuring progress or the lack thereof in the lives of Black people. The "State of Black Jacksonville Report" became an annual review of social and economic metrics, as well as prescriptive recommendations for improving the lives of Blacks in the city.

It was not unusual for Clanzel, as executive director of the Urban League, to receive invitations to meetings that dealt with job training, unemployment, under-employment, civil rights, and equal opportunities, with everyone from the Jacksonville Chamber of Commerce to the City of Jacksonville to local ministerial groups. What was striking was that, if Clanzel was not able to attend the meeting for whatever reason, there would be reluctance on the part of the meeting's conveners to proceed without their knowing if Clanzel was "on board." What a testimony to his influence!

Former president of the national Urban League John Jacobs said that Clanzel, who he had previously tapped to work with Urban League affiliates in other communities to help grow them, built the Jacksonville Urban League into the best in the nation, and, although his stay was brief, he made every minute count. Clanzel was the executive director of the Jacksonville Urban League when both Whitney Young and Vernon Jordan were the executive directors of the national organization. Young, a recipient of the 1969 Presidential Medal of Freedom, was a stalwart civil rights leader of this country until his untimely death in 1971. He would frequently refer to the Clanzel-led Jacksonville Urban League as a "star," and many felt that Young was grooming Clanzel to eventually take his place. Vernon Jordan became the national Urban League's executive director following the death of Whitney Young, and would request that Clanzel provide input and advice at meetings in New York and Washington. In 1980, President Jimmy Carter appointed Clanzel to the National Community Advisory Investment Board.

Clanzel T. Brown was a mentor before mentoring became a commonly known concept. But Clanzel was much, much more than just a mentor. Clanzel Brown was a leader, and a difference maker, who believed in people: Black people, white people, young people, old people, rich people, poor people—just people. From the day he became director of the Jacksonville Urban League in 1965, he saw the need to cultivate a cadre of young people who could be the brain trust of the local community. The list is extensive, beginning with C. Ronald "Ronnie" Belton, the City of Jacksonville's chief financial officer; Ronnie Ferguson, former president and CEO of the City of Jacksonville's Housing Authority; and Ken Johnson, former legislative aide to Congresswoman Corrine Brown, and more recently senior policy advisor for military affairs to Mayor Alvin Brown.

I sat down with three of Clanzel's four children—Clanzenetta, Clanzerria, and Clanzel II (Clanzel's youngest son, Clanzedric, was in Iraq working in a civilian job when we met and was thus unable to participate)—around the kitchen table at the home of Clanzenetta and her husband, Lee Brown, for a retrospective look at the impact their father had on the Jacksonville community. Although I have known all of them almost since birth, I wanted to hear their words and their recollection of when they recognized how significant an impact their father had on the Jacksonville community generally, and the Black community specifically. Of course, they all have the memories one would expect of children who lost their father at a young age. Yet, they were mature enough to understand what their father meant to Jacksonville as the Urban League executive director and as an advocate for the Black community.

Clanzel Brown II, Clanzel's oldest son and a licensed construc-

Clanzel Brown, 1976.

tion contractor, answered first. "One day when I was about twelve or thirteen, we were in the barber shop. It seemed like whatever conversation came up in the barber shop, the men would always ask my daddy what he thought or to explain the situation to them. Dad would take the time to explain all the scenarios of an issue. Even if the conversation had started as an argument, when he finished there was nothing left to say. I began to realize my daddy was very special."

Clanzerria is Clanzel's second daughter. "I knew my daddy was special when I realized that he always wanted to try and help everyone; he never seemed to say 'No.' My sixth-grade math teacher, Mrs. Margaret Day, and my sixth-grade English teacher, Ms. Jacque Parker, would often speak to me about some of the things Daddy was trying to do to make Jacksonville better for all people and how important education was, not only to strive, but to achieve. It was as if my dad was a teacher because everything he taught us at home was always reiterated by my teachers. As I think of my dad, he was a teacher.

"People would often come to the house to work on programs and projects through creating job-training programs, or getting involved in making their neighborhoods safer, or encouraging community consciousness through engaging dialogue and discussions about how their voice matters in their community and how economic development provides opportunities for a better quality of life in Jacksonville."

Clanzel's oldest daughter, Clanzenetta "Mickee" Brown, shared her feelings with me during the same week her son graduated from Florida A&M University. Her father had also graduated from FAMU fifty-five years ago, so it was a tearful yet significant rite of passage, a grandson following in the footsteps of his grandfather. It was even more tearful for her to share her feelings and her recollections about her father, the poignant opening up of a closed wound. She started by saying, "This was really hard to do. I thought I could whip it out, but it kind of got me down."

"When I was a young girl, I knew my father was important if not special to the community because people would be overtly attentive to him and our family. Everyone seemed to know him wherever we went, and at the beginning of my school year, teachers always asked if I was 'Clanzel Brown's daughter.' Instead of this giving me a 'princess complex' it made me determined not to embarrass my family, particularly my dad. During my teens I began to understand my father's politics and his socioeconomic worldview because he was often approached by the media. We'd see Dad on television, hear him on the radio, or see him quoted in the newspaper, regarding pressing community issues like economic disparity, police brutality, poverty, and access to quality education. He provided measured but powerful insights. After his death in 1982 I left Jacksonville to attend college and I'll admit that I missed being 'Clanzel Brown's daughter' when I was in a place where his work was not as well known. I'd go to the university library and read the *Ebony* magazine article about Jacksonville's prominence in the 'new South,' in which he was prominently featured.

"After returning to Jacksonville, I became a volunteer at Jacksonville Community Council, Inc. (JCCI), in 2001. While working at JCCI, I really began to understand the impact that my father had in the community. I was staff resource during a JCCI race-relations study. Over the course of six months, many persons who worked on the study told me how important my dad had been to the city and to them personally. The co-chair of the study committee, a prominent Black judge, told me how he had personally benefited from a Jacksonville Urban League program during my dad's tenure. I also discovered that my father had been a board member of JCCI. A signal moment for me occurred when JCCI began publishing its annual "Race Relations" report card in 2001, and I recognized that it was a successor to the annual "State of Black Jacksonville Report" that my dad had initiated back in 1977. I even had the privilege of working on the JCCI report card with my dad's good friend Rodney Hurst [the author of this book].

"As a writing, research, and planning consultant, I've had the privilege of working for a variety of organizations, including the Jacksonville Urban League, and I frequently run into individuals who worked with my dad to build a more equitable city. From time to time I'll read a snippet about him in local history books. I regularly drive past the city park that bears his name, and every year the Urban League honors a local citizen who exemplifies his spirit. My dad made a difference because he impacted the next generation of leadership in our community. Jacksonville is far from perfect, but it's a much more diverse and integrated community because of the people who fought against racial injustice and inequality during the last half of the twentieth century. My dad was one of those folks and I stand on his shoulders."

Clanzel tragically died of heart failure on July 13, 1982, much too young at age forty-nine. His enduring influence and legacy rest in his extensive work, the goals he accomplished, those whom he influenced, and his "people investments." His legacy is epitomized by the award named in his honor and given every year by the Jacksonville Urban League. (Author's note: I am a recipient of the Clanzel T. Brown Award.) His legacy is perceptible in those he mentored and impacted and those who continue to carry on an Urban League experience defined by his well-known philosophy of "helping the least among us." His legacy is also reflected in the faces and lives of four young adults who love him, cherish his memory, and understand that their father was a respected and revered community leader who simply made Jacksonville better.

Clanzel T. Brown's legacy is that of an ordinary man who simply accomplished extraordinary things! And for that, we are eternally grateful.

Ronnie Belton, 2008.

12

C. Ronald Belton

Powerful people cannot afford to educate the people they oppress . . . because once you are truly educated, you will not ask for power, you will take it.

— Dr. John Henrik Clarke
Pan-Africanist, writer, historian, professor,
pioneer in the development of Africana studies

I sat in St. Gabriel's Episcopal Church one Sunday morning, and watched Clarence Ronald "Ronnie" Belton, the first Black chief financial officer of the City of Jacksonville, Florida, introduce Alvin Brown, Jacksonville's first Black mayor. Mayor Brown was the speaker for St. Gabriel's patronal feast service that morning. Belton was appointed by Mayor Brown, and he also serves as an assistant to the mayor. The symbolism of the moment was not lost on me. I had a momentary flashback to Ronnie's mentor, Clanzel Brown. Here was Ronnie Belton, an Urban Leaguer charged with the responsibility of administering the City of Jacksonville's finance department, standing proudly with the Black mayor of Jacksonville. This was a moment I thought I would never live to see, and one that I was thankful I had lived to see.

As a cradle Episcopalian, Sundays would find the young Ronnie in St. Philip's Episcopal Church in Jacksonville, where he served as an acolyte. Ronnie's grandfather Porcher Taylor Sr., also an Episcopalian, was the editor and publisher of the *Florida Tattler*, a Black newspaper in Jacksonville. Ronnie told me fondly that one of the many positive images he had of his grandfather was his wearing a suit every day, so much so that he himself, while still in junior high, started wearing suits to school. No one told him to wear a suit, or made him wear a suit, or even suggested that he wear a suit, but his image of his grandfather wearing a suit was so motivational and inspirational that Ronnie on his own chose to wear a suit.

As a member of St. Philips myself, I knew Ronnie Belton when he was an acolyte. He was younger and several years behind me in school. Later, while I was working as a news reporter and co-host of *Feedback*, a nightly news and public affairs live interview show on WJCT Channel 7, and affiliate of Public Broadcasting Service (then National Educational Television) in Jacksonville, our paths would cross again. It was 1969, and one of my news assignments was "anchoring" live remote broadcasts from local governmental meetings, including the Jacksonville City Council. A standout track athlete, Ronnie had graduated from New Stanton High School in 1966 and enrolled in Hampton Institute (now Hampton University). Ronnie was a militant (my word), dashiki-wearing, big-afro-wearing Hampton student working as a youth advocate for the Jacksonville Urban League while home during the summer. During the public forum section of the City Council meeting, Ronnie would address the Council on the need for funding youth programs in general, and for the funding of summer youth programs specifically.

He worked under the tutelage of the late venerated Jacksonville Urban League director Clanzel Thornton Brown, whom Ronnie considers his mentor. Mr. Brown, as Ronnie always refers to Clanzel, was summarily responsible for Ronnie entering the world of finance and investments in a somewhat unusual way, but yet, in a way that represented his influence. I recently sat down with Ronnie

Unless WE Tell It . . . It Never Gets Told!

to talk about Clanzel and some of his experiences.

Ronnie first shared a story about a young freshman he befriend-ed at Hampton University, whose name was Freeman Hrabowski. Freeman was a sixteen-year-old genius, who Ronnie called "the Boy Wonder." They became close friends then, and, in fact, are close friends still. During his high school years, Freeman had attend-ed special academic programs at both the Tuskegee Institute and Hampton, courtesy of his sheer intellect. He reported to Hampton as a freshman with several college hours already in hand.

Freeman, at age sixteen, was the youngest of just three freshmen at Hampton who qualified to take a special math course. One day, the three students were to take a test; later that afternoon, a mutual friend came to Ronnie and asked whether he had seen Freeman. Ronnie said no, not recently. The friend told Ronnie that he should find Freeman, because he had last been seen crying and very upset. Ronnie looked everywhere, and finally remembered that Freeman considered the on-campus cemetery for Civil War veterans (yes, the cemetery) as a place of refuge. He found Freeman there, distraught; in between his tears he kept saying that he had made a stupid mis-take with the test earlier that day. Assuming he had failed the test, Ronnie tried to console his friend, telling him that failing a test was not the end of the world.

When it dawned on Freeman that Ronnie thought he had failed the test, he straightened up somewhat and explained why he was upset. He had not failed the test. He had taken the test with the other two freshman, and both of them had made perfect scores; Freeman was miserable because he had only scored 99.5. A 99.5! Ronnie did not make fun of his friend, but he did think that Freeman was a bit overwrought about making a score of 99.5, and he said as much. Freeman then explained that when he prepared for a class or a test, he studied to ace the test—to "win," by making a perfect score. He asked Ronnie whether, as a track athlete, he practiced to come in second. "Of course not," Ronnie told him. Freeman said the same standard applied for him when it came to taking an academic test. He said that he took the math test to win, and that his "mistake"— scoring just 99.5—was the equivalent of coming in second.

Ronnie said to me that this had been his first real eye-opener as a college student. His second eye-opener came when Freeman told Ronnie that he was "not serious enough" about his studies and needed to "keep his head in his books." Recounting this, Ronnie remarked that here had been Freeman Hrabowski, a sixteen-year-old freshman, giving him advice about how to study and to better prepare himself as a student. He came to realize that the preparation and proper study about which Freeman was so adamant was as important as anything he came to know and understand later in life.

Freeman straightened up obviously, got over his "mistake," and continued his path as a high-achieving student at Hampton. Ronnie said that he and Freeman laugh about that series of events today but that the conversation was a life-changer for him, and he often revisits that moment in time. That young genius, by the way, is now

Dr. Freeman Hrabowski III, 2009.

Unless WE Tell It . . . It Never Gets Told!

the esteemed Dr. Freeman Hrabowski, president of the University of Maryland at Baltimore County. In 2009 *Time* magazine honored Dr Hrabowski as one of the country's ten best college presidents.

In 1967, when Ronnie returned home following his freshman year at Hampton, his mother told him to contact Connie Oree, Clanzel Brown's secretary at the Jacksonville Urban League, about a job. During one of his several job-seeking visits, Ronnie finally met Clanzel himself, and told him that he had applied for a job there. Clanzel recognized Ronnie and told him that he had a new program he wanted him to organize. "It was part of the Urban League's new Green Power program for youth, involving two of the city's swimming pools, Jefferson Street pool near Blodgett Homes public housing in the Black community and Hendricks Avenue pool in the white community. Though the pools had been closed because the City of Jacksonville did not want to integrate them, the Jacksonville Urban League was given permission by the federal courts to open and operate both pools for the summer.

Ronnie continued, "My first assignment was to staff this Urban League summer swim program. As I put out flyers recruited people to work at the pools, both whites and Blacks applied, and I began putting my diverse staff together and my lifeguards in place. When I reported the progress to Mr. Brown, he said he wanted me to run the program. So I became the coordinator for Green Power's youth swimming program, placing white lifeguards at a predominantly Black pool (Jefferson Street) and Black lifeguards at a predominantly white pool (Hendricks Avenue). We thus succeeded in doing what the city fathers would not do themselves: we integrated the pools. I kept a running data count during the program of the number of kids and adults who were taught to swim, and with this "groundbreaking" effort there were no problems, no fights, no issues, and no racial incidents; no one drowned, no one called the police."

The following summer Ronnie again worked in the League's

Green Power program, but this time not in the pools. "The City had decided to run the pool program itself based on our success," he said.

Ronnie went on, "One day Mr. Brown asked me what was my major. I told him that I was majoring in psychology. Several conversations later, he suggested that I change my major to sociology, and, since I saw my future in the Urban League, I agreed to make the shift. Early in the second semester of my junior year, I applied for and received an internship in the U.S. Housing and Urban Development office in Newport News, Virginia, for that next summer, and subsequently I attended an Urban League training session in Atlanta directed by the housing director of the Atlanta Urban League. It was fast and furious, but I was learning the housing industry from the Urban League's point of view."

Ronnie received his bachelor's degree in sociology from Hampton University in 1970. He went to work for the Jacksonville Urban League, and soon found that he began to internalize Clanzel's vision around housing issues and other community concerns and projects. Clanzel was purposely involving Ronnie in many areas in order to expand his interest in and knowledge of community issues. Housing became Ronnie Belton's forte at the Jacksonville Urban League, and that entailed working with the League's first housing foundation. "I learned quite a bit about housing and urban development programs. It heightened my interest even more in the Urban League. Without my even realizing it, Mr. Brown was moving me in the direction of housing, and I was excited by that. We were helping people throughout the community with housing and mortgage problems."

"It brings to mind a light confrontation (if confrontations are ever light) that I had with the owner of one of the rental companies, which was preparing to evict a lady while we were working to help her. We visited the rental office, and, in my militant's mode, I began to dress down the rental staff about their proposed eviction actions. I asked to see the owner, and continued to tell him off, including what I thought about his business. After hearing me wax irate about how they had erred in the process of evicting our 'client,' he said something to me that stopped me in my tracks." He said, 'You are too smart to be so dumb, and if you come into my office again not knowing what you are talking about, I will have you arrested.' Ronnie said that, in his militancy, he wanted to jump on him, but in his intellect, he thought better. The man's comments were sobering . . . and he was right. Ronnie said that, with his training as a community organizer and spending time in HUD training workshops and seminars in Atlanta, he had thought he knew a lot about housing, but unfortunately he did not know enough. "I did know one thing, though. I would not make comments again without proper preparation. The next time I would definitely know what I was talking about. I went to class and studied, and received my mortgage broker's license, my real estate sales license, and my underwriter's license for property and casualty insurance."

He continued, "With housing as one of our obvious priorities, we had embarked on a housing project on Jacksonville's Eastside when the Nixon Administration eliminated the Office of Economic Opportunity and embargoed our funds, some of which were in part financing our housing project. Mr. Brown and I went to see Paul Brandenburger, a stockbroker who worked for Walsh and Company." Clanzel asked Brandenburger for help with financing to get the housing project moving again. Although he could not help them, Ronnie was impressed with Brandenburger's physical office setup—the two telephones on his desk incessantly ringing, his ticker tape machine running constantly, and the interruptions by his secretary with regard to investment issues. Ronnie said that this was all new to him, but it was obvious that Paul Brandenburger was a major stockbroker. When Ronnie inquired about the possibility of becoming a stockbroker himself, Brandenburger's response was "They are not ready for you." Ronnie told me that Brandenburger did not say it or mean it in a racist manner but "Mr. Brown and I both knew what he meant." That chance meeting and Brandenburger's words intrigued Ronnie.

A couple of years passed, and one morning Ronnie walked into Clanzel Brown's office with a copy of the *Florida Star*, a local Black newspaper, which had an advertisement from Merrill Lynch advertising for a Black stockbroker; he laughingly told Clanzel that Merrill Lynch was advertising "his" job. Clanzel suggested that Ronnie apply. Ronnie did so, filling out the necessary paperwork and proceeding with the interview and the vetting process. Of course, he did not think that Merrill Lynch would hire a Black and was certain they would not offer him the job. But still he applied.

After a series of interviews up and down the Merrill Lynch chain of command, psychological testing, and a plethora of various "testing tools," the unlikeliest of circumstances occurred: Ronnie was offered the job. So, now what?

It reminds me of the sit-in days. Even though civil rights history showed that stores like Woolworth's and Grant's would close their lunch counter rather than serve us, Mr. Pearson always cautioned us to have money in our pockets just in case Woolworth decided they would serve us. His words were, "If Woolworth would arrest us for sitting in that is one thing, but if they arrest us for not having money to pay for our food, that is a different matter." We would laugh, and then proceed with money in our pockets (or pocketbooks) to make our way to the lunch counters.

Anyway, with the job offer from Merrill Lynch staring him in the face, Ronnie decided that he did not want to accept it. He enjoyed his job at the Urban League and was reluctant to leave, nor did his family want him to part from this "good job." He went to Clanzel Brown to tell him he was not going to accept the Merrill

Lynch job offer but instead had decided to stay at the Urban League. Ronnie told me that he was taken aback when Clanzel responded by saying, "This is an opportunity of a lifetime and puts into practice what we have been preaching about upward and onward. Merrill Lynch is ready for their first step, and we must step with them. And you, Ronnie, are the right man to make that step." Then Clanzel said, "You've got to go."

Ronnie was a bit crushed that Mr. Brown did not say, "No, we want you to stay." Ronnie recalls that he even entertained the possibility that maybe Clanzel was trying to push him out of the League, though he quickly realized that this was not the case. It was quite a moment for him. Ronnie felt that, despite his curiosity about being a stockbroker, working at Merrill Lynch would be joining the "suits" and becoming a traitor to the cause of fighting for his community in the war on poverty. Yet he understood what Clanzel had preached to him from his first day at the Jacksonville Urban League: you do not open doors and then wonder, "Who is qualified enough to walk through?" It sounds idealistic, but Clanzel taught Ronnie that you are taught skills within your specific community, and that after sharing those skills with your community, you impart those skills to the larger community. You learn, and then you teach. So, finally this Urban Leaguer, this community organizer, people advocate, housing expert, dashiki-wearing Black "militant" decided to accept Merrill Lynch's offer and became Jacksonville's first Black stockbroker, not because he wanted to, but because he had to. And the rest, as we are so apt to say, is history.

Of course, it was not easy, but Ronnie Belton learned to deal with the challenges of being the first Black man in an otherwise white world of high finance. A successful stint of twenty years at Merrill Lynch led to his being invited to be a partner in an investment company by a friend from Merrill Lynch, Peter Bower, and to become executive vice president and chief compliance officer of

Riverplace Capital Management, Inc. He served in both capacities until his appointment by Mayor Brown. Ronnie, with Peter Bower, also created his own money-managing company, serving as the president and chief executive officer of Riverplace Analytics, LLC, from 2006 to 2011. These successful business ventures placed Ronnie at another level of money-managing high finance. Not only did he prove that he comprehended and belonged in this arena in which Black faces were a rarity, but he was culturally comfortable. He understood and spoke the language of this place where he had arrived.

He accumulated a bundle of experiences and a strong grasp of the world of finance. His life of preparation led him to this moment in history, where he is responsible for the City of Jacksonville's budget. Ronnie trained first in education, then in his community, and later in this stylized and at times misunderstood world of high finance.

Ronnie Belton was appointed to the Jacksonville Urban League board in 1979, and, following Clanzel's death, served as chairman

Ronnie Belton receiving the Jacksonville Branch NAACP Rutledge Pearson Award from Mrs. Rutledge (Mary Ann) Pearson and NAACP President Isaiah Rumlin.

Unless WE Tell It . . . It Never Gets Told!

Jacksonville Urban League board chair Dr. W. W. Schell, civic leader J. J. Daniel, Ronnie Belton, Father Pat Seymour, and Clanzel Brown, 1972.

of the board from 1982 to 1985. Ronnie is still very much a cradle Episcopalian, and he and his wife, Gloria, continue to worship at St. Philip's Episcopal Church.

Ronnie feels that his successes are a reflection of the time and effort that Clanzel Brown invested getting him ready, and of the fact that the good Lord is "watching over" him. But C. Ronald Belton also invested in himself. He knows and understands preparation. He has represented his place in time, and he has done so quite well. C. Ronald Belton is one of the very best that the Jacksonville Urban League had to offer. He is one of the best Hampton had to offer. He is one of the best. Clanzel T. Brown taught him well. He learned well, and the Jacksonville community is the beneficiary.

C. Ronald Belton

Alton Yates, 2000.

13

Alton Yates

We are confronted primarily with a moral issue... whether all Americans are to be afforded equal rights and equal opportunities, whether we are going to treat our fellow Americans as we want to be treated.

—President John Fitzgerald Kennedy

Alton W. Yates is a national hero. You will not, however, find his name on a monument, nor will you find a marker applauding his accomplishments in the military. Well, not yet anyway. Alton was one of the first high-speed sled jockeys during the early 1950s, conducting some of the experiments that led to the achievements of our modern-day space astronauts. That should be enough to have him and his accomplishments mentioned in the same breath with other space pioneers. It is not. Notwithstanding the dark hue of his skin, was it enough to give him an opportunity to become an astronaut? Never mind, don't answer that.

When I was president of the Jacksonville Youth Council NAACP, Alton was the vice-president and served as one of the leaders of the 1960 Jacksonville sit-ins. Those sit-ins led to the infamous Ax Handle Saturday, when two hundred white males with ax handles and baseball bats attacked us as we sat at "white" lunch counters, protesting segregation and racism.

Alton is a fourth-generation Jacksonvillian, born and raised in the Lavilla neighborhood. He is the second of seven brothers and sisters. Active in high school activities, Alton was a featured baritone soloist with the New Stanton High School glee club, under the direction of noted choir director Alpha Hayes Moore. Alton graduated from New Stanton in 1954.

In 1956, Alton, an airman second class in the Air Force, volunteered for the rocket-sled testing program at Holloman Air Force Base in New Mexico. At the beginning of the space race between the United States and the Soviet Union, little was known about how far the body could be stressed and still survive. The rocket-sled program was created for the purpose of seeking answers to that question, with sleds designed by space pioneer Colonel (and Dr.) John Paul Stapp to test a human's ability to tolerate gravitational forces or "G" forces during liftoff, re-entry, and recovery. Stapp, a famed researcher known at the time as "the fastest human on earth," attained in 1954 what was then a world-record land speed of 632 miles per hour, reached from a standstill in five seconds on a specially designed rocket sled that screeched to a dead stop in 1.4 seconds, sustaining more than forty G's of thrust, the equivalent of hitting a brick wall in a car at 120 miles per hour.[1]

Two years later, Stapp recruited a young Alton Yates. For the next few years, Holloman's pioneering program paved the way for America's first manned space flights. Yates would ride two rocket sleds, dubbed the "Daisy" and the "Bopper"; he also ascended to more than sixty-five thousand feet in balloons, testing pressure suits for astronauts. Propulsion for the Daisy was by compressed-air catapult, a similarity it shared with the popular Daisy air rifle, which gave the sled its name. It ran on the "Daisy Track," two rails five feet apart and 120 feet long. The "Bopper" ran on a track of less than thirty feet long and was more or less a slingshot, accelerating from zero to more than four hundred miles per hour in seconds,

Unless WE Tell It . . . It Never Gets Told!

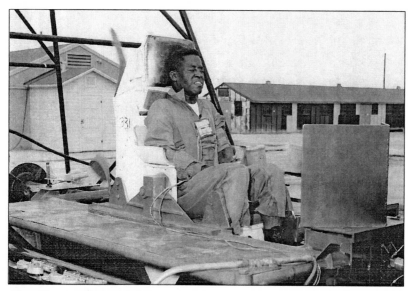

Alton Yates on the speed sled, 1958.

and then slamming to a stop. Alton confirmed that, indeed, it felt like hitting a brick wall.

Alton received national and international acclaim and was cited by the U.S. Air Force for risking his life for science. His daring and courageous story about this dangerous, pioneering testing was featured in *Ebony* and *Jet* magazines in 1959. Yet when Alton was discharged from the Air Force, he had to drive from New Mexico to Jacksonville through a belt of racial animosity and hostility. This courageous Air Force veteran could not even stop and get a sandwich or use a restroom without being insulted. It was life in these United States, circa 1959.

Alton left active duty in the Air Force in 1959 and began his long sixteen-hundred-mile drive back to Jacksonville from New Mexico. As he was underway, he stopped at a restaurant to get a sandwich and was frankly and bluntly told, "We don't serve niggers!" Traveling in his Air Force uniform apparently meant nothing to the restaurant manager; nor did risking his life many times for this country and its space science program.

He might have been a hero in his military commitment to his country; but outside of the Air Force, he was still "just a nigger." Angry and frustrated, Alton stopped at a grocery store in Texas where he purchased a jar of peanut butter, a jar of jelly, a loaf of bread, a knife, and a spoon, and then ate peanut-butter-and-jelly sandwiches all the way back to Jacksonville. He made a vow at that time to "fight racism and discrimination, even if it takes forever."

After his return home to Jacksonville, he joined the Jacksonville Youth Council NAACP. I met Alton in 1959 and we immediately developed what would become a lifelong friendship. Later that same year, I was elected president of the Youth Council, Alton was elected vice-president, and Marjorie Meeks was elected secretary. With Mr. Pearson as its advisor, the Jacksonville Youth Council NAACP became quite a formidable civil rights group.

Alton's civilian career path was also pioneering. He served as the executive director of Greater Jacksonville Economic Opportunity Inc., the city's anti-poverty agency, leading Jacksonville's war on poverty for a number of years; as administrative aide to three of Jacksonville's mayors; as executive director of the Jacksonville Community Relations Commission; as manager of administration for the Community Economic Development Center at Florida Community College; and as director of the City of Jacksonville's Regulatory and Environmental Services Department. Wherever Alton has gone, he has made a difference.

He encouraged racial diversity and equality in the military while serving from 1981 to 1996 in the Florida Air National Guard, where he worked as an equal-opportunity officer in the Guard's St. Augustine headquarters. "Lieutenant Colonel Yates is as close to a true American hero as I have met," said Major General Douglas Burnett, recently retired adjutant general of the Florida National Guard. "He was a pioneer in the early days of our nation's space effort, risking his life countless times while testing the rocket sleds used in space flight research. He also acted bravely and courageously in the civil rights struggle in his community for many years."

Alton is a Yale University / Ford Foundation graduate national urban fellow. He has held several gubernatorial appointments, including by Governor Reubin Askew to the Florida Education Council and by Governor Bob Graham to the trustee board of Florida Community College of Jacksonville (where he served as chairman from 1988 through 1990). Alton is a life member of Kappa Alpha Psi fraternity. He is a member and lecturer of Holy Rosary Catholic Church in Jacksonville, and a Fourth Degree Knight of Columbus. He is a graduate of the U.S. Department of Defense Equal Opportunity Management Institute. Alton retired from the Florida Air National Guard, U.S. Air Force, with the rank of lieutenant colonel. Among his numerous awards are: the Pro Ecclesia Et Pontifice Medal, by Pope Paul VI; the Brotherhood Award, by the National Conference of Christians and Jews; and the governor of Florida's Medal of Merit. The Medal of Merit is the highest military honor the governor can bestow and is reserved for those who gave exceptional service while on active duty.

Alton is married to former Jacksonville City Councilwoman Gwen Yates. They are the parents of two children, a son, Alton II, and a daughter, Toni, and have two granddaughters and a grandson.

Alton Yates risked his life more than sixty-five times while serving his country, and returned to his home town of Jacksonville to fight the racial injustice that has no place in "the land of the free and the home of the brave." That 1959 trip from New Mexico to Jacksonville became the start to his historic and monumental journey to fight racism and discrimination. It was if his path was pre-ordained. Certainly Alton's soul and spirit was anchored in fighting racism while improving the plight of the least of these, based on skin color and economic condition. Alton became an unsung national hero years ago. He is still a national hero today.

Bethel Baptist Institutional Church.

14

Bethel Baptist Institutional Church

*I love the pure, peaceable, and impartial Christianity of
Jesus Christ; I therefore hate the corrupt, slave-holding,
women-whipping, cradle-plundering, partial, and hypocritical Christianity of this land.*

> —Frederick Douglass
> Social reformer, orator, writer, and statesman

Bethel Baptist Institutional Church is the oldest Baptist congregation in Jacksonville. At its inception in 1838, Bethel had six members: four whites—Reverend James McDonald, the first pastor, and
his wife, plus Elias C. Jaudan, who became the first deacon, and his
wife—and two enslaved persons known as Bacchus and Peggy.

The first racially mixed congregational meetings were held in
the Government Block House, which stood near the County Courthouse. Membership quickly grew, with most early congregants
being enslaved persons who received day passes from their masters to attend. In 1840, the church purchased a lot on the northeast
corner of Duval and Newnan Streets and built its first dedicated
house of worship. The Legislative Council of the Territory of Florida
incorporated Bethel Church on February 10, 1841. William B. Kass,
Charles Merrick, Soloman Warren, Elias Jaudan, H. H. Phillips, and
A. Ossian Hart, the first trustees, participated in the incorporation.

This first church building in Jacksonville was sold to the Presbyterian Church in 1844. Elias Jaudan later purchased a lot on Myrtle Avenue between Duval and Monroe, where the second Bethel Church was built. Bethel's church leadership at that time expected a residential shift to the west of downtown Jacksonville, but that did not occur. Later Jaudan purchased another property on Church Street between Hogan and Julia Streets, and there the third Bethel Church was constructed. Soon after the congregation started worship services in the new building in the spring of 1861, the Federal Army took possession of the Bethel Church and used it as a military hospital for wounded soldiers during the Civil War.

Bethel Baptist remained one of the few interracial churches until after the war. It developed that the congregation was facing a split over which pastor to follow, and white members took the opportunity to try to force the Blacks—who were in the vast majority, the church then having 40 white members and 270 Black members— out of the church. They took their case to court, but the court ruled in favor of the Blacks, determining that they were the rightful owners of the Bethel Baptist name and property.

A short while after the court's decision, Black members sold the property on Church Street to the whites who had previously worshipped with them. There the white members established the Tabernacle Baptist Church, which was later named First Baptist Church (Downtown). First Baptist Church of Downtown Jacksonville thus developed out of Bethel Baptist Institutional Church and not the other way around.

The Black congregation, meanwhile, purchased a lot on the northwest corner of Union Street and Pine Street (now Main Street). In 1868, they erected a one-room frame building where the Bethel Baptist Church congregation would worship for twenty-seven years and grow to several hundred members.

Florida Baptist Academy, the predecessor of the Florida Nor-

Unless WE Tell It . . . It Never Gets Told!

mal and Industrial Institute, was founded on the church campus of Bethel Baptist Church in 1892 by Reverend Mathew William Gilbert, Bethel's pastor, together with Reverend J. T. Brown and Sarah Ann Blocker. Reverend Gilbert would leave Bethel to become the first president of Florida Baptist Academy. John Rosamond Johnson, Bethel's organist and choir director, and the brother of James Weldon Johnson, would accompany Reverend Gilbert and join the faculty of Florida Baptist Academy (which years later would become Florida Memorial University); there he would write the music for "Lift Ev'ry Voice and Sing."

Reverend John Milton Waldron became Bethel's pastor in 1892. Born in 1863, Waldron had been educated at Lincoln University in Pennsylvania and Newton Theological Institution in Massachusetts. In 1894 Waldron incorporated Bethel as the first Black Institutional Church in the South and enabled Bethel to provide social services and education to the surrounding communities as Protestant churches were providing in the North.[1]

Bethel's congregation grew rapidly over the years, so much so that more space was needed for worship and for training. The building could not be repaired or enlarged because of the City of Jacksonville fire code. Reverend Waldron led the congregation in replacing the one-room frame building with a larger, more attractive house of worship. In 1895, Bethel constructed the first Institutional Church building to be erected in the South by a "colored" congregation. The new structure was built of red pressed brick and trimmed with Georgia marble. It contained a main auditorium with a seating capacity of 1,150 and nine classrooms. At the time of its construction it was the most convenient and attractive church building in the city, and at a cost of $26,000. Ironically, this beautiful edifice was in use only a short time before it was destroyed by the devastating Jacksonville fire on May 3, 1901.

Following the Great Fire of 1901, Bethel Baptist Institutional

Church established temporary quarters for both church services and its Bible Institute in a building that they labeled the "Shack." Regular services continued in the "Shack" for several years.

During a time when there were no "colored" banks in Jacksonville, Reverend Waldron joined Abraham Lincoln Lewis and others in founding the Afro-American Life Insurance Company ("the Afro") to provide burial benefits for the "colored" community. The Afro also opened a savings department through which individuals could deposit ten, fifteen, twenty-five cents per week.

The congregation of Bethel Baptist Institutional Church in the meantime had grown beyond the five hundred mark, and, in order to provide for its continued growth, it was deemed necessary to find a larger site and one that was off of the main business streets. In 1903, the "Rivers' Square" was purchased, bounded by Hogan Street (now McKissick Street), Eagle Street (now First Street), Julia Street, and Caroline Street (now Bethel Baptist Street), and facing the new City Park—one of the most desirable blocks in the city for church purposes. Led by Reverend Waldron, Bethel's congregation proceeded to erect one of the most modern and spacious church buildings in the South. It was designed by architect M. H. Hubbard of Utica, New York, and combined elements of Greek Revival and Romanesque Revival architecture. Bethel's members took pride in the fact that "the church was erected by Colored workers, under the direction of Colored contractors. That now historic sanctuary still stands.

Reverend Waldron said it best when he stated that "Bethel should stand as a refutation of racial inferiority and an object lesson of the better side of Negro culture and progress in the South."[2]

Reverend Waldron left Bethel and Jacksonville in 1907 to pastor Shiloh Baptist Church in Washington, D.C., but not before establishing his leadership in the civil rights arena. When the Supreme Court

upheld the "separate but equal" doctrine in 1896, Blacks in twenty-
five cities across the South held boycotts in the ensuing decade to
protest segregated transportation. In 1901 Reverend Waldron led
Bethel in a successful boycott of the transportation system of Jacksonville in response to the city's segregation ordinances. Historians
August Meier and Elliott Rudwick described Bethel as having been
a "key church in the boycott." From 1905 through 1910 Reverend
Waldron would become one of the nation's most vocal civil rights
leaders. Waldron's crusade against racial injustice motivated him to
join with W. E. B. Du Bois and other Black leaders in the Niagara
Movement, a forerunner of the National Association of the Advancement of Colored People. He would later become the national
treasurer of the Niagara Movement. An article written by William
English Walling in 1908 entitled "Race War in the North" in *The*

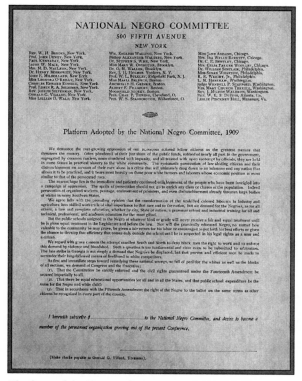

Platform of the National Negro Committee, 1909.

Independent described a massive race riot directed at black residents in the hometown of Abraham Lincoln, Springfield, Illinois, that led to seven deaths, forty homes and twenty-four businesses destroyed, and 107 indictments against rioters. Walling ended the article by calling for a powerful body of citizens to come to the aid of Blacks. Waldron and many others responded to the call, and that eventually led to the formation of the National Negro Committee, which held its first meeting in New York on May 31 and June 1, 1909. In May 1910, attendants at the second conference of the National Negro Committee established the permanent body known as the National Association for the Advancement of Colored People (NAACP). Reverend John Milton Waldron and the others who founded the National Negro Committee were also the founders of the NAACP.

Reverend John E. Ford succeeded Reverend Waldron and served as Bethel's pastor for thirty-six years, from 1907 to 1943. Although this was a long tenure, it would not be the longest. When Bishop Rudolph W. McKissick Sr., retired after serving from 1967 to 2014, his forty-seven years in the pulpit made him Bethel's longest-serving pastor. His son, Bishop Rudolph W. McKissick Jr., who served as senior co-pastor with his father, now serves as Bethel's senior pastor.

Several schools in Jacksonville are named for Bethel pastors or members of the Bethel congregation: Matthew William Gilbert Middle School (formerly Matthew William Gilbert Junior Senior High School), named for Reverend Matthew William Gilbert, pastor of Bethel and first president of Florida Baptist Academy; John E. Ford Elementary School, named for Reverend John E. Ford, pastor of Bethel Baptist Institutional Church; William Marion Raines High School, named for William Marion Raines, Bethel's Sunday School superintendent and former principal of Matthew William Gilbert High School (1938–1950); St. Clair Evans Elementary School (formerly Moncrief Elementary School), named for St. Clair Evans;

Sallye Mathis Elementary School, named for Sallye Mathis, Jacksonville City Council member (1968–1982); and Rufus E. Payne Elementary School, named for Rufus E. Payne, also one of Bethel's Sunday School superintendents.

A number of churches in Jacksonville, Florida, had their beginning in Bethel Baptist Institutional Church: First Baptist Church Downtown Jacksonville, Shiloh Metropolitan Baptist Church, Central Baptist Church, Zion Baptist Church, Greenland Baptist Church, Bethel Baptist Church (Sweetwater), Second Missionary Baptist Church, St. John's Baptist Church, Day Spring Baptist Church, Main Street Baptist Church, St. Luke's Baptist Church, Trinity Baptist Church, Harmony Baptist Church, Ebenezer Baptist Church, Bethel Baptist Church Southside, Bethel Baptist Church St. Nicholas, Second Bethel Baptist Church, and Panama Park Baptist Church.

One does not have to attend Bethel to marvel at the magnificent architecture of its historic sanctuary, which was built in 1904 and added to the National Register of Historic Places (the U.S. federal government's official list of districts, sites, buildings, structures, and objects deemed worthy of preservation) on April 6, 1978.

Bethel Baptist Institutional Church and its history have stood as a significant part of Black history in this country. From its founding, to its architecture, to the pride of being the true birthplace of "Lift Ev'ry Voice and Sing," Bethel Baptist Institutional Church is iconic. Although Florida Memorial University claims to be the birthplace of "Lift Ev'ry Voice and Sing," were it not for Bethel there would be no Florida Baptist Academy and thus no Florida Memorial University and no "Lift Ev'ry Voice and Sing."

Bethel's story is the story of a great church, with a great history. Bethel's story is the story of its impact on Jacksonville, on the state of Florida, and on this country. Bethel's story is the story of Black America, at its finest.

15

The Huston-Tillotson College Quartet

RUTLEDGE PEARSON—THE MEMO

I received this priceless memo from Priscilla Williamson, who was a member of the Stanton High School class of 1947 and Mr. Pearson's classmate:

> Congratulations! Fifty years ago you received your diplomas! That was a happy day for each of you! In 1947, you faced life as it really is; and now, this eighth day of August 1997, you again meet to share past experiences.
>
> There were some members of this class who knew me as their English teacher; some as assistant librarian (very few, walked into the room). Around 1945, you may have passed a small group of singers in the Beaver-Clay Street hallway exit. You are right—now I am teaching choral music. I began with a small group composed of largely male voices, and a few girls with Mary Lawton '47, and Lydia Dwight (Wooden) holding up that section.
>
> The Male Quartet, all members of this class—Andrew Day, first tenor; Walter Anders, second tenor; Rutledge Pearson, baritone; Nathaniel Green, bass, was the greatest then. When Mr. Pearson received an athletic scholarship to Tillotson College (now Huston-Tillotson College) in Austin, Texas, he accepted with a condition. "If you will give schol-

arships to my three buddies, we will come." The college music professor acknowledged his request, stating that it was a "first" for her. However, as time traveled on, she would always let the College Quartet sing high school repertoire.

One day in December there was a knock at my door. When I opened it, all I could see was teeth, shining eyes, and outstretched arms! After we had settled a bit, Andrew said, "Our music teacher wants you to teach us some new songs. She just loved what and how we sang. Naturally, I was flattered, but I said, "If I have to spend my Christmas holidays teaching you new material for her benefit, then she must send me a portion of her December check." We laughed but immediately got down to business. The class of 1947 has left memories that I shall never forget.

—Doris Avery Hampton-Jones

The Huston-Tillotson College Quartet

I could not thank Priscilla enough for this memo. These personal anecdotes simply show another of the many polished facets of Mr. Rutledge Henry Pearson. Of course, you could expect me to show my bias when discussing my mentor.

Mrs. Doris A. Jones was the librarian at Northwestern Junior Senior High School during my high school years, and although I never heard this particular story, Mr. Pearson would tell me many stories about the Huston-Tillotson Quartet, which he founded. Years later, my friend, classmate and fellow 1960 graduate of Northwestern Junior Senior High School, and former next-door neighbor, Catherine Patricia Marshall Massey, would become the librarian of Northwestern Middle School (formerly Northwestern Junior Senior High School).

Reverend William Holmes Borders.

16

Reverend William Holmes Borders

There is no medicine to cure hatred.
—African proverb

Between 1937 and 1988, the Reverend William Holmes Borders (1905–1993) served as pastor of Wheat Street Baptist Church in Atlanta, Georgia, where he campaigned for civil rights and distinguished himself as a charismatic spokesperson for the city's poor and dispossessed. Borders was instrumental in the hiring of Atlanta's first Black police officers in the 1940s, led the campaign to desegregate the city's public transportation in the 1950s, and established the nation's first federally subsidized, church-operated rental housing project in the 1960s.

Dr. Williams Holmes Borders gave the commencement address when I graduated from Northwestern Junior Senior High School in June of 1960. He was outstanding. Jacksonville had its share of great Black preachers at that time, but this fire-and-brimstone preacher from Atlanta was special. Ax Handle Saturday, in August of that year, was yet two months away. Reverend Borders was inspiring and motivating. Commencement speakers during those days of segregation were usually selected by the school administration and were not really that remarkable. Certainly, they were not expected to make references to the circumstances of racism and discrimination Blacks had to face. I was expecting the usual speech—"Eat your Wheaties, go to school every day, and everything will be all right" —for this first graduating class of Northwestern Junior Senior High School. Even at age of sixteen, I remember quite vividly portions of Reverend Border's speech.

Reverend Borders told us a baseball anecdote, tinged (for me) with racial achievement, about a baseball game he had attended between the Brooklyn Dodgers and the Philadelphia Phillies. That was the early 1950s, when Jackie Robinson was playing for the Brooklyn Dodgers. I was a Dodgers fan, and had met Jackie when he spoke to a mass meeting of the Jacksonville Branch NAACP. When Reverend Borders said "Brooklyn Dodgers," my ears perked up. He verbally drew this picture of three Black players for the Dodgers, pitcher Don Newcombe, catcher Roy Campanella, and Jackie Robinson, who was playing second base. Richie Ashburn, the Phillies lead-off batter and prolific base-runner was on first base after hitting a single. On Newcombe's very first pitch to the next batter, Ashburn set off attempting to steal second base; the batter swung and missed. Then, as reported by Reverend Borders: "Black Roy Campanella received the pitch from Black Don Newcombe, who threw to Black Jackie Robinson, who tagged out white Richie Ashburn. I was so glad."

What was immediately striking to me was that Reverend Borders used the term "Black." In 1960, Americans, including Blacks, had not "evolved" to the place of using "Black" as a racially descriptive term, yet here was this civil rights activist minister from Atlanta using the symbolism of a baseball game to illustrate that, for that moment, Blacks were in charge. (Yep, I thought about that at the time.)

Although many in the audience laughed, it was a strained and perhaps an uncomfortable laugh for those on the stage at Northwestern Junior Senior High School. Since this was Northwestern's first graduation, the stage was filled with white officials of the Duval

Unless WE Tell It . . . It Never Gets Told!

County school system, including the elected school superintendent Ish Brant, and the Black supervisor of Negro Education, Dr. John Irving Elias Scott. In those days of segregation, you did not joke about racial issues with whites looking on, and especially when Blacks came out on top.

Dr. Borders took his "I was so glad" comment and expanded it to talk about how proud he was to watch "his" Dodgers (and mine too) show their athletic skills. He said Negroes should strive to be the best and even "better than the rest." How his words resonated with me and my high school classmates! His anecdote and that comment—"I was so glad"—also said that Blacks working together could achieve success.

His closing comments referenced achievements. He said that when you think you have achieved a goal, then you should reach a bit higher; and when you have reached that next level, reach a bit higher yet; and then higher, and higher, and higher—and that is how he ended his splendid high school commencement speech for this historic first graduating class of Northwestern Junior Senior High School of Jacksonville, Florida. What magnificent inspiration to take into the Jacksonville sit-ins of 1960, Ax Handle Saturday, and into one of this country's most significant summers of civil rights activism!

Reverend Borders served as pastor of the Wheat Street Baptist Church in Atlanta for more than fifty years. An incessant campaigner for civil rights, he remained a civil rights stalwart and influential public figure in Atlanta until his death in 1993.

I often think back to how great it was—as I was graduating from high school—to hear his message about being Black and proud.

Dr. Barbara Williams White, 2011.

17

Dr. Barbara Williams White

Every great dream begins with a dreamer. Always remember, you have within you the strength, the patience, and the passion to reach for the stars to change the world.

—Harriet Tubman

Dr. Barbara White's inspiring professional journey began in Jacksonville, Florida, with stops in Tallahassee at Florida Agricultural and Mechanical University (FAMU) and Florida State University (FSU), before settling at the University of Texas (UT) in Austin, Texas. Although Barbara self-describes herself as an introvert, and as a person who does not need the dazzle of the limelight, her professional life is filled with luminance indeed. Her journey included her election as Miss FAMU for the 1963–64 school year. We called her "Black Jacksonville's College Queen." Barbara said she reluctantly agreed to run for Miss FAMU only after "being encouraged by her sorority sisters."

After graduating from New Stanton Senior High School in 1960, Barbara White majored in music at FAMU on the recommendation of the late Kernaa McFarlin, the venerated band director at New Stanton High School, and a seminal figure in the lives of a number of students who played in the band at New Stanton. Barbara wanted to attend college outside of Florida, but in that segregated era, scholarship money for Black students was extremely scarce. Some "Black" scholarships were awarded based on test results. Yet other "Black" Scholarships, even when merit, citizenship, and grade point average enabled Blacks to qualify, were politically based on who you were and who you knew. After suggesting she attend FAMU, Mr. McFarlin called the college's music department to recommend a work-study scholarship.

"I should not have majored in music," said Barbara, "but I didn't figure that out until my senior year. Mr. McFarlin gave me good advice at that time, but, since I was barely a teenager going to college, I really didn't know the best academic avenue to follow. I decided to minor in psychology and perhaps become a music therapist. What did I know as a nineteen-year-old? But I did stick with music. I received my bachelor's degree from FAMU. I got married and came back to Jacksonville and taught music in the school system for nine years, unhappily."

She continued, "My husband was asked to come back to FAMU in Tallahassee and work with FAMU's band. So I relocated with him to Tallahassee. I decided I would look at another field of study. I enrolled at FSU as a graduate student in sociology. I had no idea what I would do, but I did know I had an interest in the subject. After a semester of graduate studies, I discovered I did not like sociology either. Perhaps my being out of school for ten years was the reason. . . . At least that is my reason.

"I talked with one of my sociology professors, and I told him that the program did not seem like a good fit for me. He suggested that I talk with the curriculum counselors in the social work department. I took his advice and was fortunate to talk with the assistant dean, who really took the time to talk with me, and, perhaps more important, to listen to me. I told her I wanted to do something that made a difference in the lives of other people. I hated social injustice, and felt that social work was where I could make positive change. I was already behind a semester, so she suggested that I start the next semester and work on an undergraduate degree in social work which would qualify me for the one-year masters in social work program and I would not have to sit out a long period of time. My third course change.

"I completed my undergraduate requirements and all requirements for my master's degree in social work in two years. Normally it would take three years, but FSU had recently inaugurated an advanced-standing master's degree program. It totally rejuvenated me. I was now thirty years old and embarking on a new career after teaching music for nine years without a challenge. Social work is heavy on social policy and presents very worthy challenges. I had a choice between either clinical practice with an emphasis on therapy or administration. I chose administration and was selected to intern in Florida Governor Reubin Askew's office. Working in the governor's office was a great experience and a great internship, but it also let me know that you have to commit to a life of politics. It looks good, but getting there is not so fun. It reminds me of the sausage joke. Everyone likes sausage, but no one likes to see it made.

"In 1975, I went to work for the Leon County school system (Tallahassee) but left when a Title XX job—grant money but literally no benefits—came available at FAMU. About the same time, I was encouraged to run for the state president of the Florida Association of Social Work. I ran, and won by two votes. Now my work really began. My election as FASW president caught the attention of the dean of the college of social work at FSU, who asked me to apply for a faculty position in the college of social work. My interview was scheduled, and I arrived for it at the appointed time.

"I was asked to sit in an interview room and someone would come to interview me 'shortly.' No one came. No one came because they did not want me to work at FSU. The dean of the college of social work wanted me, but his staff did not. I was in fact hired, but I was hired primarily because the dean had made a decision to diversify his staff, and I was his first 'diversifier.'

"Florida State and other universities in the state of Florida had a program which allowed *one* member of the faculty to receive a year with pay to study full time for their doctorate. Through this spirited competition I was awarded one year of paid study and also won a second year, giving me back-to-back years. I received my Ph.D. from Florida State University in political science in 1984,and eventually became associate dean in the FSU college of social work, assuming the added responsibilities of assistant dean when the assistant dean quit. None of this translated to more pay—just to added responsibilities. It was truly a learning process, and I learned well.

"While serving as assistant dean at Florida State, I was elected national president of the National Association of Social Work (NASW). This entailed a very active and ambitious schedule of travel to more than thirty-eight states and a number of countries. It was not a paid position, though my traveling expenses were covered."

As the president of the 155,000-member NASW from 1991 to 1993, Dr. White joined such noteworthy and prestigious company as the late national director of the Urban League, Whitney Young, who served as president of the NASW from 1969 to 1971.

Dr. White said, "My tenure as NASW president brought me to the attention of the University of Texas. Coincidentally, my next-door neighbor from Tallahassee had taken a position at the University of Texas, and told me that Texas was conducting a search for the dean of their college of social work. I told her, quite frankly, that I did not feel like playing any affirmative-action games. Later, another colleague and my predecessor as NASW president also suggested that I apply for the position. I sent in the paperwork, not seriously expecting a reply; it was more or less to appease their wanting me to apply. I had already received a number of job offers and was seriously considering an offer from the University of North Carolina at Chapel Hill as associate dean of the college of social work. I received a call from the University of Texas to set up my interview for their position. I almost did not go for the interview, because in my mind I simply did not want to go to Texas. But, since I had sent in the paperwork to apply for the of UT job, I felt obligated to go, although I was really leaning toward the UNC position. I went to the UT interview in Austin and had an excellent interview. In fact, I considered it one of my best interviews, but I still had a feeling they did not really want me for the job.

"I fell in love with Austin, Texas, which I characterize as a real college town or city. Not a Dallas or a Houston, but to me just a bigger Tallahassee. Austin is arguably known as the "only liberal oasis" in the state of Texas. Unfortunately, the college of social work at UT had a number of challenges. After the interview, and after visiting Austin, I was intrigued by the situation and decided I really wanted the position of dean at UT. My husband and I were in the initial stages of divorce and, after discussing my wanting the deanship with my daughters, I was relieved when they reluctantly gave me their blessings. UT narrowed the applicants for dean to three finalists, and I was proud to be one of them.

"I got a call from the provost asking me to come back to Austin for an interview with the president. I was cautiously optimistic and nervously excited as I talked with the president in that interview. Whatever I was, he made the offer to me to become dean of the University of Texas School of Social Work, and I accepted. My tenure officially began in 1993. I was so 'new' to this process, and it was such a 'new' experience that I did not 'negotiate' anything—not my salary, not my staff, not the circumstances of the program, nothing.

"I immediately started the process to find some place to stay and looked at townhouses and condominiums. On several occasions, after making a deposit and when I got to the leasing offices, all of a sudden the units were no longer available. What's more, the office managers made up some of the lamest excuses as to why they had rented 'my' unit to someone else after I had paid a deposit. It was somewhat incredible, because I was in this 'liberal' college city, or so I thought. I had to threaten legal action before I was finally able to rent a place to live.

"It was only after I had accepted the position that I found out about the history of the school and that I was the first Black dean in the history of the University of Texas. In fact, had I read *Overcoming: A History of Black Integration at The University of Texas at Austin*, a book by faculty colleague Dr. Louise Iscoe, I might have instead taken the position at the University of North Carolina. Austin, this 'liberal oasis,' was only liberal to a point, and its lackluster racial history was becoming evident. Then the avalanche of hate mail came, and came—and came some more. It was amazing how many Texans were upset that the University of Texas hired its first Black dean. Let's just say that 'graphic' and 'vile' do not do justice to the nature of the mail.

"My first day as dean also came with a new university president, Robert Berdahl. William Cunningham, the president who had hired me, had become the university system's chancellor. Later that day, I met with students upset with the university and its lack of support for the school of social work. It did not take me long to determine that faculty members were somewhat apathetic. I told them that first day that we would move ahead to make the college of social work one of the best in the country and that they could join the 'team train' or get off, or jump off. My work was cut out for me. This was not the time to coddle. I also told the faculty that I would treat them as I would like to be treated unless or until they showed they did not earn that kind of treatment. Many academics are usually so individualistic that they do not understand that the whole is bigger than the sum of each individual part.

Dr. White giving remarks at her last University of Texas graduation ceremony, 2011.

"During my first year at UT, I got a call from Luci Baines Johnson Turpin, the youngest daughter of the late U.S. President Lyndon Baines Johnson, inviting me to dinner at her house with her mother, Lady Bird Johnson, and other stellar dignitaries, including Ann Richards, then governor of Texas. Once again I was nervous, and that extrovert on the outside began conflicting with the introvert on the inside. Luci's house was regal, and she was a gracious hostess. When dinner was served, I was seated next to Luci's mother, former First Lady Lady Bird Johnson, and Governor Ann Richards. Governor Richards spent most of the evening making sure I was well treated—at the dinner itself but also at the University of Texas. She was an extraordinary woman. Luci had decided that her guests would give short capsule talks about the area they represented, and had slated me first to talk about the college of social work and my experiences as the president of NASW. Of course, at this function, as with others, I was the only Black face in the place."

Of a long and extensive list of awards and recognitions, Dr. White is particularly proud of the international Rhoda G. Sarnat Award for Contributions to the Public Image of Professional Social Work, given by the NASW. A panel of international social work leaders unanimously selected Dr. White as the award recipient, stating that Dr. White "exemplifies the spirit of this award" with her inspired work on behalf of social work education, increasing awareness and respect for the profession.[1]

In 2010 Dr. White was awarded the Significant Lifetime Achievement in Social Work Education Award from the Council on Social Work Education (CSWE) for her achievements in social work education. "The leadership that Dean White has demonstrated in her immediate social work education community is an inspiration," said CSWE Executive Director Julia M. Watkins in announcing the award. "She has helped guide the profession in directions that will

Dr. White receiving the Presidential Citation at the University of Texas at Austin in 2012.

Unless WE Tell It . . . It Never Gets Told!

have a lasting, positive impact on higher education and future generations of social workers."

Dr. White is also the recipient of the prestigious University of Texas at Austin Presidential Citation in 2012, presented to her by University of Texas President William Powers Jr., in recognition of her work catapulting the college of social work into a nationally recognized leader. The award, created in 1979, is given to individuals who personify the university's commitment to transforming lives. Since the University of Texas does not give honorary degrees, the Presidential Citation is a distinct honor, the University's highest award. President Powers said that Dr. White is among those leaders at the University of Texas at Austin who have consistently lived up to the university's slogan, "What Starts Here Changes the World." "Barbara has nurtured a culture of believing in humanity's ability to make this world a better place," Powers said. "Her greatest legacy is the many graduates from the school of social work who have gone out into the world to make a difference."[2]

Under Dr. White's leadership, *U.S. News & World Report* ranked the University of Texas School of Social Work as one of the nation's best graduate programs in social work, rising from number fourteen in 1995 to number six in 2011.

Dr. Barbara White is the former president of the Council on Social Work Education, the profession's primary educational organization, which serves as the accrediting body for baccalaureate and master's degree social work programs in the United States. She is the only person in her profession to have held the presidencies of both the NASW and the CSWE. She has served on the board of directors of the International Association of Schools of Social Work, and was previously director of Florida State University's MSW program.

She was inducted into the American Academy of Social Work and Social Welfare as one of its six inaugural fellows. She has been a Fulbright Scholar on women's issues in India, and received a University Teaching Excellence Award while at Florida State University. She held a national appointment under President Bill Clinton and was inducted into the African American Women's Hall of Fame, sponsored by the National Women of Achievement, Inc.

Dr. White has authored articles and book chapters on issues dealing with cultural diversity, women, domestic violence, and social work education, and serves on numerous editorial boards and with community service organizations. She is a consultant on social work curriculum and leadership and a public speaker on a wide range of issues in social work education and practice. Among the awards and recognitions she has received are an endowment established by the UT School of Social Work advisory council and named the Dean Barbara W. White Excellence Fund in Social Work Education and Leadership. She has also received the Distinguished Alumna Award from the Florida State University College of Social Sciences.

Dr. White retired as the dean emeritus of the University of Texas School of Social Work in 2011. At her retirement dinner, Dr. Steven W. Leslie, executive vice president and provost of the University, said, "Barbara White will have led the School of Social Work for eighteen years at the completion of her deanship in August of 2011. Over these years she has overseen a march toward excellence resulting in what is now one of the finest schools of social work in the nation. Barbara has been a distinguished leader of our great university, and as she moves on to pursue her own personal and career interests she carries with her the admiration and respect of all of us who have had the privilege of working with her."

Dr. White commented, "Students come to us seeking ways to make a difference in the lives of children and families, and to provide positive interventions in areas such as health and mental health, domestic violence, substance abuse, and many other issues that touch people's lives. We proudly help them find the way.

"It takes a special individual to choose this profession. Some call it idealistic, but our mission is to see the world live up to a promise of social justice for all people. The members of our profession touch the lives of so many people, in so many ways, around the globe."

When I asked her what she planned to do during retirement, she first said, "Nothing." Then she said, "Personal time, me time, family time." She probably means it . . . for a split second. Dr. White's family time includes two of her proudest accomplishments: her daughters (with her former husband, Dr. Julian White), Tonja Mathews, an attorney in Tallahassee; and Phaedra Abbott, who works at the University of Texas in Austin. She is also the doting "grandma" of a grandson and a granddaughter.

Dr. Barbara White's life's experiences and achievements are an outstanding testimony to her commitment to purpose and making a difference to humanity. From the founding of the University of Texas, in 1883, to Dr. White's appointment as the dean of the School of Social Work, in 1993, took 110 years. That mighty journey enabled Dr. Barbara Williams White to help the many who needed her leadership, her compassion, and her integrity, so that they could learn how to make a difference in someone's life. She simply came, she saw, and she changed the world.

Joan Mattison Daniel, 2010.

18

Joan Mattison Daniel
and the Greenville Eight

*The civil rights movement was based on faith. Many of us
who were participants in this movement saw our involvement
as an extension of our faith. We saw ourselves doing the work
of the Almighty. Segregation and racial discrimination were
not in keeping with our faith, so we had to do something.*

— John Lewis
  Civil rights leader, founding member of SNCC
  (the Student Nonviolent Coordinating Committee),
  member of the U.S. House of Representatives

Joan Mattison Daniel stood with Jesse Jackson before he became
Reverend Jesse Jackson, before there was an Operation PUSH, before there was a Rainbow Coalition, and before "Run Jesse Run."
She stood with Jesse Jackson, as college students who wanted to use
the public library in downtown Greenville, South Carolina. She and
others stood with Jesse Jackson to fight the infrastructure of racism.
She stood tall and fought segregation and racism so that those who
came after her would not have to fight. She fought for freedom of
education and the freedom to read in the Greenville Public Library,
this acknowledged repository for books. Who would have thought

the public library was just another vestige of racist and vitriolic discrimination and racism?

When eight Black students entered the all-white library to extend their education by checking out books, the Civil Rights Movement began in Greenville, South Carolina. Joan Mattison was a student at Morris Brown College, and Jesse Jackson was a student at the University of Illinois. Joan, Jesse, Elaine Means, Margaree Seawright Crosby, Dorris Wright, Hattie Smith Wright, Benjamin Downs, and Willie Joe Wright were friends and high school classmates in Greenville. They became known as the Greenville Eight.

While home for Christmas in 1959, Jesse Jackson walked to the segregated "colored" library in search of research materials for school work he needed to complete during his college break. According to Joan, the Black library on McBee Avenue was "woefully small." The librarian, Jeanette Smith, worked hard to stock as many books as possible, but most books in the "colored" library were outdated, and the book inventory was tiny. Because Ms. Smith had to request books from the white library in Greenville, she told Jackson that she could not get the reference books he wanted for another six days. That would be too late. He would have to return to Illinois before he could get the books and work on his assignment.

Jesse walked to the white library on North Main to get the books himself. Jackson told Joan, "By the time I went over there to get the books, there were two policemen there. The librarian said she "did not have anyone to go to the book stacks" and "told me to come back in six days. Six days?" Jackson continued. "I was shocked. I told her I would be happy to get them myself because I needed those books right then." Jackson did not get the books. He did get what he described as a "coded message" from one of the officers. "You heard what she said," one officer told him. The message: "Leave, or get arrested." "I walked outside, and I just cried," Jackson said. "It wasn't right, and I was determined to challenge that system." The following year Jesse and Joan and other members of the Greenville Eight did challenge the system.

On the morning of July 16, 1960, they gathered at Springfield Baptist Church, which at the time was a magnet for civil rights activism, led by a charismatic young pastor, the Reverend James Hall, who was also president of the Greenville Chapter of the NAACP. They walked to the library and were told that if they did not leave, they would be arrested. They left. When they got to the church, Reverend Hall asked them why they had returned. He sent them back, telling them that going to jail was OK and, in fact, was expected. So the Greenville Eight returned to the library. After peacefully refusing to leave, they were arrested by city police. They were released after spending about forty-five minutes at the city jail, according to the Greenville County library system.[1]

Sitting in at a library might today not sound all that difficult, but it was a confrontation with the "comfortable" system of racism and segregation. Such "confrontations" were usually met with varying forms of violence. It was a further example of Black people "not

Joan Mattison (lower left), Jesse Jackson (upper left), and the rest of the Greenville Eight, at the courthouse with their attorneys (upper right), 1960.

knowing their place." In talking with Joan, I asked how she and the other members of the Greenville Eight felt at the time. "There was no fear," she said. "We all knew we were a test case against the City of Greenville's blatant racism and discrimination. But we all felt it was necessary. We also knew we had a responsibility to make society better by fighting segregation. In fact, each generation has a responsibility to fight America's wrongs no matter where or what they are. After we sat-in at the library, it ignited other demonstrations in Greenville. Our library sit-in was a pivotal point in Greenville's history, which made it all worthwhile."

Later that month, Donald Sampson, the NAACP attorney in Greenville who represented the group, filed a suit in federal court to integrate the public libraries in Greenville. On September 2, the libraries closed—"in the face of the lawsuit," as the library system put it. A few days later, Judge C. C. Wyche dismissed the suit, because the libraries were at that point "nonexistent." On September 19, the Greenville Public Library reopened as an integrated facility.

Stories such as that of the Greenville Eight did not gain the prominence of some other flashpoints in the Civil Rights Movement, such as the Montgomery Bus Boycott, school integration in Arkansas by the Little Rock Nine, or the Greensboro Four's arrest for sitting down at a Woolworth's lunch counter. Yet the work of the Eight launched demonstrations against racism in Greenville, began Jesse Jackson's journey in civil rights, and was another chapter in the struggle for human dignity and respect.[2] After the library arrests in July, there were more sit-ins and demonstrations. Demonstrators sat-in at lunch counters at Woolworth's and Kress drugstores, and staged "wade-ins" at Cleveland Park's segregated swimming pool. But the Greenville Public Library was strategic, said Reverend Hall.

Though the July 16 library sit-in wasn't the first integration action, it is distinguished by location, says Sean O'Rourke, a professor of rhetoric and oratory at Furman University. O'Rourke has done extensive research on the Civil Rights Movement in Greenville. It became what O'Rourke calls "a hinge moment," which helped pave a path, within both the Black and white communities, toward integration. The group's defiance, Greenville historian Judy Bainbridge said, was a significant piece of Greenville history, a demonstration that was the centerpiece of a busy year in the local quest for equality.

In 2000, Reverend Jesse Jackson's National Rainbow/PUSH Coalition Conference honored the Greenville Eight at its national conference in Chicago, where they were collectively presented the Coalition's Freedom Fighters Award for their sit-in at the library. In 2010 they were invited back to Greenville, where they finally received their own library cards. Also in 2010, the National Rainbow/PUSH Coalition again recognized the Greenville Eight at its national conference, this time by presenting them with its Legends Award in commemoration of the fiftieth anniversary of their sitting in. "Somehow," Reverend Jackson said during the presentation, "we all finished college and went on to replace old walls with new bridges."

Joan taught in South Carolina and Duval County public schools for five years, and at Florida Community College at Jacksonville (now Florida State College at Jacksonville) for thirty-five years, retiring in 2003. An elder in her church, True Holiness Deliverance Tabernacle, and the church's executive secretary, Joan also serves as trustee and dean of Tabernacle Bible Institute and is the assistant to the overseer. She is the proud mother, with her former husband, Mathis Daniel, of daughter Sharalyn Daniel and son Cean Daniel, and the proud grandmother of five grandsons and a granddaughter.

Joan Mattison Daniel is a pioneering hero, and America and her home town of Greenville are much better because of the courage that she and the rest of the Greenville Eight displayed. Joan decided that enough was enough. I am glad that Joan Mattison Daniel calls Jacksonville home.

Billy Daniels, 1966.

19

Billy Daniels

There are those who say to you that we are rushing this issue of civil rights. I say we are 172 years late.

— U.S. Senator Hubert H. Humphrey,
  speech at the Democratic National Convention,
  July 14, 1948

Billy Daniels is the first Black artist to have his own network television program. The *Billy Daniels Dinner Theatre* appeared Sunday evenings on ABC, premiering in 1952. A milestone in television history, the show lasted only thirteen weeks. According to television writer J. Fred MacDonald, Daniels' show was on stations in the "largest cities in the United States."

Television was an extremely difficult medium for Blacks to break into in the 1950s. One of the biggest obstacles they faced was the unwillingness of major companies to buy commercial time, although when Daniels' show was cancelled, many viewers wrote in to object. Even though the show did not enjoy a long run, it paved the way for the later success of Nat King Cole's television show.

Born in Jacksonville, Florida, Billy Daniels spent much of his early youth in the St. Philip's Episcopal Church choir. At the age of seventeen, he moved to New York City and took a job earning fifteen dollars a week as a singing waiter at a club in Harlem, Dickie Welles'

Billy Daniels on stage, 1967.

Place. At nineteen, his vocal talent and stage presence captured the interest of band leader Erskine Hawkins, who after hearing him sing quickly hired him as a featured vocalist. After a successful tour of performances across America with Hawkins' big band, Billy struck out on his own in a series of solo nightclub engagements at such night spots as the Onyx Club, the Ebony Club, and the Famous Door. He was the first of the great Black vocalists to make it as a solo performer and was one of the first Black matinee idols.

During World War II, Billy served in the U.S. Merchant Marine, and then returned to the United States to win national prominence with his 1948 recording of "That Old Black Magic." Written by Harold Arlen and Johnny Mercer, the song had been performed by many bands, and Daniels first sang it on a whim during an engagement in Atlantic City. His recording became a national hit, eventually selling more than twelve million copies. While headlining notable clubs on New York's south side such as the Latin Quarter and Copacabana, Billy Daniels was asked to appear at the London Palladium, which booked only the cream of the crop from American show business. Billy wowed his European audiences with his rendition of the "Sunny Side of the Street," a song he had performed at the MGM Studios with Dick Haymes. Billy Daniels was a consummate talented performer, but, as a Black showman who crossed into mainstream show business, was a constant target of racism.

In 1958, Daniels was the first entertainer to sign a long-term contract to appear in Las Vegas when he was hired for three years at the Stardust. He would become an entertainment pioneer in Las Vegas, making an unprecedented $26,000 a week, more than any other African American performer. In 1965, he starred on Broadway with Sammy Davis Jr., appearing in seven hundred performances of the controversial hit play *Golden Boy*. This began a fruitful series of other theatrical roles, including *Hello, Dolly!* with Pearl Bailey, and *Bubbling Brown Sugar* at the Royalty Theatre in London.

He appeared in five Royal Command Performances, and was the first singer to have performed with the National Philharmonic Orchestra at Royal Albert Hall in London. He will be forever remembered by the crowds who walk past his star on the "Walk of Fame" on Hollywood Boulevard.

In the original script for the movie *Goodfellas* (working title: *Wiseguys*) according to Daniels, the character Karen Hill was to say, "One night, Billy Daniels sent us champagne. There was nothing like it." In the final version of the movie, however, the name of the performer she invoked was changed to "Bobby Vinton." I would like not to think the obvious.

Billy Daniels died in Los Angeles on October 7, 1988. He was seventy-three years old. Billy Daniel's roots were strongly planted in Jacksonville as one of its show-business trailblazers, another great native son.

Richard Wesley Marshall in front of the Martin Luther King Jr. Memorial, 2011.

20

Richard Wesley Marshall

Hate has caused a lot of problems in the world, but has not solved one yet.

—Dr. Maya Angelou

Richard Wesley Marshall, chief financial officer of the Memorial Foundation, Inc., which was responsible for building the Martin Luther King Jr. Memorial, is another native son of Jacksonville.

Adjacent to the Franklin Delano Roosevelt Memorial on the National Mall, and situated in a direct line between the Lincoln Memorial and the Jefferson Memorial, stands the powerful and majestic memorial honoring Dr. Martin Luther King Jr. Congress passed joint resolutions in 1996 authorizing Alpha Phi Alpha Fraternity, Inc., to establish a memorial in Washington, D.C., honoring Dr. King. In 2011, the Martin Luther King Jr. Memorial was completed and dedicated.

No one can begin to imagine the sincere pride that I had in the presence of this profound—and literally monumental—recognition of the great civil rights leader. Imagine, too, how surprised I was when I saw Richard W. Marshall, chief financial officer, listed as a member of the memorial project team. It did not take me long to find out that this Richard Marshall was indeed my friend and former longtime neighbor. I could not have been prouder.

Richard Marshall, his brother, George (now deceased), and his sister, Catherine, were my next-door neighbors for more than ten years. We were also friends. During that time, I never knew Richard had a middle name. Who used a middle name back in the day?

Catherine and I graduated from Northwestern Junior Senior High School in 1960. George graduated from Northwestern in 1961, and Richard in 1964. Richard went on to Florida Agricultural and Mechanical University (FAMU), graduating with degrees in accounting and economics. He began his career in 1969 as a staff auditor for Arthur Young & Company in New York City. During his summers, Richard organized programs to help churches and daycare centers in Harlem, while also assisting them with getting help for their financial books. When he went to work for General Motors in 1972, he relocated to Detroit, and established similar programs in Michigan.

Richard began his career with GM as an internal auditor at the Pontiac Motor Division, and was promoted to divisional auditor in 1980. He progressed through the company, becoming group auditor of Buick-Oldsmobile-Cadillac and by 1985 was comptroller of the manufacturing complex in Lordstown, Ohio, a multi-billion-dollar operation of cars, trucks, and sheet metal. In 1990, Richard transferred to Pittsburgh, Pennsylvania, as comptroller to assist in converting the fabricating plant to a service parts operation. Five years later, he was promoted to finance director of the manufacturing center in Warren, Michigan, a hub of expertise for all GM manufacturing processes; and then finance director of GM Worldwide Facility Group (a multi-billion dollar operation of all GM facilities), where he assisted in the purchase of the Renaissance Center, GM's world headquarters, and set up the financial procedures.

When Richard heard about the Martin Luther King Jr. Memorial effort, he thought the project's organizers could use his expertise. He talked with Rod Gillum, the vice president of GM's community relations—and now the chairman of the Memorial Foundation's board—and Rod brought him on to work for the foundation. Richard and his wife moved to Washington, D.C., in June 2001, after GM had signed on as the Memorial's lead sponsor and committed $10 million to the foundation. And as we are prone to say, the rest is history.

Richard spent thirty-four years with the financial staff of General Motors North America. His last position with GM before joining the Foundation was as financial director of Quality, Reliability Competitive Operations Integration.

I asked Richard about the legacy of Dr. King, and what he meant to him.

From left to right: Richard W. Marshall, chief financial officer, the Memorial Foundation; Lisa Anders, senior project manager, MTTG Design-Build Joint Venture; Boris Dramov, principal, ROMA Design Group; Bonnie Fisher, principal, ROMA Design Group; 2009.

Richard Marshall: "When I was in seventh grade, my next-door neighbor was a high school senior who was a leader involved in NAACP student initiatives. He talked a lot about Dr. King and I learned from watching and listening to him at school and in the neighborhood.

My family and I started seeing a lot of civil rights marches on television, but it really brought it home that my neighbor was a young leader advocating for civil rights." [Of course, I was Richard's next-door neighbor. You never what you might do or say to impact someone.]

RH: What stories about the Memorial will you share with friends and family when they visit?

Richard Marshall: The Inscription Wall is my favorite part because it is so profound and it relates so well to current situations in our world. The wall makes the Memorial truly a living memorial. I love showing people the Stone of Hope with the image of Dr. King and how he is the first African American to be memorialized on the nation's front yard, the National Mall. I also enjoy talking about the Chinese sculptor who was so passionate about Dr. King.

I take pride in the Memorial's far-reaching impact. Washington, D.C., gets between fifteen and twenty million visitors every year from all over the world. It's estimated that more than half of those people will be coming to visit the Memorial every year.

RH: What's your favorite quote on the Inscription Wall?

Richard Marshall: My favorite quotation is one on the south section of the Inscription Wall that reads, "We shall overcome because the arc of the moral universe is long, but it bends toward justice." This is my favorite because it's all-inclusive and could serve as a key theme anywhere in our global economy.

RH: What was the highlight of the dedication ceremony for you?

Richard Marshall: One of my highlight moments was the Interfaith Prayer Service at the Basilica of the National Shrine of the Immaculate Conception. It was a service for all people and the program was very inspiring, featuring Dr. King's voice and messages.

My other favorite moment was listening to President Obama speak during the rescheduled dedication ceremony on the National Mall. It was a very historic moment, having the first Black President of the United States dedicate the first Memorial to an iconic Black civil rights figure on the National Mall. My hope has always been that the Memorial will serve as a beacon for global peace, a place for conversations that will keep the legacy of Dr. King alive to energize future generations.

Richard Wesley Marshall—pivotal in the creation of the Dr. Martin Luther King Jr. Memorial, and another Jacksonville native son.

William Stockton Surcey, left, with his brother, Waymon Surcey, 1944.

21

William Stockton Surcey, Tuskegee Airman

He who learns, teaches.

—Ethiopian proverb

I first met Mr. Bill Surcey in the late 1950s, while visiting my cousin Jimmy and his wife, Elaine, who lived across the street from the Surceys in the College Gardens neighborhood of Jacksonville, Florida. A very quiet and distinguished gentleman, Mr. Surcey appeared to me to know how to fix everything mechanical, from cars to air conditioners to all kinds of appliances. But I never heard a word during my youthful years about his serving as one of the celebrated Tuskegee Airmen. It was much later that I would find out about Mr. Surcey's ground-breaking efforts during World War II.

Bill Surcey graduated from the old Stanton High School in Jacksonville in 1939, and was in his second year at the Tuskegee Institute in Alabama when he enlisted in the Army Air Corps. After six months of training as an aircraft mechanic, he was assigned to the Tuskegee Army Air Field, and became a Tuskegee Airman.

Over the years, many have thought of the Tuskegee Airmen as being the pilots. Tuskegee Airmen, though, included not only pilots, but navigators, bombardiers, maintenance and support staff, instructors . . . and all the personnel who kept the planes in the air, the aircraft mechanics in particular. All of those involved in the so-called "Tuskegee Experience," the Army Air Corps program to train African Americans to fly and maintain combat aircraft, were Tuskegee Airmen, thus known because they received their basic and advanced pilot training near the city of Tuskegee, Alabama.

During these days of racism, and military segregation, The Tuskegee Airmen successfully fought three wars during World War II: one against our enemies overseas, one against racism within the American military, and one against racism here at home. Many historians of the Civil Rights Movement consider the actions of the Tuskegee Airmen to have been a crucial factor in the eventual full integration of the armed forces, and to have had continuing influence in subsequent civil disobedience efforts to integrate such public facilities in the South as lunch counters and schools.

Tuskegee, in rural Alabama, was at the zenith of racist cities in the country; the tragic instance of the notorious Tuskegee Syphilis Study comes immediately to mind. Most of the U.S. Army's commanders were from the South, bringing with them the region's racial stereotypes. A secret 1924 War College report titled "The Use of Negro Man Power in War" concluded: "Blacks [are] unfit for leadership roles and incapable of aviation." One senior Army commander had no hesitation in saying outright what the War College report was claiming in private. "The Negro type has not the proper reflexes to make a first-class fighter pilot," he proclaimed. As war in Europe was brewing, there were no Black pilots in the American military.

But, by 1941, pressure from the Black press and the NAACP led President Franklin D. Roosevelt to create an all African American airplane squadron based in Tuskegee. They became the Army Air Corps' 332nd Fighter Group and 477th Bombardment Group. When Roosevelt signed the law calling for the training of Black pilots, critics hoped the effort would prove a disaster. And, indeed, in many

Unless WE Tell It . . . It Never Gets Told!

ways the program was designed for failure, putting the Tuskegee Airmen through training more rigorous than that of their white counterparts, with the expectation that they could not succeed.

Stories of the Tuskegee Airmen provide snapshots of the racism of the day, yet few of them became bitter. Odds against their success were immense, but the unrealistically harsh training regimen had an unforeseen effect. The great expectations that they were not supposed to be able to live up to ended up developing great airmen in spite of—and to a considerable extent because of—the challenge of succeeding with the deck stacked against them.

Public perception changed dramatically when First Lady Eleanor Roosevelt took it upon herself to visit Tuskegee. Despite the protests of her Secret Service protectors, she climbed into the back seat of an open-cockpit plane and insisted that the plane take off for a short flight with a broadly smiling Chief Civilian Flight Instructor Charles Alfred Anderson at the controls. "That one picture in the plane did it," an elderly Airman remembers fondly. "She wasn't afraid of flying with these so-called 'inferior beings.'" And, with that, the "Tuskegee Experiment" took off.

First Lady Eleanor Roosevelt's 1941 flight piloted by Charles Alfred Anderson helped to change public opinion.

William Stockton Surcey, Tuskegee Airman

Bill Surcey, this distinguished veteran of World War II, never talked about his time as a Tuskegee Airman, said daughter Katherine Surcey. "People began to call checking the facts" as HBO prepared to release its 1995 film *The Tuskegee Airmen*, Katherine said. "So I asked, 'Why are so many people calling you?' He said, 'Because I was one,' and it just blew me away. He told me, 'It was just a job. I served my country and I did what I was supposed to do.'" This was how she found out that her father was a member of one of the most revered groups of Black trailblazers in the history of this country.

During the 1944 invasion of Italy, the 99th Fighter Squadron (originally the 99th Pursuit Squadron) shot down a number of German aircraft. Surcey earned a Bronze Star for distinguished service for supervising and completing weekly major repairs on P-40 aircraft during the fighting.

Surcey and the rest of the 99th Fighter Squadron were considered heroes overseas, but back at home they were not, purely because of the color of their skin. The combat record of the Tuskegee Airmen, though, speaks for itself:

- more than 15,000 combat sorties
- 111 German airplanes destroyed in the air
- 150 aircraft destroyed on the ground
- 148 aircraft damaged
- 1 destroyer sunk by P-47 machine-gun fire
- 950 railcars, trucks, and other motor vehicles destroyed
- 179 bomber escort missions
- 66 pilots killed in action or accidents
- 32 pilots downed and captured, POWs
- 96 Distinguished Flying Crosses awarded
- 744 Air Medals
- 8 Purple Hearts
- 14 Bronze Stars

Discharged as a master sergeant in 1945, Bill Surcey completed his studies at the Tuskegee Institute. He later worked as an aircraft mechanic at Jacksonville Naval Air Station, and then spent twenty-seven years with the U.S. Postal Service. He also ran an air-conditioning and refrigeration repair business, until he retired at age eighty-seven. "He was an impressive person who accomplished a lot, but always maintained a quiet demeanor," Katherine said. "A friend recently put on Facebook that she will always think of him as the perfect Southern gentleman, and I thought, 'Gosh, that says it all.'"

After the HBO movie was released and Bill Surcey was "discovered," he came into demand as a speaker. He had requests throughout Jacksonville to talk about World War II and the Tuskegee Airmen, which he did, though somewhat reluctantly.

On March 29, 2007, in a long-overdue national observance, the Tuskegee Airmen were collectively awarded a Congressional Gold Medal at a ceremony in the U.S. Capitol rotunda; the medal is on display at the Smithsonian Institution. Mr. Surcey was unable to attend the ceremony because his wife was ill, but two years later the Congressional Gold Medal was presented to Master Sergeant William Stockton Surcey by Major Trent Johnson, in a ceremony in Jacksonville's city hall on April 21, 2009.

On May 6, 2011, William Surcey died at the age of ninety-two. His daughter Melody Surcey and his brother Waymon Surcey, a Tuskegee Airman pilot, predeceased him. Future Surcey, his wife of sixty-two years passed in December 2012. Bill and Future Surcey are survived by their daughters Katherine and Renee, and Waymon by his daughter Angela; as descendants of Tuskegee Airmen they are now Tuskegee Airmen Heritage members, charged with continuing the legacy of the Airmen for future generations.

You might not have known of William Stockton Surcey nor recognized his name, but his deeds are enshrined in history. Thank you, Mr. Surcey.

Welton E. Coffey II, 2012.

22

Welton E. Coffey II

Change does not roll in on the wheels of inevitability,
but comes through continuous struggle. And so we must
straighten our backs and work for our freedom. A man
can't ride you unless your back is bent.

—Dr. Martin Luther King Jr.

Welton E. Coffey is a refreshing young man of integrity. He is a
family man with a very sound and firm religious anchoring. He is a
role model and a leader on the athletic field, in the classroom, and
just walking down the street. And although he may have missed
major coaching assignments and opportunities because of the color
of his skin, what he has attained is a testament to his preparation,
his hard work, his spirit, and his exemplary accomplishments.

His stated objective is to foster an attitude of pride and a sense
of excellence in the classroom as well as on the playing field among
student-athletes, which says a lot about a teacher and a high school
football coach and a young leader working to influence the young
minds who will lead this country one day.

Welton E. Coffey II was born November 13, 1967, in Jacksonville,
Florida. He attended local schools in Duval County and graduated
from William M. Raines Senior High School in 1985. Welton attended Tennessee State University on a baseball scholarship. After

transferring to Georgia's Valdosta State College, he received his bachelor of science degree in mental retardation K–12 education in 1990. Later, in 2008, he would earn a master's degree in postsecondary education from Troy University in Alabama.

After several key assignments coaching high school baseball and football in Duval County, Coffey returned to William M. Raines High School in 1997 as head football coach. In his first season as head coach of the William Raines Vikings, Coffey's team compiled a record of 15 and 0. In what was arguably the strongest division in high school football in the state, Coffey coached the Vikings to Florida's 1997 4A championship, making Raines only the second Duval County high school to win a state championship since the formation of the Florida High School Athletic Association in 1920.

The first Duval County public high school to win a Florida state championship was Matthew William Gilbert High School, which won the segregated Black state football championship in 1958. I thought it interesting and a bit of a coincidence that Coffey's father and mother, Welton E. Coffey Sr. and Cheryl A. Daise Coffey, both attended Matthew William Gilbert High School. Just as the football team at his parents' high school brought pride to the segregated Black community on the Eastside of Jacksonville forty years earlier, the stellar achievement of the younger Coffey's 1997 Raines' team brought pride to the predominantly Black William M. Raines High School in a predominantly Black Jacksonville community.

While at Raines, Coach Coffey coached a number of gifted players who eventually continued their football careers in the National Football League, among them Lito Sheppard, Jabar Gaffney, and Ryan Freel. Of particular note, during Coffey's six seasons as head coach at Raines, his team's average grade point average was 3.2.

Coffey's leadership—both on the athletic field, and in the classroom—led to his being named as the NFL's regional director of Junior Development for Jacksonville in 1999, which he took on in addition to his duties as head coach at Raines. Junior player development, designed to help inner-city youth lacking access to structured football programs was first tried in New York City earlier that year. Coffey was supported for the position by Tom Coughlin, who at the time coached the Jacksonville Jaguars. "Welton came highly recommended," said Scott Lancaster, who helps coordinate the program for the NFL from his New York office. "As well as his football coaching, he has done youth clinics in the Jacksonville area, and he stands out as an enthusiastic, charismatic leader."

After six years with the Vikings, Coffey was recruited by Georgia's renowned Valdosta High School to coach quarterbacks and wide receivers. In his first season there, the Valdosta Wildcats went to the 5A state championship, where they lost to the Camden County High School Wildcats. He stayed in Valdosta for three years.

Coffey later joined the equally legendary football program at Camden County High as its offensive coordinator and quarterbacks coach. The Wildcats won the Georgia 5A state title in 2008 and 2009; and in the 2008, 2009, and 2011 seasons, Coffey's offense led the state in scoring and total yards. He is one of the few high school coaches to have won a state football championship in both Florida and Georgia. What a great follow-up for the offspring of graduates of Matthew William Gilbert High School.

Coffey has received countless community awards and a number of "Coach of the Year" honors. He is particular proud of the Florida state award for being top performing coach in an amateur sport. He also received the Man of the Year Award from Strong Men for Christ and is a member of the William Raines High School Hall of Fame. He is a popular speaker at youth rallies, churches, athletic camps, businesses, and coaching clinics. Welton and his wife Keenya have a daughter, Kelsey Patrice Coffey. On March 28, 2013 Welton Coffey became the new head football coach of the Camden County High School Wildcats.

SECTION II

Confronting Racism

TO BE SOLD & LET

BY PUBLIC AUCTION,

On MONDAY the 18th of MAY. 1829,

UNDER THE TREES.

FOR SALE,

THE THREE FOLLOWING

SLAVES,

VIZ.

HANNIBAL, about 30 Years old, an excellent House Servant, of Good Character.
WILLIAM, about 35 Years old, a Labourer.
NANCY, an excellent House Servant and Nurse.

The MEN belonging to "LEECH'S" Estate, and the WOMAN to Mrs. D. SMIT

TO BE LET,

On the usual conditions of the Hirer finding them in Food, Clot in. and Medical　ancε,

THE FOLLOWING

MALE and FEMALE

SLAVES,

OF GOOD CHARACTERS.

ROBERT BAGLEY, about 20 Years old, a good House Servant.
WILLIAM BAGLEY, about 18 Years old, a Labourer.
JOHN ARMS, about 18 Years old.
JACK ANTONIA, about 40 Years old, a Labourer.
PHILIP, an Excellent Fisherman.
HARRY, about 27 Years old, a good House Servant.
LUCY, a Young Woman of good Character, used to House Work and the Nursery.
ELIZA, an Excellent Washerwoman.
CLARA, an Excellent Washerwoman.
FANNY, about 14 Years old, House Servant.
SARAH, about 14 Years old, House Servant.

Also for Sale, at Eleven o'Clock,

Fine Rice, Gram, Paddy, Books, Muslins, Needles, Pins, Ribbons, &c. &c.

AT ONE O'CLOCK, THAT CELEBRATED ENGLISH HORSE

BLUCHER,

ADDISON PRINTER GOVERNMENT OFFICE.

Ad announcing the public sale at auction of enslaved Africans, 1829.

23

Slavery

It demands great spiritual resilience not to hate the hater whose foot is on your neck, and an even greater miracle of perception and charity not to teach your child to hate.

—James Baldwin
  Novelist, essayist, playwright, poet, and social critic

American slavery is the greatest tragedy and most immoral failing in the history of this country.

Slavery, not states' rights, birthed the Civil War. The Civil War was fought to maintain slavery. Everything about the Civil War revolved around slavery. Period. End of story.

Dr. James Loewen's book *The Confederate and Neo-Confederate Reader* clearly shows that the secessionist papers of the Confederate States of America gave slavery as their reason for seceding from the Union.[1] Many white Southerners and white historians give every other reason but slavery and claim that the South was defending its "Southern heritage" or defending "states' rights," and refer to the Civil War as either the "War for Southern Independence" or the "War of Northern Aggression."

Yet for some it is misnamed the "Civil War." The South seceded because of Slavery and organized an enemy government—the Confederacy and not the Confederate States of America—which sought to overthrow the United States of America. It was not the North against the South. There was no North Division of the U.S. government, and no South Division. The Confederacy was an enemy government fighting to defeat the United States of America so that its white citizens could continue to live the life made possible by a free-labor economy, and continue to receive all the lavish perks and benefits of enslaved people working for them without ever having to pay them a dime. All of the Confederacy's enemy government combatants—all of its government officials, terrorist army generals, officers and soldiers—should have been tried for treason. President Andrew Johnson, a Confederacy sympathizer and a slavery supporter, gave them all a presidential amnesty. They got off scott-free for their treason, another historical fact not discussed in high school history classes, nor on college and university campuses. The next time someone refers to the "Civil" War, correct them and tell them the Confederacy was an enemy government committed to overthrowing the United States of America.

Let's expand a bit on this basic myth about the reason for the Southern states seceding. Across America, 60 percent to 75 percent of high school history teachers believe and teach that the South seceded for states' rights, according to Dr. Loewen, who puts it this way: "It's complete B.S., And by B.S., I mean 'bad scholarship.'"

In fact, Loewen says, the original documents of the Confederacy show quite clearly that the war was based on one thing: slavery. On December 24, 1860, delegates at South Carolina's secession convention adopted a "Declaration of the Immediate Causes Which Induce and Justify the Secession of South Carolina from the Federal Union." It noted "an increasing hostility on the part of the non-slaveholding States to the institution of slavery," and protested that Northern states had failed to "fulfill their constitutional obligations" by interfering with the return of fugitive slaves to bondage.

Similarly, in its declaration of secession, Mississippi held that,

One of the restraints used to prevent enslaved people from escaping. Note also that this man's forehead has been branded to identify him as being enslaved.

"Our position is thoroughly identified with the institution of slavery —the greatest material interest of the world. . . . A blow at slavery is a blow at commerce and civilization." And in its declaration of secession, South Carolina actually came out *against* the rights of states to make their own laws—at least when those laws conflicted with slaveholding. "In the State of New York even the right of transit for a slave has been denied by her tribunals," the document reads. The "right of transit" was the right of slaveholders to bring their slaves with them on trips to non-slaveholding states.

The trade in enslaved persons, from the middle of the fifteenth century to the end of the nineteenth, was responsible for the kidnapping of between twelve and fifteen million people, forcibly removed from Africa to the Western Hemisphere. The trafficking of Africans by the major European countries during this period is sometimes referred to by African scholars as the "Maafa," Swahili for "great disaster." The slave trade led to the violent transporting of those millions of Africans, and to the deaths of many millions more. Nobody knows the actual number of Africans who died during slave raids and associated wars in Africa, during transportation and imprisonment, or in the horrendous conditions of the so-called "Middle Passage," the voyage from Africa to the Americas.

Some historians conclude that the total loss in persons removed, together with those who died on the arduous march to the coastal slave marts and those killed in slave raids, exceeded the sixty-five to seventy-five million inhabitants remaining in Africa at the trade's end. More than ten million died as direct consequence of the Atlantic slave trade alone. After being kidnapped from their homelands rich in culture and history and forced to become "chattel or property" on their way to an alien land, many Africans chose to jump overboard during those horrific trips aboard the slave ships and succumb to a death by drowning rather than succumb to death in slavery.

They were turned into nameless human beings, kidnapped and herded like cattle. Packed as human cargo and brought to foreign shores. Stripped of their identity and history. Stripped naked in the public square and inspected like livestock. Sold at auction to the highest bidder. Beaten and brutalized and dehumanized with searing regularity. Forced under unimaginable penalty to work under horrific conditions for no pay. Raped and marginalized with absolute impunity. Hunted like animals when they dared to rebel and seek freedom. Denied basic human rights. And yet they survived.

There are those—including noted Black historian and scholar Dr. Henry Louis Gates—who would argue that slavery was largely coordinated and assisted by Africans. Professor Gates' op-ed in *The New York Times*, "Ending the Slavery Blame-Game" (April 22, 2010) essentially said that, because some members of the African hierarchy were involved in the transatlantic slave trade as commercial partners with Europeans, blame must be equally assigned to them as well, spreading guilt around so much as to render it meaningless. Not surprisingly several equally noted scholars responded to Dr. Gates. Dr. Michael A. Gomez is currently professor of history and Middle Eastern and Islamic studies at New York University. His response to Gates: "It is difficult to imagine assigning equal culpability to a community fending off the slave trade with the European nations bankrolling and in ultimate control of the entire affair, when those European nations were providing the weaponry—and especially since it was Europe and America who were responsible for the broad design and implementation of the slave trade in the first place."

From Dr. Molefi Kete Asante, professor and chair of the Department of African American Studies at Temple University: "First, we must get the terms of the argument straight. There is no African slave trade, no transatlantic slave trade; there is only European slave trade across the ocean, as there is the Arab slave trade across the

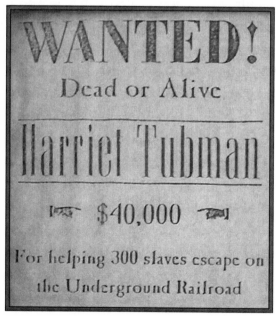

One of many "Wanted" posters for Harriet Tubman, "Conductor" of the Underground Railroad.

desert. I say 'European slave trade,' because the motive for kidnapping and transporting Africans across the ocean was a European initiative." According to Dr. Asante, one only has to ask these questions: "Who traveled to Africa in search of captives? Who created an entire industry of shipbuilding, insurance, outfitting of crews and ships, and banking based on the slave trade? Who benefited enormously from the evil and vile project of human kidnapping?"

For those kidnapped Africans, America's self-proclaimed foundation on Christian ethics—"love one another"—was a stark contrast with reality. America simply ignored "life, liberty, and the pursuit of happiness" in order to enslave men, women, and children based on the color of their skin. American history textbooks do not accurately describe the horrors of slavery—the killings, the inhumanity, the decimation of the Black family unit, and the horrors of torturous bondage.

More recently, in January of 2012, the Tennessee Tea Party petitioned the Tennessee Educational System to stop teaching about slavery. In other words: remove all references to slavery or genocide from American history textbooks, so as not to sully the reputation and eminence of the Founding Fathers. Dr. Michael Eric Dyson, noted author and professor of sociology at Georgetown University, states that the effect of slavery continues to exert its brutal influence in the untold sufferings of millions of everyday folk, and is responsible for the high level of residential separation of Blacks from whites today.

And this from Noam Chomsky, linguist, political philosopher, and one of the world's most prominent public intellectuals: "American culture is imbued with fears that African Americans will someday repay the violence and oppression that has marred their history in this country. Chomsky was speaking with philosopher George Yancy about the roots of American racism as part of an ongoing *New York Times* series of discussions around race. Yancy noted that contemporary American conversations about terrorism often omit "the fact that many black people in the United States have had a long history of being terrorized by white racism." Chomsky emphasized the ongoing impact of Black suppression in the United States, saying that "fears that the victims might rise up and take revenge are deeply rooted in American culture, with reverberations to the present." Chomsky cited the fact that slaves had arrived in the colonies four hundred years ago, and were largely responsible for America's early economic strength.

In *The Half Has Never Been Told: Slavery and the Making of American Capitalism*, historian Edward E. Baptist asserts that slavery was woven inextricably into the fabric of early nineteenth-century capitalism.[2] Banks and financiers fed slavery with the investment it needed to continue expanding, and were rewarded with handsome profits from the labor of enslaved millions. Baptist pointed out how slave owners were able to boost productivity to a higher degree than other industries by working their slaves almost to death.

In the 1820s, slave owners held two million enslaved persons worth $1 billion—a third of all U.S. wealth at the time. The number of those enslaved in the United States had swelled to about four million at the time of the Civil War. In slavery, Africans were considered less than human, with no worth except as faceless "vessels" to carry out demeaning biddings, to work, to procreate and thereby generate children to be themselves enslaved.

Many contemporary textbooks, though, give a sanitized and historically inaccurate account, claiming that Africans were better off in American slavery than they were in Africa. Slave owners and slave traders would boast that slavery was "natural" because of race. Africans were not human beings, and therefore, they were born to be slaves. As historian Eric Williams writes in his book *Capitalism and Slavery*, "Slavery was not born of racism; rather, racism was the consequence of slavery."

Reparations? Surely You Jest!

Yes! Magazine calls America "A Nation Built on the Back of Slavery and Racism."[3] Ta-Nehisi Coates, in his article for *The Atlantic*, makes "The Case for Reparations."[4]

In the part of the "I Have A Dream" speech that no one seems to remember, Dr. Martin Luther King Jr. declared: "It is obvious today that America has defaulted on this promissory note insofar as her citizens of color are concerned. Instead of honoring this sacred obligation, America has given the Negro people a bad check, a check which has come back marked 'insufficient funds.'"

Legalized slavery allowed America to extract wealth from the lives of four million African Americans. "Slaves were the single largest, by far, financial asset of property in the entire American economy." The sale of these slaves—"in whose bodies that money congealed," writes Walter Johnson, a Harvard historian—generated even more ancillary wealth. Loans were taken out for purchase, to be repaid with interest. Insurance policies were drafted against the untimely death of an enslaved person and the loss of potential profits. Sales of enslaved persons were taxed and notarized. The selling of enslaved Black bodies and the sundering of countless enslaved Black families became an economy unto themselves, estimated to have brought in tens of millions of dollars to antebellum America. In 1860, because of the enslavement of Black human beings, there were more millionaires per capita in the Mississippi Valley than anywhere else in the country.

The institution of slavery created the economic basis for modern capitalism and turned the United States into the wealthiest nation in the world. New York was built on cotton—the crop that dominated the international markets in the 1800s—as the city collected forty cents of every dollar earned in the cotton trade, transforming it into a financial center. Moreover, at the start of the Civil War, slaves were worth 48 percent of the wealth of the South, more than all of the banks, factories, and railroads in the country *combined*. These figures set the parameters for engaging in conversation about reparations.

When considering what sort of reparations are appropriate, it is important to keep in mind that the institution of slavery did not just set Black people back—it also greatly enriched white people. It is not just that when slavery ended, Black people were starting from much farther behind—white people were, in fact, starting from much farther ahead, having reaped enormous profits for hundreds of years by stealing the fruits of Black peoples' labor. If the public refuses to calculate the cost of slavery on human lives and souls, at least calculate this: money was stolen. Enormous amounts of it! Broadly speaking, white Americans today have benefited from the great infusion of wealth that slavery provided to their ancestors, and Black Americans have lost out on that wealth to at least the same degree—if not actually to a greater degree, given the opportunity cost of all the wealth-building activities that slaves never had the chance to undertake.

Just how much of white America's historic wealth was derived directly from the exploitation of Black people? "In the seven cotton states, one-third of all white income was derived from slavery," Coates writes. "By 1840, cotton produced by slave labor constituted 59 percent of the country's exports."

If you were to guess how much the United States owes Black people in economic damages—reparations—for slavery, how much would that amount be? While some people would conclude that no dollar amount can make up for the centuries that Black people were kidnapped, enslaved, and forced to work without pay, the fact remains that Black America's misfortune made white America quite wealthy. Yet few will admit that slavery built the system of U.S. capitalism that we know today.

Time magazine columnist Jack White estimated that Blacks are owed $24 trillion, which amounts to unpaid wages denied to ten million slaves, doubled for pain and suffering, with interest. Further, Dr. Denis G. Rancourt, a former physics professor at the University of Ottawa, concluded that the minimum amount of reparations is $59.2 trillion. He calculated that value of the stolen labor was $3.7 trillion, based upon two million slaves working ten hours a day, 365 days a year for seventy years (from 1790 to 1860) at a rate of $7.25 an hour. Applying a 2 percent interest rate compounded annually, he reached the $59.2 trillion figure.

Following the end of the Civil War, the government paid reparations to slave owners, but not to Black people themselves. Instead, America maintained a convict-lease system that swept up Black men and created a new form of slavery in the Southern prisons. The Black Codes, laws passed by Southern states immediately following the war, had the effect of restricting Blacks' freedom, and of compelling them to work in a labor economy based upon low wages or debt. These laws were designed to impede Black progress and keep whites ahead of the game through discriminatory practices. Special fees for Black people discouraged us from owning businesses, and high interest rates hindered the building of Black wealth. In addition, segregation and racist policies prevented Black people from benefiting from government programs that were made available to whites. As a result, the Black share of national wealth changed only a tiny amount between 1865 (0.5 percent) and 1990 (1.0 percent), meaning that there has always been very little for us to pass down to future generations. Moreover, the wealth gap between Blacks and whites has not changed since 1970. Policies have kept Black people underwater and whites afloat and thriving, on purpose.

This is why reparations make so much sense, and this is what white privilege looks like. True racism exists not solely in the offensive remarks and epithets hurled by individual whites at Black people on a daily basis, but, more importantly, in the systems of oppression that stack the deck and rig the game. Whites mistakenly believe that racism is a thing of the past, and that slavery is something that occurred long ago from which they derive no benefit. But the fact is that there is a continuum of racial discrimination that extends from slavery times up until now, with mass incarceration and the war on drugs creating a new form of enslavement for Black people. White folks have inherited the wealth and privilege derived from free Black labor, which they willingly enjoy today. Black folks inherited nothing and received nothing when freed, and they continue to face the effects of this rigged game, which continues into the present day, even as they have struggled, and resisted this system, and attempted to build for themselves.

Every year since 1989, Representative John Conyers (D-Michigan) has introduced a bill that calls for a federal commission to study reparations. In April 2015, the Institute of the Black World 21st Century, led by Dr. Ron Daniels, held an international conference in New York, with participants from twenty countries and throughout the Diaspora discussing global reparations strategies.

As for estimating the price tag, here is one way to continue the discussion and bring home the gravity of the issue: More than two hundred and fifty years of slavery. Ninety-plus years of Jim Crow. Sixty-plus years of separate but equal. Thirty-five-plus years of racist housing policy. Until we reckon with our compounding moral debts, America will never be whole. As Dr. Martin Luther King Jr. said, "They owe us a lot of money."

To add the proverbial insult to injury and to further justify not apologizing for slavery, the State of Texas recently approved new social studies textbooks that will "barely address racial segregation," nor will the textbooks make mention of the Ku Klux Klan, nor the Jim Crow laws put in place to continue what began with slavery. This is called Revisionist History.

Ku Klux Klan members.

24

The American Institution of Racism

The truth is that Jim Crow may be dead, but racism is alive and well.

—Julian Bond,
Civil rights activist, former board chair of the NAACP,
University of Virginia history professor,
distinguished professor in residence at
American University, Washington, D.C.

Slavery created racial segregation and institutionalized racism. Most dictionaries define "racism" as racial hatred based on the color of one's skin. As Dick Gregory said, "White is not a color; it's an attitude." Some add that racism is racial prejudice plus the institutional and systemic power to dominate, exclude, discriminate against, or abuse targeted groups of people based on a designation of race. Racism is an insidious cultural disease.

In their book *Black Power: The Politics of Liberation in America*, the late Black activist Kwame Ture (formerly Stokely Carmichael) and university professor Charles V. Hamilton introduce the term "institutional racism," which they define as being any system of inequality based on race.[1] It can occur in public government bodies, private business corporations (such as media outlets), and universities (public and private). All of racism's many definitions trigger misrepresentations, lies, anger, frustration, self-defense, and denial.

America's "prove it" syndrome requires Blacks to provide irrefutable proof of racism. Dr. Melissa Harris-Perry, the holder of the Presidential Endowed Chair in the department of politics and international affairs at Wake Forest University and the host of her own network television show on MSNBC, addressed the "if you can't definitively prove racism, it isn't so" phenomenon quite well in what she calls the "epistemology of race talk." Dr. Harris-Perry said, it "is a common strategy of asking any person of color who identifies a racist practice or pattern to 'prove' that racism is indeed the causal factor. This is typically demanded by those who are certain of their own purity of racial motivation. The implication is if one cannot produce irrefutable evidence of clear, blatant, and intentional bias, then racism must be banned as a possibility. But this is both silly as an intellectual claim and dangerous as a policy standard. In a nation with the racial history of the United States, I am baffled by the idea that non-racism would be the presumption and that racial bias must be proved beyond reasonable doubt."[2]

A Chinese proverb says: "The beginning of wisdom is to call things by their proper name." Use of the term "progress" when addressing racism implies that congratulations are in order for a "race-relations" job well done, that we live in a "post-racial" society as some like to say. Fifty years after his assassination, Malcolm X's analysis remains perceptive: "If you stick a knife nine inches into my back and pull it out three inches that is not progress. Even if you pull it all the way out, that is not progress. Progress is healing the wound, and America hasn't even begun to pull out the knife." Half a century on, this quotation still captures America's attitude toward race, and congratulations are still not in order.

Racist forces in America today would like to revise American history by "prettying up" the repulsive and sordid practices of slavery, by denying the historical impact of Jim Crow laws, by obscur-

Unless WE Tell It . . . It Never Gets Told!

The Confederate battle flag.

ing the historical impact of segregation and racism, by forgetting the many abhorrent years that followed the end of slavery, and by rewriting and ignoring the obscene violence that was perpetrated on people in the Civil Rights Movement.

Many Americans begrudgingly admit that racism still exists. When they do admit it, the caveat is usually "things used to be like that, but things are changing"; "I don't look at the color of one's skin, I look at the content of their character"; "The Confederate flag is not a symbol of hate, just a symbol of Southern heritage"; and of course the well-worn classic: "Some of my best friends are Black." Then there is this insincere quest to determine where to find this despicable racism thing. Looking in the mirror is never an option.

It has been more than 395 years since 1619, when the first African slaves were brought to the North American colony of Jamestown, Virginia, to aid in the production of such lucrative crops as tobacco; more than 157 years since the landing of the last slave ship (on November 28, 1858, *The Wanderer* was the last documented ship to bring a hold full of slaves from Africa, discharging its cargo at Jekyll Island, Georgia); more than 150 years since the end to legal slavery with the end of the so-called "Civil" War; more than 137 years since the beginning of Jim Crow in 1877; more than 50 years since the Civil Rights Act; and more than 49 years since the Voting

Rights Act. Even these laws passed to ensure equality are constantly challenged before the U.S. Supreme Court, once a respected bastion of fairness that now does not understand racial equality or chooses not to understand racial equality. And still Blacks are asked to wait to be afforded the most basic human rights provided to whites?

Honest dialogue about racism interferes with social comfort levels and blurs the neat lines of socially integrated and professional friendships. Many Blacks and whites feel that talking about race and racism can only cause frustration, and serves to polarize the races even further. They disingenuously feel that discussing racism and issues of race and discrimination would threaten their white friends or Black friends, making them feel uncomfortable. Or, as a person told me during a presentation I made on race and racism, "Talking about those things in the past, Mr. Hurst, opens wounds which have been slowly healing or are healed." Oh, really? Why is it that Blacks are made the victims twice: first, in the way that they are treated in this country based purely on the color of their skin, and second, by being made to feel guilty when they discuss that treatment? Another comment I hear is, "Leave things in the past and let us move on." But how do you move on from who you are and what you have experienced? Move on to what?

I am reminded of a colloquial phrase Eric Daniel Johnson would use when discussing Black folks and others who simply do not get it: "Been down so long 'til getting up ain't crossed yo' mind." Those words are prophetic.

And this from Mychal Denzel Smith: "Racism is not simply personal prejudice and bigotry that only manifests in the form of being unkind to someone on the basis of their skin color or calling them a derogatory name. Racism is a system of oppression, one that creates a society of first- and second-class citizens by denying rights and access to resources to non-white people. Racism is a system of power created by and maintained through public policy. Racist rhetoric or

Unless WE Tell It . . . It Never Gets Told!

action is anything that reinforces and upholds that system. So until the day comes when the U.S. government enacts laws aimed specifically and purposefully at ensuring that white people are shut out of education / healthcare / jobs / housing, and shuttled into prison and poverty, I don't want to hear any more about the growing discrimination against white Americans. It is nonexistent. Additionally, I will be more conscious about not using softer, ambiguous phrases when referring to racism. There is no more "race relations" or "conversations about race" or "racial issues / discrimination." There is racism. We have to name it before we face it."[3] I saw a great comment the other day that simply said "Racism is taught."

Conversations about race and racism also intimidate both whites and Blacks. They do not want to remind each other of the American holocaust called slavery, nor of the period in the South after Reconstruction during which this country initiated a violent and terroristic brand of American-style apartheid to keep recently freed Africans "in their place." Whites are uncomfortable hearing how they treated Blacks historically for political and financial gain; Blacks are uncomfortable talking about how they were treated historically for political and financial gain.

Revered civil rights activist and U.S. Representative John Lewis (D-Georgia), recently commented about racism, "I've never seen this country as mean-spirited as it is today." Racists today do not wear a robe, but you can see them and hear them in America's pulpits, in elective offices at all levels, hosting television talk shows and radio shows, and spouting vitriolic messages of hatred and derision.

As writer, poet, and musician Eric Wattree has put it: "This entire nation, and the future of our children, is being threatened by the desperate attempt of a handful of insecure bigots to maintain their delusions of superiority, and as far as they're concerned, if the country has to be sacrificed for that cause, so be it."

A lynching in Litchfield, Kentucky, in 1913. Note that the "lynching tree" is in front of a church.

25

Racism and Violence

*Brave men do not gather by thousands to torture and murder
a single individual, so gagged and bound he cannot make
even feeble resistance or defense.*

— Ida B. Wells-Barnett
  Journalist, newspaper editor, suffragist, sociologist,
  civil rights activist

A lynching is a killing by a mob of people. A lynching in the South usually meant the killing of a Black man by the Ku Klux Klan, with a Bible and the Christian cross in one hand and the lynching rope in the other. A lynching was originally a system of punishment used by whites against slaves; even whites who protested against lynchings were themselves in danger of being lynched. On November 7, 1837, Elijah Parish Lovejoy, the editor of the *Alton Observer,* in Alton, Illinois, was killed by a White mob after he had published articles criticizing lynching and advocating the abolition of slavery.

Lynching was a local community affair. Black civil rights activist Ida B. Wells-Barnett found that Blacks had been "lynched for anything or nothing"—for wife-beating, for stealing hogs, for being "sassy" to white people, for sleeping with a consenting white woman—essentially, for being in the wrong place at the wrong time. It was American terrorism, carried out routinely in the American

South, year after year, decade after decade. It has been estimated that between 1880 and 1920, an average of two to three Blacks a week were lynched in the United States.

Dr. Rayford Logan wrote that during this period many Blacks (mainly men), were harassed, mutilated, and lynched in the United States. Dr. James Loewen further notes that lynching emphasized the helplessness of Blacks: "[The] defining characteristic of a lynching is that the murder takes place in public, so everyone knows who did it, yet the crime goes unpunished."

After it was founded, the Ku Klux Klan's numbers and the lynching of Blacks increased dramatically. In 1924, the Klan had four million members. It controlled the governorship and a majority of the state legislature in Indiana, as well as exerting powerful political influence in Arkansas, Oklahoma, California, Georgia, Oregon, and Texas. Those whites who would argue the Klan was just an organization "protecting state's rights" simply ignore the obvious. The Ku Klux Klan was a terrorist organization whose main objective was to keep former slaves on plantations as cheap labor, to incite fear, promote violence, and maintain white supremacy in the South.

As Rayford Logan has written: "So determined were white Southerners to maintain and return to their own way of life after the Civil War they resorted to fraud, intimidation, and murder to control state governments. This new civil war within the Southern states stemmed from an adamant determination to restore white supremacy. Regulators, Jayhawkers, the Black Horse Cavalry, the Knights of the White Camellia, the Constitutional Union Guards, the Pale Faces, the White Brotherhood, the Council of Safety, the '76 Association, the Rifle Clubs of South Carolina, and above all the Ku Klux Klan terrorized, maimed, and killed large number of Negroes. In some instances, Northern soldiers sided with the gangs that terrorized and killed Negroes."

Emmett Till

In August 1955, fourteen-year-old Chicagoan Emmett Till visited relatives in Mississippi. At Bryant's Grocery and Meat Market, a store owned by a white couple, Roy and Carolyn Bryant, it was claimed that Till whistled at Mrs. Bryant. Several days later, on August 28, Till was kidnapped, brutally beaten, shot, and dumped in the Tallahatchie River, his mutilated corpse barely identifiable. Emmett Till's mother insisted on leaving the casket open for the funeral and on having people take photographs because she wanted everyone to see how badly her son's body had been disfigured. She has famously been quoted as saying, "I wanted the world to see what they did to my baby." As many as fifty thousand people viewed Emmett Till's body.

Roy Bryant and his half-brother, J. W. Milam, were arrested for the murder. The all-white male jury in Sumner, Mississippi (some of whom actually participated in Till's torture and execution), took only an hour to return a verdict of "not guilty." One juror said that

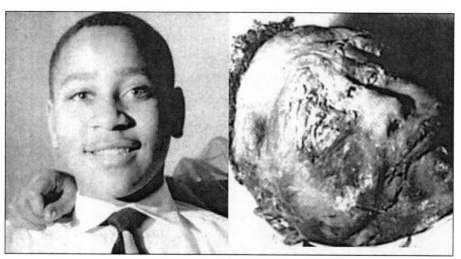

Emmett Till. His mother, Mamie Elizabeth Till-Mobley, insisted on leaving his casket open for the funeral and on having people take photographs, because she wanted the world to see what had been done to her son and how badly his body had been disfigured.

they took a soda-pop break during the deliberations to stretch them out and "make it look good."

To add insult to injury, knowing that they would not be re-tried, and with double jeopardy protecting them from being tried a second time, Bryant and Milam later boasted in a *Look* magazine interview about committing the murder. (William Bradford Huie, *Look* magazine, 1956).[1]

Keith Beauchamp is a dynamic young documentarian who honed his behind-the-camera skills during the day and spent his evenings doing research and reaching out to anyone who might have information on the Emmett Till case, a story told to Beauchamp when he was just ten years old. It was at this young age that Beauchamp saw a copy of *Jet* magazine that contained a picture of Emmett Till's dead body and was told the story behind his murder.

Although it was long believed that Bryant and Milam (both now deceased) acted alone, new evidence—much of it provided by Beauchamp's documentary *The Untold Story of Emmett Louis Till*— indicates that numerous other individuals may have been involved.[2] The death of eighty-six-year-old Juanita Milam barely made head-lines. Her brief obituary ran in the Biloxi, Mississippi, *Sun Herald*, but few noticed her passing, despite her being the widow of a killer.

Keith came to Jacksonville in February 2009 to join the Jacksonville Branch NAACP commemoration of the hundredth anniversary of the NAACP with a showing of his documentary.

On May 10, 2004, the U.S. Department of Justice reopened this fifty-year-old murder case, calling the 1955 prosecution a "grotesque miscarriage of justice," and citing Beauchamp's documentary as the starting point for their investigation. In May of 2005, Emmett's body was exhumed and the FBI turned over their evidence to the appropriate district attorney in Mississippi.

Two years later, however, the FBI and Mississippi prosecutors closed the book on the Till case. The statute of limitations prevented federal charges from being filed, and state prosecutors determined they did not have sufficient evidence to go after other suspects. Witnesses claimed that Mrs. Bryant was on the truck the night Emmett Till was kidnapped, though she denies any involvement. Some of Emmett's family members still hold out hope that Mrs. Bryant will be held accountable for her role in the horrific murder, while other relatives say the lengthy investigation has allowed them to put the matter to rest.

In 2007, Tallahatchie County finally issued a formal apology to Till's family: "We the citizens of Tallahatchie County recognize that the Emmett Till case was a terrible miscarriage of justice. We state candidly and with deep regret the failure to effectively pursue justice. We wish to say to the family of Emmett Till that we are profoundly sorry for what was done in this community to your loved one."

Georgia congressman John Lewis, whose skull was fractured when he was beaten during the 1965 "Bloody Sunday" march in Selma, Alabama, sponsored a bill that provides a plan for investigating and prosecuting unsolved murders from the civil rights era. The Emmett Till Unsolved Civil Rights Crime Act was signed into law in 2008.

Bolstered by his ability to connect with potential witnesses who otherwise might not come forward in communities where such Civil Rights crimes have occurred, Beauchamp has become a passionate advocate for survivors seeking justice, and has assisted the FBI by developing new leads for some of the still unsolved cases from this shameful troubled chapter in American history. His television series, *The Injustice Files*, allows him to comb through records; interview family members, witnesses, and investigators; and piece together the known facts of civil rights murder cases. Beauchamp recently announced a new film project about the Emmett Till story, in partnership with Whoopi Goldberg.

Although many of the laws that legitimized racism are no longer in place, the basic structure still stands. Institutional racism is responsible for school segregation, school "re-segregation," job discrimination, housing discrimination, "redlining," and Jim Crow laws, just for starters. Jamelle Bouie of the *Nation* website wrote in a column, "Public schools teach the basics of slavery, the Civil War, Reconstruction, and the Civil Rights Movement, but there's no attempt to go deeper with the material, and move away from the notion that racism is something reserved for the Bull Connors and Klansmen of the world. It's not just that students leave history education with a skewed, and often benign, view of American apartheid (in my experience, Jim Crow is reduced to its cultural signifiers—there's no attempt to deal with the reality of state-condoned terrorism against Black Americans), but that they come away with the belief that racism is the sole province of bad people."

Nearly four thousand Black people were lynched in the American South between the end of the Civil War and World War II, according to a report by the Equal Justice Initiative in February, 2015. The report, *Lynching in America: Confronting the Legacy of Racial Terror*, says that the number of victims in the twelve Southern states was more than 20 percent higher than previously reported.[3]

Lynching steadily increased throughout the South in the years following the Civil War, as whites kept Black neighborhoods in a perpetual state of fear. The U.S. government did nothing to stop the terror—and we have already documented through the work of James Weldon Johnson that Congress incredibly refused to pass a law to ban lynching. From the Equal Justice Initiative report: "Not a single white person was convicted of murder for lynching a black person in America during this period, and of all lynchings committed after 1900, only 1 percent resulted in a lyncher being convicted of a criminal offense." According to Bryan Stevenson, executive director of the Equal Justice Initiative, "The lynching of African Americans was really a direct message to the entire African American community. It was designed to traumatize and terrorize. "

Pulitzer Prize-winning columnist and author Carl Hiaasen details some of the horrific examples of man's inhumanity to man and woman: "A Black man named Luther Holbert and a woman thought to be his wife were snatched by a lynch mob on suspicion of killing a white landowner. No prosecution, no trial, no finding of guilt. They were first tied to a tree. Their fingers were hacked off and given out as souvenirs. Next their ears were chopped from their heads. A mob beat the man while a crowd of hundreds watched. A large corkscrew was then used to mutilate both captives, who were tossed onto a fire and burned. While all this was happening, the onlookers—which included women and children—were served lemonade and deviled eggs. This homegrown American atrocity took place in 1904 in Doddsville, Mississippi."[4]

These deaths were just two of the 3,959 documented "racial terror lynchings" in twelve Southern states between 1877 and 1950, according to the Equal Justice Initiative. The Alabama-based legal-rights group spent five years researching such murders, and how they were used to terrify African American communities.

Charles M. Blow, a *New York Times* op-ed columnist who writes about politics, public opinion, and social justice once wrote, "Violence is weakness masquerading as strength. It is a crude statement of depravity voiced by the unethical and impolitic. It reduces humanity rather than lifts it."

Some whites and Blacks say discussing lynchings and slavery are not worth the energy. I vehemently beg to differ. You cannot whitewash American history to ignore the inhumane treatment of enslaved Africans by the Founding Fathers, and the dastardly and cowardly way of racist, terrorist violence.

The American institution of racism uses the Confederate flag as its cherished symbol of heritage. Referred to as the Confederate battle flag, and the "Southern Cross" (or the cross of St. Andrew), the Confederate flag has been described both as a proud emblem of Southern heritage and as a shameful reminder of slavery, segregation, and the violence of racism. If the Confederate battle flag were merely a historical curiosity, someone might argue that it illustrates a quaint past. But the fact is that the flag is a symbol of hatred exemplified by its usage for more than one hundred fifty years, and as an instrument for lynchings. According to the Southern Poverty Law Center, more than five hundred extremist groups use the Southern Cross as one of their symbols.

Tonyaa Weathersbee, award winning columnist for the *Florida Times-Union*, wrote an excellent column and response to a young Black male embracing the Confederate flag: "Recently, Byron Thomas, a nineteen-year-old Black student from Augusta, Georgia, stirred controversy for hanging a Confederate flag from the window of his dorm room. He took it down before Thanksgiving, but for the wrong reasons: He told the *Augusta Chronicle* that he did so because the conversation had shifted from 'holding to traditional

Byron Thomas with "his" Confederate flag.

Unless WE Tell It . . . It Never Gets Told!

views' to his right to free speech. So, Byron Thomas claims that he hung a Confederate flag outside of his dorm room at the University of South Carolina Beaufort because he wants his generation 'to start forming our own opinions about things.' I say he's been exposed to too many GOP talking points, which imply that Blacks who don't acquiesce to their recasting of this nation's racial history, or who don't ignore racial reality, are brainwashed illiterates who don't know any better. For that, as well as a number of other reasons that caused him to fly the Confederate flag as some sort of symbol of him being liberated from his own history, Thomas ought to be ashamed. Especially since the flag he's defending represents a heritage that viewed people like him as a better fit for the cotton fields than for a state university. Talk about twisted."

The defenders of the Confederate flag often claim that it represents "heritage, not hate," even though white supremacists use that flag as their ideological symbol. The "corner-stone" address, which was delivered by Confederate Vice-President Alexander Stephens at the Athenaeum in Savannah, Georgia, on March 21, 1861, set forth the fundamental differences between the constitution of the Confederacy and that of the United States, and defended slavery: "Our new government is founded upon exactly the opposite idea; its foundations are laid, its corner-stone rests, upon the great truth that the negro is not equal to the white man; that slavery subordination to the superior race is his natural and normal condition. This, our new government, is the first, in the history of the world, based upon this great physical, philosophical, and moral truth." No amount of revisionist history can hide the true meaning of this "heritage."

Would we see the public glorification of the Nazi swastika as a cherished symbol of "heritage"? Yet the mainstream media, historians, and historical societies somehow see the Confederacy as having fought for an honorable and noble cause. There are "Southern heritage" groups that glorify the Civil War—or as many of them

The Southern Poverty Law Center's Civil Rights Memorial.

call that conflict, "the War of Northern Aggression." Is it honorable to fight a war in order to maintain slavery? Is it honorable to call Southern states courageous because they decided to secede from the United States of America to maintain their heritage of an economy based upon free labor of enslaved human beings? Or is it just more racist Confederate mental debris?

On the Southern Poverty Law Center's Civil Rights Memorial in Montgomery, Alabama, are inscribed the names of civil rights martyrs, individuals who lost their lives during the modern Civil Rights Movement—1954 to 1968—incurring the wrath of the white Southerners and reaping the whirlwind of the "Southern strategy." Those listed include activists who were targeted for death because of their civil rights work; random victims of vigilantes determined to halt the movement; innocent citizens like Johnnie Mae Chappell from Jacksonville, Florida; and individuals who, in the sacrifice of their own lives, brought new awareness to the struggle.[5]

Unless WE Tell It . . . It Never Gets Told!

Two names not included on SPLC Civil Rights Memorial list are Harry T. Moore and his wife, Harriette Moore. They were murdered on the night of their twenty-fifth wedding anniversary, December 25, 1951, when a bomb exploded under their home in Mims, Florida. It was the first killing of a prominent civil rights leader, but because their deaths occurred before 1954, they are not included among those listed on the SPLC Civil Rights Memorial. This was not a slight by the SPLC; it is in accord with the fact that many consider 1954, the year that Emmett Till was murdered, to have been the beginning of the modern Civil Rights Movement.

I, though, agree with those who feel that the deaths of Harry T. Moore and Harriette Moore in 1951 was the spark that ignited the Civil Rights Movement, and we must position them at the top of the list of civil rights martyrs. They are the only husband and wife killed during the struggle, an unfortunate distinction, but a distinction defined by their courage and bravery.

Harriette Moore and Harry T. Moore were inducted into the Florida Civil Rights Hall of Fame in April 2013. (Author's note: It was my honor to serve as the keynote speaker for that 2013 Florida Civil Rights Hall of Fame induction ceremony.)

Dr. James Cone, in *The Cross and the Lynching Tree*, describes America's quandary: "The cross has been transformed into a harmless, non-offensive ornament that Christians wear around their necks. Rather than reminding us of the 'cost of discipleship,' it has become a form of 'cheap grace,' an easy way to salvation that doesn't force us to confront the power of Christ's message and mission. Until we can see the cross and the lynching tree together, until we can identify Christ with a 'recrucified' black body hanging from a lynching tree, there can be no genuine understanding of Christian identity in America, and no deliverance from the brutal legacy of slavery and white supremacy."[6]

NAACP Executive Secretary Roy Wilkins and the author (at age sixteen), at the Jacksonville Youth Council NAACP Mass Meeting in Jacksonville, Florida, December 1960.

26

"Ruby, we cannot guarantee Rodney's safety"

*I love America more than any other country in the world
and, exactly for this reason, I insist on the right to criticize
her perpetually.*

—James Baldwin

Following the August 27, 1960, race riot in Jacksonville that became
known as Ax Handle Saturday, I was invited by NAACP branches
in Alabama and Mississippi to visit them and tell the story of civil
rights in Jacksonville. There was nothing unusual about that—during those turbulent times, members and officers of NAACP branches, youth councils, and college chapters who were involved in the
struggle, were regularly invited to come and tell their civil rights
story. You would speak at NAACP "mass meetings," usually held
at churches. Churches were the spiritual base of the movement, but
during those days of segregation they were also the only venues of
size available to us, and thus the places where you could disseminate
news of current activities in the Civil Rights Movement.

In 1960, Roy Wilkins, executive secretary of the national
NAACP, issued a memo to all NAACP branches requesting that no
representative of the organization travel to Mississippi or Alabama.
Mrs. Ruby Hurley, regional director of the Southeast Region of the
NAACP, eventually contacted Mr. Wilkins about my invitations to

speak in those states. Not that it was the NAACP'S responsibility, but with the violence in the South directed toward anyone related to the Civil Rights Movement, Mr. Wilkins' memo was timely. In those days it was necessary for the NAACP to provide a modicum of protection to those involved in NAACP business.

Roy Wilkins said to Mrs. Hurley, "Ruby, we cannot guarantee Rodney's safety." My case was not an isolated one. Violence was that predictable—and violence in Alabama and Mississippi was especially predictable—but of course we never knew where the next incident of violence would erupt. I did speak in North Carolina, Georgia, South Carolina, and Virginia, but not in Alabama and Mississippi. Almost a hundred years after the end of slavery, in this country of freedom and equality, this richest country in the world, violence reigned supreme because America simply would not protect its Black citizens. Violence became the Southern racist response to freedom and equality, to the Civil Rights Movement: the retributive "Southern strategy." And Southern law-enforcement officers were not only complicit in the violence, but many led the charge.

I met Roy Wilkins during the 1960 annual convention of the Virginia State Conference of NAACP Branches, held at the Richmond Mosque in Richmond, Virginia. He was the keynote speaker, and during his talk he invited me to the podium to tell the "Jacksonville Story." I count that as one of the great honors of my life. In December of that year, when the Jacksonville Youth Council NAACP was boycotting downtown businesses, Mr. Wilkins would come to Jacksonville as the featured speaker at one of our mass meetings. He did not just speak and leave, but spent time talking with us and encouraging our participation in the fight against racism.

Mr. Wilkins began his career in St. Paul editing a small Black newspaper called the *Northwest Bulletin*. Before long, a larger Black weekly in Kansas City—the *Kansas City Call*—hired him as a reporter and columnist; later, he became managing editor. By 1931 the

NAACP—National Association for the Advancement of Colored People—which was the most prominent civil rights organization at the time, took notice of the young Wilkins and brought him on board. Between 1931 and 1934 he was assistant NAACP secretary under Walter Francis White. When W. E. B. Du Bois left the organization in 1934, Wilkins replaced him as editor of *The Crisis*, the official magazine of the NAACP. After serving in various high administrative positions with the NAACP, he became executive secretary in 1955 (the position would be renamed "executive director" in 1964).

From that post he fought for such signal legislation as the 1964 Civil Rights Act, the 1965 Voting Rights Act, and the 1968 Fair Housing Act. Wilkins also held various leadership and consulting positions outside of his NAACP duties, as an advisor to the U.S. War Department (1945), a consultant to the American delegation to the U.N. Conference in San Francisco (1945), chair of the American Delegation to the International Conference on Human Rights (in Teheran, 1968), and president of the Leadership Conference of Civil Rights (1969). For his civil rights work, the NAACP awarded him the Spingarn Medal in 1964; in 1967, President Lyndon B. Johnson bestowed upon him the country's highest civilian honor, the Presidential Medal of Freedom.

Roy Wilkins retired in 1977. He died four years later, at age eighty. On May 17, 1984, Mr. Wilkins was posthumously awarded the Congressional Gold Medal. Minnesota's St. Paul Civic Center Auditorium was renamed the Roy Wilkins Auditorium in 1984, and the Roy Wilkins Center for Human Relations and Human Justice was established in the University of Minnesota's Humphrey Institute of Public Affairs in 1992. A memorial to this stalwart of the Civil Rights Movement was erected on the Minnesota State Capitol mall in 1995. Roy Wilkins is the twenty-fourth African American honored in the U. S. Postal Service's long-running *Black Heritage* commemorative stamp series. A great civil rights fighter!

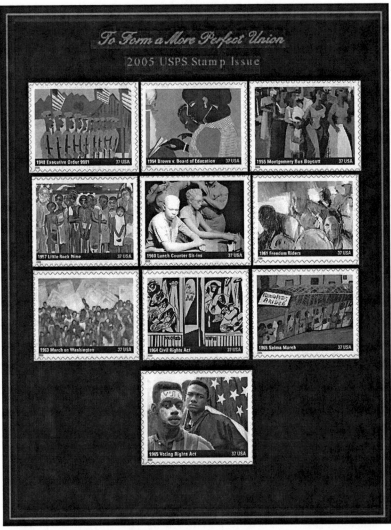

To Form A More Perfect Union, *a 2005 stamp issue of the U.S. Postal Service.*

27

Talking Black History
and the Civil Rights Movement

History is not everything, but it is a starting point. History is a clock that people use to tell their political and cultural time of day. It is a compass they use to find themselves on the map of human geography. It tells them where they are, but more importantly, what they must be.

—Dr. John Henrik Clarke
Historian, scholar, and Pan-African activist

Fighting for civil rights is not a fight of might, but a purposeful fight in the ongoing struggle against racism and discrimination. We marched to fight racism; we sat down at lunch counters to fight racism; we walked picket lines to fight racism; we boycotted stores and newspapers to fight racism; we registered to vote to fight racism; we withstood the ridicule and threats to go to school to fight racism; we joined civil rights organizations to work with their membership to fight racism; we survived vicious racial epithets and water hoses and baseball bats and ax handles to fight racism; and some died from the bullets and the bombs and the lynching ropes, fighting racism.

It has been well documented that the consistent response to the Civil Rights Movement was violence. Nonviolent passive resistance was arguably the answer to violence, and many were determined that nonviolence could overcome violence—although my good friend Charlie Cobb makes the case in his book *This Nonviolent Stuff'll Get You Killed: How Guns Made the Civil Rights Movement Possible* that the threat of violence, and the fact that some Black folks had guns, helped as well.[1]

I was struck by a statement that another friend, Wendy Clarissa Geiger, once made about making a difference and doing your part to register your protest on a personal basis. "Perhaps, it is in a small way why I do not buy Coca-Cola products because of apartheid in South Africa," Wendy said. "I also do not eat table grapes in honor of Cesar Chavez and the farm workers. It is the 'little' ways that keep our integrity from corroding, perhaps, more widely than it has already." Wendy is a Quaker and committed to the struggle, and those comments come from her heart.

Bob Dylan's "Blowin' in the Wind" begins with the words, "How many roads must a man walk down, before you call him a man?" This moving and poignant song is a tribute to the Civil Rights Movement and its focus on human dignity and respect. In a story that symbolizes the ways in which American popular music intersected with and helped sustain the civil-rights movement, Sam Cooke was motivated to write "A Change Is Gonna Come" by Bob Dylan's "Blowin' in the Wind." When Cooke first heard that song, Peter Guralnick writes in his 2005 volume *Dream Boogie: The Triumph of Sam Cooke*, he "was so carried away with the message, and the fact that a white boy had written it, that . . . he was almost ashamed not to have written something like that himself."[2]

Half a century ago, on March 7, 1965, state troopers gassed and beat a number of men and women (including future Congressman John Lewis) who were participating in a peaceful march for voting rights in Selma, Alabama. That same day, radio listeners around the country might have heard Sam Cooke singing a lyric he'd writ-

Unless WE Tell It . . . It Never Gets Told!

ten and recorded several months earlier, but which could have been describing the "Bloody Sunday" confrontation on the Edmund Pettus Bridge: "Then I go to my brother and I say, 'Brother, help me please.' But he winds up knockin' me back down on my knees."

Sam Cooke's powerful civil rights anthem recently marked its fiftieth anniversary, and it passed without much commemoration, which is surprising, since "A Change Is Gonna Come" remains as timely as ever. The entire issue of Black Lives Matter, as articulated by Shaun King, senior justice writer for *The New York Times*—the ongoing serial shootings of unarmed Black men by law enforcement; the continued brutalization of Black women by law enforcement; the Justice Department reports on police abuse and corruption in Ferguson, Missouri, and other communities; the Supreme Court gutting of a provision of the Voting Rights Act that was a key consequence of the Selma marches—these and other facts have signaled the relevance of Sam Cooke's classic song. If Cooke were alive to write a follow-up to "A Change Is Gonna Come" based on the current political scene, he might decide to call it "The More Things Change, the More They Remain the Same."

I spoke to a group of curriculum developers and supervisors about Black history and the Civil Rights Movement, and asked them why the study of American history cannot recognize salient contributions to the history of the country by Black people. One supervisor responded by saying, "Mr. Hurst, we can't include everybody." And therein lies the problem. You cannot justify the exclusion of Black history and the historical events of the Civil Rights Movement by simply saying, "We can't include everybody." As a Black student, if I cannot read about the historical contributions of my Black ancestors, the educational playing field is kept uneven.

Many Blacks and whites consider the civil rights fight against racism and segregation and discrimination and Jim Crow laws to be a significant piece of America's history. Unfortunately, other Blacks and whites suffer from varying degrees of amnesia when it comes to civil rights and understanding its impact, so the U.S. Postal Service acknowledging major civil rights events and recognizing important civil rights pioneers in two separate stamp issues is a good thing.

In 2005, the U.S. Postal Service issued ten stamps to commemorate some of the milestone events of the Civil Rights Movement. They named the stamp series *To Form a More Perfect Union.*

- On July 26, 1948, President Harry S. Truman's issued Executive Order 9981 mandating full integration in all branches of the U.S. military. By the time the Korean conflict ended in the early 1950s, integration was on its way to being achieved. Noted Black artist William H. Johnson's "Training for War," a silkscreen print created circa 1941, recalls President Truman's Executive Order. Johnson, who died in 1970, would himself become the subject of a stamp.

- *Brown vs. Board of Education* honors the unanimous ruling of the U.S. Supreme Court that separate educational facilities for Black and white children are inherently unequal. The landmark ruling is suggested by Romare Bearden's 1984 lithograph, "The Lamp."

- The Montgomery Bus Boycott is represented by a detail from "Walking," a 1958 painting by Charles Alston. After Rosa Parks was arrested on December 1, 1955, for refusing to move from the front of the bus to the rear of the bus, Blacks began a 381-day boycott of Montgomery's city bus line. They walked or carpooled for more than a year and finally on November 13, 1956 won their case before the U.S. Supreme Court. The boycott officially ended on December 20, 1956. On December 21, 1956, Black passengers once again rode Montgomery city buses, and this time they sat anywhere.

- The Little Rock Nine stamp is based on George Hunt's 1997 painting "America Cares." After the Supreme Court declared segregated schools unconstitutional in the 1954 decision in *Brown vs.*

Board of Education, many Southern public school systems adamantly resisted integration. In 1957, nine courageous students became the first Blacks to attend Central High School in Little Rock, Arkansas, where they withstood racist and virulent harassment on a daily basis before they received the protection of federal troops.

• "Lunch Counter Sit-Ins" recalls the sit-in effort to integrate "whites-only" lunch counters with a photograph of a civil rights exhibit created by Studio EIS, a New York design and fabrication firm, for the National Civil Rights Museum. When four Black college students from North Carolina Agricultural and Technical College entered a "whites only" lunch counter in Greensboro, North Carolina, in 1960 and tried to place an order, they sparked acts of civil disobedience in many other cities.

• "Freedom Riders," a 1963 gouache by May Stevens, honors the Freedom Riders, racially integrated groups of men and women who volunteered to take bus rides through the South, using the "wrong" facilities at stops to test a ruling that outlawed segregation of bus stations and terminals serving interstate travelers. Several Freedom Riders were injured because of mob violence instigated by segregationists, eliciting an outpouring of support.

• "March on Washington," painted in 1964 by Alma Thomas, commemorates the great march by more than 250,000 people in Washington, D.C., for racial justice in 1963, when Martin Luther King Jr. delivered his historic "I Have a Dream" speech from the steps of the Lincoln Memorial.

• The Civil Rights Act of 1964, designed to provide broad protections against discrimination on the basis of race, is suggested by "Dixie Cafe," a brush-and-ink drawing made in 1948 by Jacob Lawrence. Signed into law by President Lyndon B. Johnson, the Civil Rights Act prohibited discrimination in public accommodations such as hotels, restaurants and theaters.

- "In the spring of 1965, demonstrators demanding an end to discrimination gathered in Selma, Alabama, to march to Montgomery, the state capital, fifty miles away. The march is represented by "Selma March," a 1991 acrylic painting by Bernice Sims.

- President Johnson signed the Voting Rights Act into law in 1965, strengthening the federal government's ability to prevent state and local governments from denying citizens the right to vote because of their race. The event is suggested by Bruce Davidson's photograph of Bloody Sunday, "Youths on the Selma March, 1965."

Four years later, in 2009, the U.S. Postal Service issued six stamps to commemorate the hundredth anniversary of the Civil Rights Movement and the founding of the NAACP. Each stamp in this issue, *Civil Rights Pioneers*, featured a pair of stalwarts in the fight, a total of twelve individuals so recognized.

- Ella Baker (1903–1986) was one of the unsung heroes in the struggle from the 1940s through the 1960s. In early 1960, in the aftermath of the wave of student sit-ins, Baker signed the call for the student conference that met at Shaw University in Raleigh, North Carolina, and resulted in the founding of the Student Nonviolent Coordinating Committee.

- Ruby Hurley (1909–1980) was a leader of the movement in the South during the 1950s and 1960s. Hurley aided in all of the major school desegregation cases of the period, took part in the investigations of the murder of Emmett Till, and worked closely with statewide field organizers around the South, including Medgar Evers and Vernon Jordan. (As director of the NAACP's Southeast Region, Mrs. Hurley spent several months in Jacksonville after the 1960 sit-ins and the riot on Ax Handle Saturday. Those of us in the 1960 Jacksonville Youth Council NAACP considered Mrs. Hurley our NAACP "surrogate mother.")

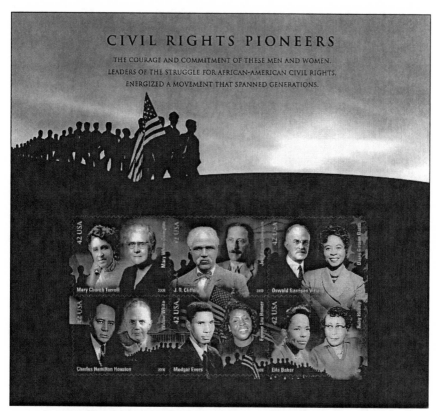

Civil Rights Pioneers, *a 2009 stamp issue of the U.S. Postal Service.*

• J. R. Clifford (1848–1933) was a Union Army veteran and West Virginia's first African American attorney. In 1905, Clifford joined W. E. B. Du Bois, William Monroe Trotter, and twenty-seven Black men in founding the Niagara Movement, the foundation for the National Association for the Advancement of Colored People.

• Joel Spingarn (1875–1939), a literary critic and Columbia University professor, was among the leading figures in the NAACP during its first three decades, serving as president and chairman of the board. The NAACP's Spingarn Medal is named for him.

• Medgar Evers (1925–1963), World War II veteran and civil rights leader in Mississippi, was assassinated on June 12, 1963. After the 1954 *Brown* decision, Evers applied to the University of Mississippi Law School, but was denied admission. The NAACP subsequently hired him as the first field secretary for Mississippi. Evers organized protests in Jackson, including a boycott of merchants in the early 1960s, and led the effort to have James Meredith admitted to the University of Mississippi. (In 1963, Evers spoke in Jacksonville, Florida, at the invitation of Rutledge Pearson.)

• Fannie Lou Hamer (1917–1977) worked as a sharecropper for most of her life. In 1964, she won national attention during the Democratic Convention when she represented the Mississippi Freedom Democratic Party before the Credentials Committee in a challenge to the all-white Mississippi delegation.

• Mary Church Terrell (1863–1954) was born in the year of the Emancipation Proclamation and died just months after the 1954 *Brown* decision. Throughout her life, as a writer and lecturer, Terrell was a leading voice for racial justice and women's rights in the United States and abroad.

• Mary White Ovington (1865–1951) was one of the founders of the NAACP and a leading figure in the organization for nearly four decades.

• Charles Hamilton Houston (1895–1950) is often referred to as the "architect" of the Civil Rights Movement. Houston, born and raised in Washington, D.C., was the first African American elected to the *Harvard Law Review*. At a time when most Blacks were barred from voting, he believed that Black lawyers had a unique role to play by using the law as a tool for social change.

• Walter Francis White (1893–1955) was one of the most important civil rights leaders of the twentieth century. In 1917, as a young college graduate, he helped establish the first NAACP branch in Atlanta and soon caught the attention of NAACP executive secretary James Weldon Johnson, who created the position of assistant secretary for White. White, a blue-eyed man with a fair complexion, could easily pass for white and used this to his advantage in his daring under-cover investigations and exposés of lynchings.

- Oswald Garrison Villard (1872–1949) was one of the founders of the NAACP and served as the first chairman of the organization's board.

- Daisy Bates (1914–1999). In 1957, Daisy Bates became a house-hold name when she fought for the right of nine Black students to attend the all-white Central High School in Little Rock, Arkansas. (See Chapter 7.)

There are many Blacks who have made contributions throughout the development of this country, yet their names and their ac-complishments remain elusively outside the purview of authors of American textbooks, and of those curriculum supervisors and co-ordinators who approve American textbooks.

- Dr. Daniel Hale Williams performed the first successful heart surgery.

- Benjamin Banneker, mathematician and mapmaker, laid out the city of Washington, D.C.

- Garrett Augustus Morgan Sr. invented both the automated traffic signal and the gas mask.

- Matt Henson was the first person to set foot on the North Pole.

- Toussaint Louverture was a slave who led slave revolts and the freeing of slaves in Haiti, where he also defeated Napoleon's armies in the hills of that country. He was betrayed and tricked by the French army under a flag of truce, but his defeat of Napoleon's troops directly led to the United States purchasing the Louisiana Territory. Toussaint Louverture is known as "the Father of Haiti."

• Granville T. Woods was an inventor with patents for more than sixty inventions, particularly for trains and street cars. Although other inventors including Thomas Edison made spurious claims to his inventions, he was able to successfully defend many of those claims. Perhaps his most noted inventions were the electro-mechanical brake and the "telegraphony."

• Norbert Rillieux invented a sugar-processing evaporator for making sugar from sugar beets or sugar cane.

• Richard Spikes received a patent for an automatic gear shift for cars.

• Otis Boykin invented a variable resistor for guided missiles, IBM computers, and heart pacemakers.

• Frederick McKinley Jones patented more than sixty inventions, and is best known for inventing an automatic refrigeration system for long-haul trucks in 1935, a roof-mounted cooling device. Jones was the first to invent a practical, mechanical refrigeration system for trucks and railroad cars, eliminating the risk of food spoilage during long-distance shipping trips. The system, for which Frederick Jones was issued the patent on July 12, 1940, was, in turn, adapted to a variety of other common carriers, including ships.

• Dr. Percy Julian developed a way to synthesize cortisone, a sterol that has eased the sufferings of millions. Prior to his work, sterols cost several hundreds of dollars per gram; his process brought them down to twenty cents per gram. Dr. Julian also developed a soy protein solution that put out gas and oil fires that were not affected by water. This material, known as "bean soup" aboard U.S. Navy ships, saved the lives of countless sailors during World War II.

• Dr. Mark Dean started working at IBM in 1980 and was instrumental in the invention of the personal computer. He holds three of IBM's original nine personal computer patents and currently holds more than twenty patents altogether.

Unless WE Tell It . . . It Never Gets Told!

• Lewis Howard Latimer invented a method of making carbon filaments for the electric incandescent lamp.

• Jan Ernst Matzeliger invented a machine that would sew the sole of a shoe to the upper part in about a minute. His machine changed the process of how shoes were made by mechanizing a part of their manufacture that previously had to be done by hand, thereby cutting the cost of making shoes in half.

• Elijah McCoy invented an automatic lubricator system that continues to be used in large industry today. It was one of fifty-seven patents received by McCoy; many believe that when you say "the real McCoy," you are talking about Elijah McCoy.

• George Washington Carver invented more than three hundred products derived from the peanut and numerous products derived from the sweet potato.

• Dr. Charles Drew is famous for his pioneering work in blood preservation and is included in a 2002 list of the One Hundred Greatest African Americans.

There is a scarcity of Black history in American history textbooks, and you cannot teach American history in an accurate and truthful way without teaching Black history. Dr. Carter G. Woodson created Negro History Week in 1926 to highlight the overlooked accomplishments of Blacks. It has evolved to Black History Month. Black History Month does not say that Blacks are superior to other groups; there is no White History Month because the accomplishments of whites and their contributions to American history are showcased all year long.

If a race has no history, it has no worthwhile tradition, it becomes a negligible factor in the thought of the world, and it stands in danger of being exterminated.
—Dr. Carter G. Woodson

28

"We are not hiring Blacks at this time, but . . ."

I served four years in the Air Force and was honorably discharged in April, 1965. After a month or so of soaking up a little of the Florida sun that was a relief after being baked for almost four years in the Texas sun, it was time to hunt for a job. I say "hunt" because I that is how the job market felt in Jacksonville in 1965. I went to an insurance company owned by a man for whom my stepfather, William "Joe" Wilson, had worked for a number of years. In fact, Daddy Joe (that was the affectionate name that my sister and I had for him) arranged for me to have an interview with the personnel director. The interview went well, or so I thought. Near the conclusion of the interview, the personnel director said to me, "Look Mr. Hurst, we are not hiring Blacks at this time, but if you go and apply at Prudential's South Central Home Office, they are hiring Blacks."

It is amazing how things just stay with you over the years. I wanted to ask him, "Well if Prudential Insurance is hiring Blacks, why aren't you?" Obviously, that was not the time nor the place.

Later that same day, I made my way to Prudential's South Central Home Office, located on the near Southside of Jacksonville. After my experience with the other insurance company, I was somewhat leery about what I could expect, and here I was walking in cold. No prearranged interview. What I received, though, was not what I expected. I was greeted by one of the most gracious white ladies I had ever met. Her name, in fact, was Betsy White. Her professional manner was outstanding, and it was neither condescending nor patronizing. She gave me an application, and scheduled me to take a test—an aptitude test, I guess.

I did well on the test, and few days later received a call for an interview. This time it was with Prudential's personnel director. I had already prepared myself for his response: "Don't call us; we'll call you." In fact, before the interview I had checked my bus schedule to see when I could catch the next Jacksonville Transportation Authority 36B Moncrief bus home. Imagine my surprise when, at the end of the interview, he offered me a job! Which, of course, I accepted. He told me he would call me in a couple of days to give me a start date. And then he said, "Welcome to Prudential." I walked out of there in a daze. This was not supposed to happen. I had not expected a call back when I first applied at Prudential. Not only did I get a call back, but then came this job offer. Mrs. White called me two days later and was as gracious and professional on the phone as she had been in the office. She then said those magical words: "Congratulations, Mr. Hurst. Please report to Prudential's personnel office on June 17. Welcome to the Prudential family. "

I reported to Prudential at 7:45 AM on Monday, June 17, 1965. After working my way through and signing a blizzard of forms, I was escorted to the manager's office of the department where I would work. I knew that several Black females worked in Prudential's secretarial pool. What I did not know when I was hired was that I would be the first Black male to work in Prudential's South Central Home Office.

Several white colleagues later told me that prior to my starting there, Prudential's administration had a series of meetings with the other men in the Home Office to advise them to "watch their language." This was Jacksonville, Florida, circa 1965.

Movie poster for The Birth of a Nation, *1915.*

29

Racism and the American Presidency
Part I

Racism is a way of life for the vast majority of white Americans, spoken and unspoken, acknowledged and denied, subtle and sometimes not so subtle—the disease of racism permeates and poisons a whole body politic.

—Dr. Martin Luther King Jr.

Our history has always deified Presidents of the United States as idealistic leaders of this country. Despite the fact that it is not openly discussed and almost never written about in most high school history textbooks, many U.S. Presidents owned slaves and exemplified the deeply racist attitudes that accompanied that vile practice. How many Presidents owned enslaved persons? Glad you asked:

The first U.S. President: George Washington owned 317 slaves (and owned slaves during the time that he was President).

Third President: Thomas Jefferson owned 237 slaves (and owned slaves while he was President).

Fourth President: James Madison owned 117 slaves (and owned slaves while he was President).

Fifth President: James Monroe owned seventy-five slaves (and owned slaves while he was President).

Seventh President: Andrew Jackson owned two hundred slaves (and owned slaves while he was President).

Eighth President: Martin Van Buren owned one slave.

Ninth President: William Henry Harrison owned eleven slaves.

Tenth President: John Tyler owned seventy slaves (and owned slaves while he was President).

Eleventh President: James K. Polk owned twenty-four slaves (and owned slaves while he was President).

Twelfth President: Zachary Taylor owned 145 slaves (and owned slaves while he was President).

Thirteenth President: James Buchanan owned two slaves.

Seventeenth President: Andrew Johnson owned eight slaves.

Eighteenth President: Ulysses S. Grant owned five slaves.

The second, John Adams; sixth, John Quincy Adams; thirteenth, Millard Fillmore; fourteenth, Franklin Pierce; and sixteenth President, Abraham Lincoln, did not own slaves. Thirteen of our first eighteen Presidents owned slaves—and eight of them owned slaves while serving as President of these United States of America.

President Thomas Jefferson took it several steps further. At the age of twenty-one, Thomas Jefferson inherited five thousand acres of land from his father, and fifty-two slaves. By 1773, at age thirty, he owned sixteen thousand acres and more than two hundred slaves. Jefferson would become the largest slaveholder in Albemarle County, Virginia. Despite his documented affair with his slave Sarah "Sally" Hemings, which resulted in six offspring (a fact that was denied by most historians until DNA testing proved it), President Thomas Jefferson's words in the Declaration of Independence are contrary to the principles he supposedly held so dear in the founding of America. We know his words all too well: "We hold these truths to be self-evident, that all men are created equal." But these were hypocritical words from a slave-owning future President. According to a *New York Times* article, and quoting Paul Finkelman, "Jefferson was always deeply committed to slavery, deeply hostile to the welfare of Blacks, slave or free," and was known to be a cruel slave master. He would separate slave family members as punitive punishment. He regarded free Blacks as "pests in society" who were as incapable as children of taking care of themselves, and believed that Blacks were "inferior to whites in the endowments of body and mind."

Following the Civil War, Blacks were able to vote and to participate in politics, and some were elected to public office. With the Compromise of 1877 and the election of President Rutherford B. Hayes, these gains were reversed. During the 1880s, Black civil rights and voting rights were once again dismantled. Elected politicians from both the North and the South simply agreed that Black civil rights would no longer matter. Racism and Jim Crow steadily became the order of the day.

The election of Theodore Roosevelt in 1904 initiated a presidential administration that was openly hostile to civil rights for Blacks. Roosevelt believed Blacks were intellectually inferior. He reduced federal appointments of Blacks, and promised Southerners that he would not appoint local federal officials who would disrupt the South.

President Howard Taft, a Republican elected in 1908, believed that Blacks should not participate in politics, and perpetuated the racist party line adopted by Theodore Roosevelt.

Woodrow Wilson and *The Birth of a Nation*

Woodrow Wilson, who won both the 1912 and 1916 presidential elections, is often held up as an example of a "progressive" President, but many consider him to have been a racist in presidential clothing. In order to win the African American vote, Wilson made the campaign promise that he could be counted on "for absolute fair dealing, for everything by which I could assist in advancing the interests of [the African] race in the United States." But following Wilson's election, his first Congress sent him some of the most racist legislation in the history of that body, and Wilson promptly signed it.

Woodrow Wilson was born in 1856 in little Staunton, Virginia. Though his family had recently relocated from famously abolitionist Ohio, his father, a Presbyterian minister, was pro-slavery and a supporter of the Confederacy. Wilson was still a boy when the family moved to Augusta, Georgia, where he grew up during the Civil War and Reconstruction. As president of Princeton University, Woodrow Wilson would not hire Black applicants; during that time, Princeton was the only major northern university that refused to admit Black students. In the White House, he continued the racist practices of Presidents Roosevelt and Taft.

Woodrow Wilson's election gave the South license to pursue its racist practices without concern about the possibility of federal interference. On taking power in Washington, Wilson brought his own brand of racism with him, which included telling "darkie" jokes during his Cabinet meetings. He appointed many pro-segregation Southerners to his Cabinet, which allowed them to quickly change the way the federal government handled racial issues, and he used the power of the Presidency to impose widespread segregation in the federal government.[1]

Having said during his campaign that he would improve the conditions of Blacks in the country, President Wilson, after he was elected, did nothing to make good on his campaign promises. In fact, he acted to re-segregate the federal workplace. Following the Civil War, Blacks had been employed in various federal jobs in Washington, D.C., and often the offices they worked in were integrated; in many departments, white clerks worked under Black

Unless WE Tell It . . . It Never Gets Told!

supervision. Wilson's Cabinet put an end to that, and in fact ended Blacks having access to federal jobs. Moreover, his Administration made it mandatory to include a photograph with any application for a federal position, which further facilitated the exclusion of Blacks from government jobs. President Wilson allowed officials to segregate work areas of their departments, even segregating the lavatories. One reason given was that white government workers had to be protected from various contagious diseases, particularly venereal diseases, which Wilson claimed were widespread among Blacks. Black supervisors and a number of Black diplomats were replaced with whites. A number of Black federal officials in the South were removed from their posts. Even the local Washington police force and the fire department stopped hiring Blacks.[2]

Wilson claimed that segregation was an act of kindness. He actively supported racist legislation, such as a bill passed by the House of Representatives that made interracial marriages a felony in Washington, D.C. President Wilson pushed for segregation of federal workers, systematically demoted Black civil servants, and claimed that nothing could be done to improve the situation of Blacks in the country. He refused to meet with Black leaders, to appear at Black conferences on issues of race, or to publicly denounce lynching. During World War I, President Wilson's administration relegated Black soldiers to non-combat labor billets, claiming that they were incapable of fighting courageously. Under Wilson, the Navy allowed Blacks only to serve as "mess boys," and the Marines did not accept Blacks in any capacity.[3]

William M. Trotter (1872–1934) was a journalist and civil rights advocate and a founder of the Niagara Movement, who was described by James Weldon Johnson as "an implacable foe of every form and degree of race discrimination." On Nov. 12, 1914, Trotter led a delegation from the National Independent Political League to the White House to meet with President Wilson and to protest his policy of segregation in federal employment.[4] To their amazement, Wilson defended segregation as "what was best" to manage racial tensions, and suggested that the Jim Crow system was "not a humiliation and ought to be so regarded by you gentlemen." Wilson's explanation—that integrated workplaces would inevitably lead to tension between "colored" clerks and white ones, and that segregation was "not done to injure or humiliate the colored clerks, but to avoid friction"—infuriated Trotter and others in the delegation.

When Trotter disputed the President's viewpoint, Wilson thought that Trotter was calling him a liar. But the crux of the matter was that Woodrow Wilson could not deal with a Black man offering his own opinion; a Black person should just be seen and not heard. "Your manner offends me," Wilson was reported to have said to Trotter. Trotter asked what had offended the President; Wilson replied, "Your tone, with its background of passion." Trotter responded, "But I have no passion in me, Mr. President. You are entirely mistaken; you misinterpret earnestness for passion." The two men continued to interrupt each other for another forty-five minutes, until Wilson bluntly instructed Trotter that he was the only one who could interrupt. Needless to say, the delegation left the White House thoroughly disappointed in their hopes for federal backing in their quest for opportunity and equality.[5]

The aftermath of this failed meeting with President Wilson was even more disheartening, as the national press inflamed public prejudice by portraying the visit and the "confrontation" as a case of impudent Blacks not knowing their place. This "incident" made national news and the story ran on the front page of *The New York Times*. As one might expect, the mainstream press sided with Wilson and characterized Trotter as a poor representative of his race, possessed of "superabundant untactful belligerency." A Texas newspaper went further. "The Tucker darkie who tried to sass the President" wrote the newspaper, getting Trotter's name wrong, "is not a

Booker T. Washington type of colored man. He is merely a nigger." Wilson banned Trotter from the White House for the remainder of his term, saying furiously: "If this [Black] organization were to ever have another hearing before me, it must have another spokesman."

William Trotter and his allies learned a lesson that Nelson Mandela would come to know and articulate many decades later: "There is no easy walk to Freedom anywhere, and many of us will have to pass through the Valley of the Shadow of Death repeatedly before we reach the mountaintop of our desires."

On February 8, 1915, two years into Wilson's presidency, D. W. Griffith's silent film celebrating the rise of the Ku Klux Klan had its premiere in Los Angeles at Clune's Auditorium. *The Birth of a Nation* is an unconscionably racist film of epic proportions, and President Woodrow Wilson was one of its most outspoken fans. This reprehensible movie portrays the so-called "overthrow" by the Ku Klux Klan of Reconstruction in the South. Griffith had white actors in blackface portray Black characters as savages, and characterized Klan members as brave, courageous, and patriotic.[6]

The movie was based on the equally offensive book *The Clansman*, which was authored by Wilson's close friend Thomas F. Dixon Jr., an American Baptist minister and a North Carolina state legislator.[7] James Weldon Johnson, doing battle against the pernicious effects of *The Birth of a Nation*, wrote, "*The Clansman* did us much injury as a book, but most of its readers were those already prejudiced against us. It did us more injury as a play, but a great deal of what it attempted to tell could not be represented on the stage. Made into a moving picture play, it can do us incalculable harm." Sadly, this was an understatement.

President Wilson's own earlier two-volume work, *A History of the American People*, was so racially biased that D. W. Griffith quoted him in *The Birth of a Nation*: "The white men were roused by a mere instinct of self preservation, until at last there had sprung into existence a great Ku Klux Klan, a veritable empire of the South, to protect the Southern country." Not only did Wilson, as President of these United States, proudly stand by those words, but he also had a private showing of the movie at the White House. If that was not enough, D. W. Griffith's movie showed Jesus Christ blessing the founding of the Ku Klux Klan. After seeing the film, an enthusiastic Wilson reportedly remarked, "It is like writing history with lightning, and my only regret is that it is all so terribly true."

The NAACP would fight to prevent the showing of *The Birth of a Nation* or to excise the most offensive scenes. Their efforts resulted in no success. The public endorsement and unwavering support of the film by President Woodrow Wilson as a sitting President was an important factor in undermining the NAACP's struggle against it. Dr. James Loewen writes, in *Lies My Teacher Told Me*, that the resurgence of the Ku Klux Klan during this period is attributable to the success of *The Birth of a Nation*. After all, this movie had the en-

Klan parade in Washington, D.C., 1925.

Unless WE Tell It . . . It Never Gets Told!

dorsement of the President of the United States. Wilson's endorsement is still affixed to prints of the film that are screened for film students studying Griffith's advances in editing.

Woodrow Wilson, the twenty-eighth President of the United States, is often lauded as a progressive and as a "high-minded idealist" and held up as a shining example of presidential leadership. After all, he is known for advocating the League of Nations as a deterrent to war. But why should we applaud him? It is far more accurate to understand Woodrow Wilson's two terms leading this country as an eight-year era of Presidential racism.

The Birth of a Nation accomplished exactly what it was intended to. With the wholehearted support of President Wilson, it inflamed the racist attitudes of white America against Blacks in this country and helped popularize the second incarnation of the Ku Klux Klan, which gained its greatest power and influence in the mid-1920s. Blacks, just a few years out of slavery and not remotely considered equal by whites, were portrayed as the villains of this racist Hollywood story.

Although the Ku Klux Klan used *The Birth of a Nation* as a recruitment tool, many film scholars now acclaim the movie as groundbreaking because of its many cinematic innovations, refinements, and technical effects, including a color sequence at the end. Some are so effusive in their praise as to call it one of the greatest American films of all time. One biographical summary of D. W. Griffith included these words: "Griffith's use of intricate editing and film techniques, such as alternating close-ups and long-shots from varying camera angles, were revolutionary and inspired a generation of directors." As a result of all this misplaced admiration, in 1993 *The Birth of a Nation* was voted into the National Film Registry, and in 1998 the American Film Institute ranked it as number forty-four of the "Top 100 American Films."

The exaltation of *The Birth of a Nation* to the height of film royalty is a monument to the racism that is embedded in this country. Can you overlook the movie's repulsive and overtly racist theme because it is considered by some "groundbreaking" and "innovative"? Hollywood and President Woodrow Wilson said "yes" when they chose to support this arrogantly racist film. Why should any person, Black or white, proclaim *The Birth of a Nation* a great film? Do we celebrate, or even try to justify, Leni Riefenstahl's *Triumph of the Will*, a movie created for Hitler's campaign of Nazi propaganda? Some also consider Riefenstahl's films "groundbreaking," but should we ignore their anti-Semitic theme? Knowing the content and intent of the film's story line about Adolf Hitler and Nazism, do we laud and embrace its impact on moviemaking, and disregard the broad-brushed stereotyping of Jews throughout the world?[8]

So tell me why I should like or appreciate *The Birth of a Nation*. No thinking person should respect D. W. Griffith for making such a vile film, nor should they respect the actors who appeared in it.

The Republicans' Southern Strategy

One can make the case that the last fifty years have been another "Nadir of American Race Relations," based on changes in the political landscape in the South that began during the Civil Rights Movement. According to journalist Bill Moyers, President Lyndon Johnson remarked, after he signed the 1964 Civil Rights Act, "We have probably lost the South for some time."

He was right. Republicans, their Southern strategy playbook at the ready, have successfully exploited racially driven fear to win political campaigns across the region. In the mid-1960s, Richard Nixon and the Republican Party began employing what they called the "Southern strategy" to retake the Presidency by appealing to white Southerners' anger over desegregation. There are amazing parallels between the periods after 1865 and 1964: the South is now a bastion of Southern conservative Republican philosophy, while following the Civil War and Reconstruction, it was home to a conservative Democratic philosophy.

When Ronald Reagan kicked off his presidential campaign in 1980 he did so in Philadelphia, Mississippi. Yes: *that* Philadelphia, Mississippi! The Philadelphia, Mississippi, where twenty-one-year-old Black Mississippian James Chaney, and two white New Yorkers, twenty-year-old Andrew Goodman and twenty-four-year-old Michael Schwerner, were brutally murdered for trying to register Black people to vote. The Philadelphia, Mississippi, that most people in this country had never heard of until those senseless, racially motivated killings. The Philadelphia, Mississippi, where Reagan never spoke one word about the civil rights murders, but did tell an overwhelmingly white crowd of his devotion to "states' rights." The Philadelphia, Mississippi, where Reagan sounded his racist dog whistle signal to Southern Democrats with the message that the Republican Party should be their home.

This was the Ronald Reagan who publicly stated that he would have voted against the 1964 Civil Rights Act—the Ronald Reagan who would, as President, oppose the establishment of a federal holiday honoring Dr. Martin Luther King Jr., and who signed the bill creating the holiday only after vast majorities in both the House of Representatives and in the Senate voted to pass it.

While campaigning for President in 1980, Ronald Reagan also told tales of Cadillac-driving "welfare queens" and "strapping young bucks" buying T-bone steaks with food stamps. In trumpeting these phony claims of welfare allegedly run amok, Reagan never needed to mention race, because he was blowing his dog whistle—sending a message about racial minorities that was inaudible to many people, but clearly heard by his intended audience. In doing so, he tapped into the scurrilous political tradition that was given new life by Richard Nixon and is more relevant than ever in the age of the Tea Party and the first Black President.[9]

President Barack Hussein Obama.

30

Racism and the American Presidency
Part II

*As it stands, our society is not yet colorblind, nor should it
be, given the disparities that still afflict and divide us. . . .
We must be willing to acknowledge the problems we face, to
talk frankly about inequality, and to examine its causes and
its impacts and, most importantly, to act to eradicate it.*

— U.S. Attorney General Eric Holder

America rejoiced in 2008 with the historic and triumphant election of America's first Black President, Barack Hussein Obama. Many were those who, with enthusiasm and great relief, believed that America had finally turned a corner in its racial history with President Obama's election.

Yet, three years later the Southern Poverty Law Center reported that, "fed by antagonism toward President Obama, resentment toward changing racial demographics, and the economic rift between rich and poor, the number of so-called hate groups and anti-government organizations in the nation has continued to grow from 602 in 2000 to 1018 in 2011."[1] What has become painfully obvious is that America has not moved very far from its historic racist rhetoric, notwithstanding the election of its first Black President.

According to police and monitoring organizations, "Barack Obama's election as America's first Black President has unleashed a wave of hate crimes across the nation," and "has further highlighted the stubborn racism that lingers within some elements of American society as opponents pour their frustration into vandalism, harassment, threats, and even physical attacks."

When the history books are finalized about the 2008 and 2012 presidential campaigns, they should easily reveal the most racially divisive presidential elections in the history of this country. What was also quite evident to many in this country, and especially to Blacks, is that the country's core racism continues unabated.

GFK Custom Research, under the supervision of the Associated Press polling unit, interviewed 1,071 adults in August and September 2012. In all, 51 percent of those polled expressed *explicit* anti-Black attitudes, compared with 48 percent in a similar 2008 survey. When their responses were measured for *implicit* racial attitudes, the number of Americans with anti-Black sentiments jumped to 56 percent, up from 49 percent during the election cycle four years earlier. "As much as we'd hope the impact of race would decline over time . . . it appears the impact of anti-Black sentiment on voting is about the same as it was four years ago," said Jon Krosnick, a Stanford University professor who worked with AP to develop the survey.

During and after President Obama's successful 2012 re-election campaign, in which he defeated former Massachusetts governor Willard "Mitt" Romney, racism was again working overtime:

• There was an abundance of hate speech on Twitter following Obama's re-election, with people hurling violent and racial epithets such as this one: "Can't wait for Mitt Romney to win the election and kick that filthy nigger Obama and his family out of the White House (Our House)." Many of those tweeters were teenagers whose public Twitter accounts feature their real names and advertise their participation in the sports programs at their various high schools. Principals and superintendents of those schools had little to say about how calling the President—or any person of color, for that matter—a "nigger" or a "monkey" accords with their student codes of conduct.

• November 7, 2012: According to local reports, as many as four hundred students from the University of Mississippi staged a riotous protest at the news of Obama's re-election. The Jackson *Clarion-Ledger* reported that "students were heard shouting 'nigger' and other racial epithets about President Obama and Blacks in general. Police were called to the scene and the crowd broke up around 12:30 a.m." Similar incidents occurred at Hampden-Sydney College in Virginia, and hundreds more were documented throughout the country.

• Right-wing talk show host Rush Limbaugh had this to say: "The Associated Press said that this nation is more racist today than it was in 2008. AP, that's been a theme of theirs: 'We're more racist today than 2008.' Yet we just gave the first African American president a mulligan. We just gave him a do-over. What a racist nation this is. Ho, man!"

• NBCNews.com reported that twenty-two-year-old Denise Helms was fired from Cold Stone Creamery after calling the president "a nigger" on her Facebook page. The Turlock, California, native, who was a manager at the ice cream chain, had added, "Maybe he'll get assassinated this term!"

• The vice-presidential running mate of Mitt Romney, Republican Congressman Paul Ryan in a post-election interview commented, "The surprise was some of the turnout, some of the turnout especially in urban areas, which gave President Obama the big margin to win this race." Ryan's saying that he was "surprised" that urban areas (read: Black and Latino) voted, implied that he and Governor Romney somehow thought that "minority voters" would not show up on Election Day.

- As if that was not enough, Governor Romney waded in himself. According to reports in the *Los Angeles Times* and *The New York Times*, the former Republican nominee said during a call with donors on the Wednesday a week after the election that Obama had been "very generous" throughout his first term in doling out "big gifts" to "the African American community, the Hispanic community and young people" as well as to women. Benefits such as access to "free health care," guaranteed contraceptive coverage, more affordable student loans, and "amnesty for children of illegals," all combined to give the President a decisive edge in popularity.

- Conservative radio host Glenn Beck declared that Mitt Romney's loss to President Barack Obama proved that "sometimes God really sucks."

- The Southwest Shooting Authority in Pinetop, Arizona, took out an advertisement in the local newspaper, the *White Mountain Independent*, that spelled out the store's new policy in explicit terms. According to Cope Reynolds, the store's owner, "If you voted for Barack Obama your business is not welcome at Southwest Shooting Authority," the ad reads. "You have proven that you are not responsible enough to own a firearm."

- Eventually General Colin Powell, perhaps the senior Black Republican in this country and certainly one of the most admired, felt compelled to respond to the parade of racist comments that his fellow Republicans had directed at the President during the 2012 campaign. In an appearance on the *Meet the Press* television news show on January 13, 2013, Powell called out former Alaska governor and 2008 Republican vice-presidential candidate Sarah Palin, together with John Sununu, former New Hampshire governor and the national co-chair of Mitt Romney's presidential campaign, for directing racist comments at the President, and for representing a racist element that Powell said has taken over the Republican Party. Quoting their comments on national television after the first 2012 presidential debate, Powell said that Palin saying that the President was "shucking and jiving" and Sununu calling President Obama "lazy" were racist, and represented a "dark vein of ignorance" in the Republican Party. Powell directly accused both former governors of riling up the admitted racist element of the Republican Party.

The list is forever long, but you get the picture. These events are a nasty throwback to those ignorant and venom-filled days of Jim Crow laws and segregation. What they reinforce is that we must understand that no matter how much we want to live in a so-called "post-racial" society, a racist element remains that will never consider Blacks, not even a Black President, as being accomplished or worthy, and certainly not as equal.

When asked about the ignorant nature of racism, Dr. Martin Luther King Jr. said, "Ignorance is not bliss; it is just ignorance." And, referring to America's violent response to the Civil Rights Movement, "Nothing in the world is more dangerous than sincere ignorance and conscientious stupidity." That is, nothing is more dangerous than acid hatred based on the color of one's skin! Dr. King knew and understood that racism is ignorance in its purest, raw, and unadulterated form. Dr. King knew that equality of Blacks would continue to take a back seat in this country. He knew that the fight for justice and equality was worth the battle. Yet this champion of justice, freedom, equality, and civil rights also knew that the struggle to overcome hatred would surely continue. This winner of the 1964 Nobel Peace Prize took the fight to those who would not accept human dignity for Blacks.

One school of thought says that we must protect young people from discussing racism. However, many experts agree that more sincere conversations about race relations and racism in the home, church, and school are keys to changing attitudes. It sounds so simple, but it is not easy. Experts generally agree that dealing with racism at a young age is the right thing to do—and that the earlier those conversations occur, the better.

Recent studies indicate that most whites believe they are discriminated against more than Blacks are. Perhaps one of the most overworked but true comments about American society is, "Those who do not know the past are doomed to repeat it."

During the presidency of Barack Obama we have quite fittingly seen the fiftieth anniversaries of historic civil rights events, starting in 2010 with Ax Handle Saturday (which took place in 1960 in Jacksonville, Florida); in 2013, the assassination of Medgar Evers and the 1963 March on Washington, and the bombings and murders in Birmingham, Alabama; in 2014, the 1964 riots in St. Augustine and the 1964 Civil Rights Act; in 2015, the 1965 Selma marches and the 1965 Voting Rights Act; and many others. Remember that these events were punctuated with horrific violence and senseless deaths.

With the Edmund Pettus Bridge in the background, President Obama spoke in Selma, Alabama. It was the fiftieth anniversary of the Selma marches and Bloody Sunday, during which future Congressman John Lewis almost lost his life, and on this day the President and the Congressman walked across the bridge together. These are a few of President Obama's comments:

"In one afternoon fifty years ago, so much of our turbulent history—the stain of slavery and anguish of civil war; the yoke of segregation and tyranny of Jim Crow; the death of four little girls in Birmingham, and the dream of a Baptist preacher—met on this bridge. The Americans who crossed this bridge were not physically imposing. But they gave courage to millions. They held no elected office. But they led a nation. They marched as Americans who had endured hundreds of years of brutal violence, and countless daily indignities—but they didn't seek special treatment, just the equal treatment promised to them almost a century before.

"We gather here to celebrate them. We gather here to honor the courage of ordinary Americans willing to endure billy clubs and the chastening rod, tear gas and the trampling hoof—men and women who, despite the gush of blood and splintered bone, would stay true to their North Star and keep marching toward justice. What they did here will reverberate through the ages. Not because the change they won was preordained; not because their victory was complete; but because they proved that nonviolent change is possible—that love and hope can conquer hate.

"As we commemorate their achievement, we are well-served to remember that at the time of the marches, many in power condemned rather than praised them. Back then, they were called

President Barack Obama and First Lady Michelle Obama on either side of Congressman John Lewis, retracing the 1965 march across the Edmund Pettus Bridge, 2015.

Communists, half-breeds, outside agitators, sexual and moral degenerates, and worse—everything but the name their parents gave them. Their faith was questioned. Their lives were threatened. Their patriotism was challenged.

"What greater expression of faith in the American experiment than this, what greater form of patriotism is there, than the belief that America is not yet finished, that we are strong enough to be self-critical, that each successive generation can look upon our imperfections and decide that it is in our power to remake this nation to more closely align with our highest ideals?

"That's why Selma is not some outlier in the American experience. That's why it's not a museum or static monument to behold from a distance. It is instead the manifestation of a creed written into our founding documents: 'We the People . . . in order to form a more perfect union.'

"'We hold these truths to be self-evident, that all men are created equal.'"

Thank you, Mr. President.

As we commemorate these historic events, let us keep in mind that racism is still the order of the day today, as it was then. America is not warm or accepting of civil rights *now* any more than America was warm or accepting of civil rights *then*. Racists in those days responded with ax handles and baseball bats and bullets and bombs directed to anyone standing for human dignity and respect.

Two quotes from Tim Wise, anti-racism activist and writer, sum it up: "To believe that the United States is post-racial requires an almost incomprehensible inability or unwillingness to stare truth in the face." And: "If you want to know if racism is a problem in your country, you might not want to ask white people."

Consider, also, this from Abraham Joshua Heschelm, rabbi, theologian, and participant in the marches from Selma to Mont-

President Obama sat in Rosa Park's seat on the historic Montgomery bus in April 2012. He said, "I just sat in there for a moment and pondered the courage and tenacity that is part of our very recent history but is also part of that long line of folks who sometimes are nameless, who oftentimes didn't make the history books, but who constantly insisted on their dignity, and their share of the American dream."

gomery: "Racism is man's gravest threat to man—the maximum of hatred for a minimum of reason."

The late Curtis Mayfield, one of the great music lyricists of our time, penned a very moving song that addresses our birthright and why we must continue the fight. The lyrics begin: "Some people think we don't have the right / to say it's my country. / Before they give in, / they'd rather fuss and fight, / than say it's my country. I've paid three hundred years or more, / of slave driving, sweat, and welts on my back." Mayfield called it simply, "This Is My Country."

Violence was the mindset as racists always responded to the Civil Rights Movement, and though violence today may be expressed in tweets and the hateful words of right-wing talk show hosts, real violence always lurks below the surface. That is what the American institution of racism is all about. Even though it is uncomfortable history, it is nonetheless American history . . . Black history . . . Civil rights history. It is the history we must tell over and over and over again, because *unless we tell it, it never gets told!*

Demonstrators in support of changing the name of Nathan Bedford Forrest High School.

31

The Story of Nathan Bedford Forrest High School

We live in a country whose population has acquired the habit of not taking historical memory seriously and therefore we tend to assume that something that happened ten years ago, or twenty years ago, or thirty years ago, or one hundred years ago, is a part of a history that remains securely in the past. But histories never leave us for another inaccessible place. They are always a part of us. These histories inhabit us and we inhabit them even when we are not aware of our relationship to history.

— Angela Y. Davis
  Author, educator, and activist

In 2010, during a question-and-answer period after giving a speech for Black History Month in Orlando, Florida, I was asked, "Is it true that there is a school in Jacksonville named for Nathan Bedford Forrest, the founder of the Ku Klux Klan?" I replied that indeed there was, and proceeded to discuss the "whys" of such an insulting and racist political decision. Prior to the school opening in 1959, its name was to be voted on at a School Board meeting, and many Jacksonville organizations suggested names for the new school.

After many ballots, a name that had been proposed by the United Daughters of the Confederacy was chosen. The new school would be named "General Nathan Bedford Forrest High School."

Nathan Bedford Forrest? What an insult! Prior to the Civil War, Nathan Bedford Forrest was a slave trader. Confederate General Nathan Bedford Forrest's men were responsible for the massacre of three hundred Blacks who were at Fort Pillow under a flag of surrender. Nathan Bedford Forrest was a founder of the Ku Klux Klan, and he was the Klan's first Grand Wizard. Did these accomplishments warrant giving his name to a high school in Jacksonville?

In 2008, almost fifty years later, college sociology professor Lance Stoll and some of his students petitioned the Duval County School Board to change the name of Nathan Bedford Forrest. But when the members of the School Board could have righted that horrific wrong, they declined to do so.

The news story said it all: "A Florida school board voted late Monday night to keep the name of a Confederate general and early Ku Klux Klan leader at a majority Black high school, despite opposition from a Black school board member who said the school's namesake was 'a terrorist and a racist.'"[1] The vote was 5 to 2, with five white members of the Duval County School Board voting to keep the name Nathan Bedford Forrest. The two votes against came from the two Black board members, Betty Seabrooks Burney, and my niece, former board chair Brenda Priestly Jackson.

It is unfathomable that this viciously racist and insulting decision to name a public school for Nathan Bedford Forrest should even warrant discussion today, let alone that the name should still stand. It is tremendously insulting to Jacksonville's Black community—as it should be to the entire community—that there is a school in Jacksonville named for one of the founders of the Ku Klux Klan. Yet, over the years, those who are in the position of being Jacksonville's civic leaders have not demanded that the name be changed. This is one of the reasons that some refuse to include Jacksonville in the same sentence with the word "progressive."

Five years further on, in August 2013, Duval County School Board member Dr. Constance Hall submitted a letter to the board and to the school superintendent formally asking them to change the name of Nathan Bedford Forrest High School. At about the same time, Omotayo Richmond of Jacksonville started a petition, "Rename Nathan Bedford Forrest School," which garnered more than 160,000 signatures. The existence of Richmond's petition led to a letter being sent to the School Board by a Klan chapter from Missouri, saying that Forrest and the organization he helped found following the Civil War were not necessarily racist, and asking the board not to change the name.

The ball had started rolling, though. Over the next several months, there were a series of community and student meetings about the name change. I was asked to participate in the final meeting, a panel discussion at the school on December 11, 2013. The four-person panel discussion had been established as part of the process for potentially changing the name, in order to allow students at Nathan Bedford Forrest High School to hear from those in the community on both sides of the issue. I gladly accepted, as did Professor Lance Stoll, the sociology professor who with his students had raised the issue with the School Board five years earlier, and the two of us spoke in favor of changing the name of the high school. The other two members of the panel would speak in favor of keeping the name of the school as Nathan Bedford Forrest. The discussion, which began at 8:00 AM, was held in the school auditorium; it was only for students and correspondingly closed to the public and the media. After the panel discussion, the students would vote to keep the name of Nathan Bedford Forrest for their school, or to change it.

When I arrived that morning at 7:15, standing outside of the school were three individuals waving Confederate flags. Of course, they really did not have to get up that early just to acknowledge our presence. One of the Confederate flag wavers was H. K. Edgerton, a Black activist on behalf of Southern "heritage" and a member of the Sons of Confederate Veterans. Go figure. Edgerton is often given a prominent place at rallies for the Confederate flag, and in this instance he was demonstrating on behalf of keeping the high school named after Nathan Bedford Forrest.

The panel was interesting, to say the least, and without going into great detail, let me just say that Professor Stoll and I handled our responsibilities on the panel well. The reasons for renaming Nathan Bedford Forrest High School remained the same as they were for not naming the school in this racist way back when it first opened in 1959; and they were the same as when Professor Stoll and his students brought their concerns to the School Board in 2008. The issues are knowledge and truth. There is nothing honorable about the deeds and misdeeds of Nathan Bedford Forrest. The sup-

H. K. Edgerton is an African American activist for Southern heritage and a member of the Sons of Confederate Veterans. He is often given a prominent place at rallies for the Confederate flag.

porters of Nathan Bedford Forrest, though, including those on the panel, sought to recast his memory from the appalling to the sublime. We know Nathan Bedford Forrest was a slave trader, the Fort Pillow butcher, a founder of the Ku Klux Klan, and its first Grand Wizard. His supporters had a different spin on those facts:

- "Yes, Forrest was a slave trader, but slavery was legal during that time."

- "This was war and General Forrest was simply getting in his payback when he and his soldiers massacred 300 black United States Army soldiers and women and children." (This was actually said by a college history professor.)

- "Yes, he was the first Grand Wizard of the Ku Klux Klan, but the Klan was different then from what it is now."

- "I appreciate General Forrest because he found the Lord in 1875." (Of course, he died in 1877, and by the time of his born-again conversion had accomplished all the evil he would be able to do.)

- The most recent Forrest apologist position is that somehow Nathan Bedford Forrest (who died in 1877) was one of the early founders of the NAACP (which was founded in 1909), through his support of an outfit called the "Jubilee of Pole Bearers," an organization unfamiliar to most historians.

After explaining racism and in particular the racism that led to naming a school for Forrest, Professor Stoll and I were able to put a face on slavery for the current Forrest students. We also explained why every label given Forrest and his support of slavery and dealing in the sale of Black human beings was anathema to everything decent and fair, and in total opposition to human dignity and respect.

Of course, the overriding question is why the 1959 Duval County School Board chose to name the school Nathan Bedford Forrest in the first place. I explained that that long-ago School Board had to know that there was no redeeming value in putting his name on a school, but did so anyway on the recommendation of the United Daughters of the Confederacy as a racist response to the epic Supreme Court decision in *Brown vs. the Topeka, Kansas, Board of Education*. Handed down on May 17, 1954, the Court's unanimous decision stated that "separate educational facilities are inherently unequal." As a result, *de jure* racial segregation was ruled a violation of the Equal Protection Clause of the Fourteenth Amendment of the U.S. Constitution. This ruling paved the way for integration and was a major victory of the Civil Rights Movement.

Following the panel discussion, one of the Black students thanked me for explaining the issues and making "real" the history of Nathan Bedford Forrest. She told me she was graduating the next year and would be embarrassed to put her diploma on her wall or in her dormitory room, since everyone would see that she graduated from a school named for the founder of the Ku Klux Klan. I spent some time talking with her and told her: "Do not let the name of your school define who you are."

Soon thereafter, Dr. Nikolai Vitti, superintendent of the Duval County public school system, announced that he would make a recommendation to the School Board in five days. If the students voted to change the name, then the board would begin the process to select a new name for the school. According to the current "Naming or Renaming Schools or School Facilities" policy, schools could not be named for persons (living or deceased) nor could they be in conflict with an existing school or district facility name.

Prior to the school board receiving the students' vote, one of Jacksonville's local news stations led off its news hour with this question: "How much could the cost run to rename Nathan Bedford Forrest?" Not: "Why was a local school named for a slave trader?" Not: "Why was a local school named for a war criminal responsible for the massacre of three hundred U.S. soldiers and women and children?" Not: "Why was a local school named for the first Grand

The "new" Westside High School in 2014, following the name change from Nathan Bedford Forrest High School.

Wizard of the Ku Klux Klan?" Not: "Why would the 1959 Duval County School Board name a school for a racist miscreant in the first place? No, the burning question was how much would it cost to remedy this awful act. But given Jacksonville's sordid history of race relations, costs to eliminate a longstanding racist symbol should not even be a consideration.

On December 16, 2013, the news was this: "The Duval County School Board voted 7–0 tonight to rename Nathan Bedford Forrest High School. School board members followed the recommendations of the Forrest students who voted last Wednesday 67% to 33% to change the name. School Superintendent Dr. Nikolai Vitti will have Forrest students vote on a new name, which will go into effect July 1, 2014."[2] Now, finally, papers across the country blared: "FLORIDA SCHOOL NAMED AFTER KKK LEADER GETS NEW NAME."[3]

"A Jacksonville high school named in 1959 after a former Confederate general and the co-founder of the Ku Klux Klan has a new name. Following the vote of the students attending Nathan Bedford Forrest High School, the Duval County School Board voted on January 7, 2014, to change the name of Nathan Bedford Forrest

High School to Westside High School effective July, 2014, thus ending a fifty-four-year battle to remove the name of the first Imperial Wizard of the Ku Klux Klan from a Duval County public school. Forty-three years after it was integrated by court order, Nathan Bedford Forrest High School in Jacksonville, Florida, will drop the name of the Confederate general who ran an infamous antebellum slave yard, presided over the massacre of surrendering black Yankee troops, and was the first national leader of the Ku Klux Klan."

It was a long time coming. I thank God I was able to play a part with the name change. School Superintendent Nikolai Vitti, who supported the change, said it could end a "cloud of divisiveness" and would now "allow us to focus on what matters most—student achievement." "We recognize that we cannot and are not seeking to erase history," said Duval County School Board member Dr. Constance Hall, whose letter had urged the board to take up the issue. "For too long and to many, this name has represented the opposite of unity, respect, and equality—all that we expect in Duval schools. Our board has [been] and is guided by a set of core values that promote equal opportunity, honors differences, and values diversity." Westside High School, formerly Nathan Bedford Forrest High School, is located in the school district represented by Dr. Hall.

Professor Stoll was glad that the change was finally accomplished, but continued to be astounded at the stiff defense of the name that had been put up by many locals. "Their argument was so shallow and so ridiculous," he told Hatewatch. "You can't defend Nathan Bedford Forrest. He was a miserable, despicable human being. And the Confederacy was a horrible place. Why do we allow our schools to be named after treasonous people? It's just amazing."

Thank you, Professor Lance Stoll. Thank you, Dr. Constance Hall. Thank you, Omotayo Richmond. Thank you, Duval School Superintendent Dr. Nikolai Vitti. And: thank you, students of the newly named Westside High School, for your bravery and your courage, and for making the decision that so many adults refused to make. So thank you, also, students of Westside High School, for giving the adults political cover.

The Jacksonville Branch NAACP, at its 2014 Freedom Fund Dinner, presented Dr. Constance Hall the Rutledge Pearson Award for Outstanding Leadership, and presented the Willye Frank Dennis Award for Leadership in Civic Engagement to the students of the new Westside High School.

Although the times were different and the circumstances different, the students' vote and actions in bravely taking a stand gave me a moment of pause. I thought back more than fifty years to 1960, and to the sit-ins and other activities of the Jacksonville Youth Council NAACP. Without considering the political ramifications or those who did or did not agree with their decision, students at Forrest High School decided they needed to do the right thing and removed the name of Nathan Bedford Forrest from their school building. They decided they would be a part of the solution and not part of the problem. They should be very proud. Youth leadership emerged in Jacksonville during the Civil Rights Movement of the 1950s and 1960s. Youth leadership emerged again in Jacksonville in 2013.

There will be School Board issues and school system issues about which the Black community will not agree with Dr. Vitti, as has occurred with past superintendents of Duval County's public schools. But we were on the same page with the issue of the renaming of Nathan Bedford Forrest High School.

As my own junior high school history teacher, Mr. Rutledge Henry Pearson, always told us: "Freedom is not free." It comes with the price of challenge and sacrifice in this ongoing struggle for human dignity and respect. Justice begins when one person stands up to injustice, and then takes the first step in the journey that eventually leads to human dignity and respect.

The author's mother, Janelle "Jan" Wilson.

32

"Janelle, you need to do something about that boy."

The unsung heroes of the civil rights movement were always the wives and the mothers.

— Andrew Young

I am often asked about my time participating in sit-in demonstrations. Why were you involved in sit-in demonstrations? Were your parents afraid for you? Were you afraid? My answers, invoking favorite sayings of Mr. Pearson, are "Freedom is not free", and "If you are not a part of the solution, you are a part of the problem." Corny perhaps, but many Black youths felt it was our time to fight racism and discrimination. True, my mother and my grandmother and later my stepfather were anxious for me, but they totally supported my involvement in the sit-ins and the Civil Rights Movement. I can honestly say I was not afraid.

I joined the Jacksonville Youth Council NAACP at age eleven. If you were Black and lived in this country you knew racism. Age did not make a difference. You could not miss signs which read "Colored" and "White." You could not miss signs identifying separate "Colored" and "White" restrooms. When my sister and I visited our cousins in Aiken, South Carolina and we went to the white movie theatre, we had to sit upstairs in the "Colored" balcony section.

White lunch counters were visible vestiges of segregation, which we were able to use to dramatize opposition to this racist symbol of American society. Demonstrations were evidence that young people knew how to use nonviolent direct action as a weapon in the war against racism. Young Blacks became an emerging new leadership force in the Black community.

I was raised a Baptist and attended church with my grandmother at West Friendship Baptist Church in Jacksonville. With my mother I later attended St. Philips Episcopal Church, a segregated but not a segregating Black Episcopal church. Some Black churches supported the Civil Rights Movement, and some did not. Some Episcopalians supported the Civil Rights Movement, and some did not. Some members of St. Philips supported the Civil Rights Movement, and some did not. The priest at St. Philips at that time was Father Toussaint Vincent Harris, who was Black and quite supportive of the Civil Rights Movement.

Following Ax Handle Saturday there was a two-week cooling-off period, requested by the U.S. Civil Rights Commission. When that concluded, and with the obvious racial fallout in Jacksonville, everyone had an opinion about the Youth Council NAACP resuming demonstrations, boycotting downtown stores, and continuing to keep the pressure on retail stores and the political establishment in Jacksonville. After a bi-racial committee had been appointed, and after much acrimony, these activities culminated in Marjorie Meeks (Brown) and myself integrating the white lunch counters in downtown Jacksonville. Weeks earlier, though, and one Sunday morning after church service no less, a Black attorney and a member of St. Philips—in a voice that would not be considered appropriate for church—confronted my mother and said: "Janelle, you need to do something about that boy. He is making it uncomfortable for all of us. He is stirring up a lot of racial strife."

His tone attracted attention from other church members. Responding to ill-advised comments was something my mother could handle. I saw her do it on several occasions. But before she could reply—and before he could say another word—he was unceremoniously physically "jacked-up" in a very unchristian fashion by my stepfather, William "Joe" Wilson, and several male church members. It was quite the talk of the church for a couple of Sundays.

As a youngster, I thought that all Black lawyers were heroic. Thurgood Marshall led the list. This lawyer—let's just call him "Mr. T"—was no hero. He was far from it. The only thing he saw was an agitating teenage president of the Jacksonville Youth Council NAACP upsetting the carefully laid out apple cart of his dealings with white businessmen in Jacksonville. And the only thing I saw, even then, was an unfortunate example of one of those Blacks who thought they were different because white folks told them they were different and gave them a little pat on the head. They felt that if they showed that they were willing to go along to get along, everything would be all right. What such people did not understand was that the Civil Rights Movement was not going away, that this emerging Black youth leadership would not be denied, and that the mothers and fathers of those civil rights youngsters would stand tall and support them. Those memories of my mother's support are as vivid today—and my gratitude just as deep—as they were more than fifty years ago. Thank you again, Mother.

Joe Madison, one of my favorite radio talk-show hosts, opens his program every morning with this quote from civil rights icon Fannie Lou Hamer: "You can pray until you faint. But if you don't get up and start to do something, God is not gonna put it in your lap. And there's no need of runnin' an' no need of sayin' 'Honey I'm not gonna get in the mess.' Because if you are born in America with a Black face, you are born in the mess."

Some Blacks will never understand Mrs. Hamer's wisdom.

"Janelle, you need to do something about that boy. . . ."

President Barack Hussein Obama taking the oath of office while being sworn in as the forty-fourth President of the United States in January 2009. First Lady Michelle Obama is holding the same Bible used by Abraham Lincoln when he became President.

33

The 2009 Inauguration
of President Barack Hussein Obama

Let it be said by our children's children that when we were
tested we refused to let this journey end, that we did not turn
back nor did we falter; and with eyes fixed on the horizon
and God's grace upon us, we carried forth that great gift of
freedom and delivered it safely to future generations.

— President Barack Obama, 2009 Inauguration address

My thoughts about a great day and the pride of the moment.

My son Rodney II and I left Jacksonville on Friday morning,
January 16, driving north for the Inauguration of President Barack
Obama on Tuesday, January 20, 2009. In the course of our driving, which took about twelve hours, we watched the SUV computer
register the drop in temperature. When we left Jacksonville it was
in the range of 50 degrees; in North Carolina it dropped to 35; and
in Virginia the outside real temperature was registering 14 degrees.
When we arrived in Maryland, it was 9 degrees — not the wind-chill
temperature but the actual thermometer reading, which made it
bone-chilling cold.

But what the heck, the cold is not a deterrent to being here for
this historic occasion. Still, skull caps, sweaters, big coats with lin-

ings, small coats with linings, jackets with linings, gloves with linings, scarves with linings, anything that can keep you warm (with
a lining), and, of course, thermals are a necessity if you want to
enjoy the Inauguration and all the festivities in a relative mode of
comfort. (Note to winter travelers: clothing purchased in the South
to wear in the North during winter will not do the job.)

It is worth making the round-trip drive to Washington to wit-
ness and share in this grand Inauguration of the most powerful person in the world, who this year happens to be Black.

It is Sunday morning here in Glenn Dale, Maryland and my
son I are staying with my nephew, Cassius Priestly. Cassius has a
beautiful well-appointed three-story house (shameless plug) including a fully furnished basement. In addition to Rodney and myself,
several of Cassius and Rodney's Young Turk friends are staying over
for the Inauguration, Rudy Jamison, Irvin Pedro Cohen, Stephanie
Boykins, and Tan Mayhew.

As a veteran of the Civil Rights Movement and living through
and being a part of history, I want young Blacks to understand the
significance and the impact of history. My son and my nephews
have heard sermons from my soap box over the years. They were too
young (or not born) for the March on Washington in 1963, which
I attended as a member of the military on leave, and they did not
attend the Million Man March with me in 1995. This is their moment, and the moment for many young Blacks to understand the
historical significance. President Obama's Inauguration does not
revolve around balls and gowns and celebrities and who attended
what ball with whom. It revolves around some promises made and
some promises kept. It represents another station along the Civil
Rights Journey. I thank God that he allowed some of us old-timers,
veterans of the Civil Rights Movement, to see this day and to see it
with our children and our grandchildren. The March on Washington and the Million Man March were events I sacrificed to attend,

and that I thanked God for the insight to understand. Rudy, Rodney, Cassius, Tan, Stephanie, and Irvin get it, and they listen when CRMV's (Civil Rights Movement Veterans) discuss the significance of Black history and the Civil Rights Movement. After all, they are important problem solvers of this country.

The Inauguration of this country's first Black President is significant for a number of additional reasons. And interestingly, many of the reasons we don't openly discuss. The Inauguration of President Barack Hussein Obama was this country's first payment on an IOU due to Black folk who were stolen and kidnapped from Africa, then made to suffer in the torturous and stench filled trips from Africa, and finally compelled to sweat and toil for free— developing and underwriting a free-labor economy of this country.

This country, founded on freedom of religion and freedom of

On a brutally cold January morning in 2009, hundreds of thousands of people assembled on the National Mall for this historic event in the nation's history.

The 2009 Inauguration of President Barack Hussein Obama　　283

choice, quickly tossed aside the ethical substance of Christianity when it decided that it needed to hold a race of people in torturous physical bondage and keep them there by violence and intimidation and terrorist acts. This country then took the Christian Bible and tore it to shreds by insisting that the enslaved Africans that it kept in bondage were property and were not human. The execrable actions by the founding fathers of this country belied the hypocritical assertion that "all men are created equal and are endowed by their creator with certain inalienable rights, that among these rights are Life, Liberty, and the Pursuit of Happiness."

Prior to Abraham Lincoln, no one in this country's leadership was absolved of guilt. Presidents, corporate heads, universities, colleges, and most religious denominations were all guilty of violating the United States Constitution. In fact, most of the Presidents prior to Abraham Lincoln owned slaves. And don't try to tell me that there were good slave owners. Don't even go there. That is perhaps the ultimate oxymoron. Remember too, that this country has never officially apologized for slavery, nor has it even attempted a national dialogue on reparations.

Even with the abolition (both legally and physically) of slavery, during the advent of the so-called Reconstruction era one of the original terrorist groups was organized, the Ku Klux Klan, with its sole purpose being to keep "niggers" and their sympathizers in check. Blacks by the thousands were lynched by the Klan and other groups with such regularity that lynchings became a social event. They were as common in parts of the South as the sun rising. American history texts do not do justice to that evil and wickedly vile part of our past in the way they should—but do the research, it is there. Better still; discuss some of these issues in your American history and world history classes and in your Sunday Schools.

Millions of Africans were taken from their homes, with many Africans choosing to jump overboard to drown themselves rather than to be slaves. Yet through all these hardships in the wilderness, God's chosen people fought and struggled and kept their faith in His masterful plan.

The history and the significance are inescapable. The substance of the moment is the stuff of which legends are made. The importance of President Obama's taking the reins of this mighty country should never be lost in ancillary issues. This is one historical event, one major, major Black history event, which historians will not be able to trivialize or overlook as they have done with the historical accomplishments and contributions of most Black Americans. For God has written this moment in the Eternal History Book of Time.

Though this is a moment and a time of great pride, it is not enough just to revel in the moment. It is a time to reassess who we are and to challenge our young people to take up the mantle of freedom and continue the struggle. This first payment on that long overdue IOU is only for those prepared to understand the future based upon the knowledge and the experiences of our great past.

And when you think that you have it made, that there is no longer a mission, that the challenge is minor, that the struggle is over, or that racism has somehow magically disappeared, then look in the mirror every day and make sure you really know the complexion of the face looking back at you.

The Struggle Continues.

Notes

Introduction

1. Logan, Rayford, *The Negro In American Life And Thought; The Nadir, 1877–1901*. New York: Dial Press, 1954.

2. Loewen, James W., *Lies My Teacher Told Me: Everything Your American History Textbook Got Wrong*. New York: Touchstone Publishing, 2007.

1: James Weldon Johnson

1. http://www.english.illinois.edu/maps/poets/g_l/johnson/life.htm.

2. Bond, Julian, and Sondra Locke, *Lift Every Voice and Sing: A Celebration of the Negro National Anthem, 100 Years, 100 Voices*. New York: Random House, 2000.

3. McWhirter, Cameron, *Red Summer: The Summer of 1919 and the Awakening of Black America*. New York: St. Martin's Griffin, 2012.

2: Augusta Savage

1. http://blackhistorynow.com/augusta-savage.

3: Asa Philip Randolph

1. Pfeffer, Paula, *A. Philip Randolph: Pioneer of the Civil Rights Movement*. Baton Rouge, Louisiana: Louisiana State University Press, 1996.

2. http://www.aphiliprandolphmuseum.com/evo_history4.html.

3. James, Dante, director, *A. Philip Randolph: For Jobs and Freedom*. Documentary produced by WETA, Arlington, Virginia, 1996.

4. Theoharis, Jeanne, *The Rebellious Life of Mrs. Rosa Parks*. Boston: Beacon Press, 2013.

4: Robert "Crow" Hayes

1. http://www.fhsaa.org/news/2007/1211.

2. Curry, George E., *Jake Gaither: America's Most Famous Black Coach*. New York: Dodd, Mead, 1977.

3. http://espn.go.com/page2/s/wiley/020920.html.

4. http://www.nytimes.com/2002/09/26/sports/football/26RHOD.html.

5. http://www.profootballhof.com/hof/member.aspx?PlayerId=276.

6. http://jacksonville.com/news/metro/2011-03-14/story/look-back-day-bullet-bob-hayes-came-home-olympic-champion.

5: Dr. Mary McLeod Bethune

1. Zrinyi Long, Nancy Ann, *The Life and Legacy of Mary McLeod Bethune*, Second Edition. Boston: Pearson Custom Publishing, 2006.

2. http://ncnw.org/about/bethune.htm.

3. http://www.aaregistry.org/historic_events/view/cookman-institute-right-place-and-time.

4. http://www.cookman.edu/about_BCU/history/index.html.

7: *Brown vs. Board of Education* and the Struggle for School Integration

1. http://www.notablebiographies.com/Lo-Ma/Marshall-Thurgood.html.

2. http://blackhistorynow.com/daisy-gatson-bates

3. http://archive.firstcoastnews.com/news/article/425/3/Time-for-change-The-story-of-one-of-the-first-black-students-in-Jacksonville.

4. http://jacksonville.com/tu-online/stories/021003/met_11705962.shtml#.Va6BmPnmt No.

5. http://openjurist.org/378/f2d/561/rosecrans-v-united-states.

6. http://www.biography.com/people/ruby-bridges-475426#synopsis.

8: Charlie E. Cobb Jr.

1. http://www.freedommosaic.com/charles-cobb-jr.

2. http://www.sncclegacyproject.org/index.html.

3. Cobb, Charlie E. Jr., *This Nonviolent Stuff'll Get You Killed: How Guns Made the Civil Rights Movement Possible*. New York: Basic Books, 2014.

9: Dr. Norma Ruth Solomon White

1. http://www.thehistorymakers.com/biography/norma-white-41.

10: Dr. Arnett E. Girardeau

1. http://archive.flsenate.gov/data/Publications/Archive/SenateHandbooks/pdf/88-90%20Senate%20Handbook.pdf.

13: Alton Yates

1. http://www.npr.org/2014/08/29/343988510/a-teenager-in-the-1950s-extreme-sledding-for-the-air-force.

14: Bethel Baptist Institutional Church

1. http://www.shilohbaptist.org/pages/page.asp?page_id=245533.

2. http://www.waymarking.com/waymarks/WMC396_1904_Bethel_Baptist_Institutional_Church_Jacksonville_FL.

17: Dr. Barbara Williams White

1. http://www.naswfoundation.org/awards/sarnat.asp.

2. http://www.utexas.edu/president/citation/past.html.

18: Joan Mattison Daniel and the Greenville Eight

1. http://articles.chicagotribune.com/2010-07-16/opinion/ct-edit-revjackson-20100716
_1_library-woolworth-s-lunch-counter-arrest.

2. http://www.blacklegalissues.com/Article_Details.ASPX?ARTCLID=ad942a68bf.

23: Slavery

1. Loewen, James W., *The Confederate and Neo-Confederate Reader: The "Great Truth" about the "Lost Cause."* Jackson, Mississippi: University Press of Mississippi, 2010.

2. Baptist, Edward, *The Half Has Never Been Told: Slavery and the Making of American Capitalism.* New York: Basic Books, 2014.

3. Coates, Ta-Nehisi, "The Case for Reparations." *The Atlantic*, June 2014.

4. http://www.yesmagazine.org/issues/make-it-right/infographic-40-acres-and-a-mule
-would-be-at-least-64-trillion-today.

24: The American Institution of Racism

1. Ture, Kwame, and Charles V. Hamilton, *Black Power: The Politics of Liberation.* New York: Vintage Books, 1992.

2. Harris-Perry, Melissa, "The Epistemology of Race Talk." *The Nation*, September 26, 2011.

3. Smith, Mychal Denzel, "Three Ways to Fight Racism in 2014." *The Nation*, January 3, 2014.

25: Racism and Violence

1. http://www.history.com/this-day-in-history/emmett-till-murderers-make-magazine-confession.

2. http://www.emmetttillstory.com.

3. http://www.eji.org/lynchinginamerica.

4. Hiaasen, Carl, "Racial lynchings, our own history of terrorism." *Miami Herald*, February 21, 2015.

5. http://www.splcenter.org/civil-rights-memorial.

6. Cone, James, *The Cross and the Lynching Tree.* Peabody, Massachusetts: Beacon Press, 2013.

27: Talking Black History and the Civil Rights Movement

1. Cobb, *This Nonviolent Stuff'll Get You Killed.*

2. Guralnick, Peter, *Dream Boogie: The Triumph of Sam Cooke.* New York: Back Bay Books, 2006.

29: Racism and the American Presidency, Part I

1. Link, Arthur, *The Road to the White House*. Princeton, New Jersey: Princeton University Press, 1947.

2. Yellin, Eric. *Racism in the Nation's Service: Government Workers and the Color Line in Woodrow Wilson's America*. Chapel Hill, North Carolina: University of North Carolina Press, 2013.

3. http://www.worldfuturefund.org/wffmaster/Reading/war.crimes/US/Wilson.htm.

4. http://www.biography.com/people/william-monroe-trotter-9510831.

5. Lunardini, Christine A., "Standing Firm: William Monroe Trotter's Meetings With Woodrow Wilson, 1913–1914." *The Journal of Negro History*, Vol. 64, No. 3 (Summer 1979).

6. http://www.rogerebert.com/reviews/great-movie-the-birth-of-a-nation-1915.

7. Dixon, Thomas, *The Clansman: An Historical Romance of the Ku Klux Klan*. New York: Doubleday, Page & Co., 1905

8. https://leniriefenstahl.wordpress.com/triumph-of-the-will.

9. Lopez, Ian Haney, *Dog Whistle Politics: How Coded Racial Appeals Have Reinvented Racism and Wrecked the Middle Class*. New York: Oxford University Press, 2014.

30: Racism and the American Presidency, Part II

1. http://www.nytimes.com/2012/03/08/us/number-of-us-hate-groups-on-the-rise-report-says.html?_r=0.

31: The Story of Nathan Bedford Forrest High School

1. http://www.nbcnews.com/id/27530588/ns/us_news-life/t/fla-high-school-retains-klan-leaders-name/#.VasP1fnmtNo.

2. 1 http://www.washingtonpost.com/blogs/answer-sheet/wp/2013/12/16/school-named-after-kkk-grand-wizard-to-be-renamed-finally.

3. http://www.huffingtonpost.com/2014/01/08/westside-high-kkk-school_n_4563336.html.

Photograph Credits

Index

Unless WE Tell It . . . It Never Gets Told!

Index

About the Author

Rodney L. Hurst Sr. is a civil rights activist and the author of *It was never about a hot dog and a Coke®!* In that personal account of civil rights demonstrations in Jacksonville, Florida, Hurst recounted with clarity the bloody events of August 27, 1960 — the day that came to be called Ax Handle Saturday — when two hundred whites with ax handles and baseball bats attacked members of the Jacksonville Youth Council NAACP who were peacefully sitting in at segregated lunch counters. *It was never about a hot dog and a Coke®!* is the winner of more than a dozen awards, including the USA Book News Book First Place Gold Medal Award for Multicultural Nonfiction, and the Florida Book Awards Bronze Medal in Nonfiction.

Hurst speaks extensively on civil rights, racism, and Black history. In addition to his involvement in the Civil Rights Movement, he served two four-year terms on the Jacksonville City Council, was the first Black to co-host a television talk show in Jacksonville (on PBS Channel WJCT), and was one of the original thirteen national recipients of the Corporation for Public Broadcasting Television Fellowships. He loves classic rhythm and blues and Motown music.

Rodney and Ann Hurst have been married for five decades. They have two sons, Todd and Rodney, and two granddaughters, Marquiette and Jasmine.